Lincoln's LITTLE WAR

WEBB GARRISON

RUTLEDGE HILL PRESS
NASHVILLE, TENNESSEE

Published in Nashville, Tennessee, by Rutledge Hill Press, 211 Seventh Avenue North, Nashville, Tennessee 37219. Distributed in Canada by H. B. Fenn & Company, Ltd., 1090 Lorimar Drive, Mississauga, Ontario L5S 1R7. Distributed in Australia by Millennium Books, 33 Maddox Street, Alexandria NSW 2015. Distributed in New Zealand by Tandem Press, 2 Rugby Road, Birkenhead, Auckland 10. Distributed in the United Kingdom by Verulam Publishing, Ltd., 152a Park Street Lane, Park Street, St. Albans, Hertfordshire AL2 2AU.

Typography by E. T. Lowe, Nashville, Tennessee.

Library of Congress Cataloging-in-Publication Data

Garrison, Webb B.
    Lincoln's little war / Webb Garrison.
       p.   cm.
    Includes bibliographical references and index.
    ISBN 1-55853-460-1
    1. United States—History—Civil War, 1861–1865. 2. Lincoln, Abraham, 1809–1865. 3. United States—History—Civil War, 1861–1865—Causes. 4. Fort Sumter (Charleston, S.C.)—Siege, 1861.
I. Title.
E471.G37   1997
973.7'11—dc21   97-12348
                                                    CIP

Printed in the United States of America.

1 2 3 4 5 6 7 8 9—99 98 97

Contents

Introduction   *5*

Part 1: Prelude to Inferno

1   A Southern Officer and a Southern Fort   *9*
2   No Foreign Presence   *19*
3   Washington Humiliated   *29*
4   A New Commander in Chief   *41*
5   He Says We Don't Exist   *51*
6   Keep Your Slaves and Come Back   *59*

Part 2: Firestorm at Sumter

7   Bread Enough for Five Days   *69*
8   An Intolerable Offer   *77*
9   Success in Failure   *87*
10   A Continuous Bombardment   *93*
11   The Heroes of Fort Sumter   *97*
12   Point of No Return   *107*
13   The Call   *115*
14   War on the Water   *123*
15   Citizen Rights Suspended   *131*

Part 3: The President Loses Control

16   The Loss of a General   *141*
17   Four More States Are Lost   *149*

18 The Loss of an Armory and a Naval Base   *157*
19 Many Lives Are Lost in Baltimore   *167*
20 Personal Safety Is Lost in Saint Louis   *175*
21 Lincoln Loses His Reins on the Slavery Issue   *185*
22 The Tremendous Loss of Life Begins   *195*

Conclusion   *205*
Notes   *209*
Bibliography   *225*
Index   *233*

Introduction

THE LEGACY OF THE American Civil War haunted the rural South for seventy-five years, from Appomattox to Pearl Harbor. It took a global conflict to push the memories of the past from everyday consciousness. Until World War II, the person identified most as the one behind all this bitterness and resentment was the sixteenth president. In what was once the Cotton Belt, Abraham Lincoln was widely held responsible for the war and Reconstruction that followed.

Southern public opinion, however, was not quite right because it overlooked a significant variable: Lincoln was the moving spirit behind the war as it was fought—its timing and many of its consequences—but he was not responsible for the fact that in 1861 civil war was seen by many as inevitable. Neither did he shape the course of Reconstruction.

Sectional differences between the North and the South were distinct long before the former British colonies came together to form a "more perfect union." Money and industry tended to gravitate toward the North, while the agrarian South was dependent upon the soil. Crops required a large labor force, and in the American South in the mid-eighteenth century, that meant slavery—the great unsettled question left over from the founding of the country and the framers of the Constitution. The increasing cost of maintaining a slave population almost eliminated the peculiar institution. Short-staple or "green" cotton was almost too expensive to harvest by the time a visitor from the North designed a machine that could separate cotton fibers from seeds, thus cutting costs and making slavery economically feasible.

Eli Whitney's cotton gin allowed upland cotton to be planted and harvested in ever-increasing quantities. Once the gin was available, cotton and slavery expanded together at an incredibly fast rate.

At least as early as the Jacksonian era it was clear that while the new United States shared a weak central government, it was constituted of two separate cultures. With the influence of abolitionists growing rapidly in the North, the people's representatives in Washington engaged in a series of delicate balancing acts. Each new compromise was intended to settle forever the North-South quarrel between free states and slave states, but none did.

Many in the Cotton Belt were confident that the region's world monopoly would last indefinitely, and this attitude was the seedbed in which the dreams of secession and independence flourished. In the North, alarm at the rapid expansion of the slave population was at least as dynamic a factor as was the humanitarian movement for abolition.

Secession or attempted secession would have come sooner or later, just as long-smoldering differences have led to hope for independence from Canada on the part of many in French-speaking Quebec. Whether or not secession would have inevitably led to civil war, however, is another question.

Lincoln's speeches en route to his inauguration, coupled with his first inaugural address, offer abundant insight into his views. Clearly, he expected to initiate a sectional clash somewhere soon and was confident that a short struggle would bring "so-called seceded states" back into the Union. His ideas concerning the role of fate in his life and that of the nation helped to insulate him from possible consequences of his actions.

Fatalism on the part of the new president was justified at least in part. Events thrust him center stage at a moment when all long-simmering sectional animosities were on the verge of exploding. Lincoln had comparatively little to do with his being the Republican nominee for the presidency in 1860. Neither was he responsible for the fact that in the South all Republicans were considered to be ardent abolitionists.

Once in office, the man dedicated to the preservation of the Union—not the abolition of slavery—soon took the steps without which war would not have come precisely when and as it did. Lincoln's seemingly adroit handling of the Fort Sumter issue was the match that lit a fuse. Once ignited, nothing could be done by the president or his opponents to extinguish it.

When the full story of the beginning of the Civil War is put together, it demands a new look at many long-established conclusions. The purpose of this volume is to show that our conventional wisdom is not necessarily valid.

Part 1

Prelude to Inferno

Maj. Robert Anderson of the U.S. Army led his small band of men into empty Fort Sumter and occupied it. *(Illustrated London News)*

1

A Southern Officer and a Southern Fort

IN MANY WAYS, THE election of Abraham Lincoln in November 1860 did not bode well for the country. The first Republican chief executive, to southerners his ascension to the White House symbolized a shift in the national power structure in favor of the abolitionists who would drastically alter the way of life that had developed in the cotton fields of the autocratic society. The compromises of the past were now in danger, and the people were caught up in the vociferous states' rights rhetoric of a far-flung party of secessionists.

Maj. Robert Anderson of the First Artillery Division of the U.S. Army dreaded returning to duty. Mounting sectional tensions indicated that he might have to choose soon between loyalty to Kentucky and fidelity to the Union. On leave at the plantation of his birth near Louisville, he hoped, but did not expect, to stay there until the end of the year. He was surprised when a message came from Lorenzo Thomas, the assistant adjutant general.[1]

Acting in the name of Gen. Winfield Scott, Thomas directed the Kentucky native to proceed immediately to South Carolina's Fort Moultrie, an installation on Sullivan's Island, four miles east of Charleston. Upon his arrival, he was to relieve Col. John L. Gardner, commandant of a string of forts in the harbor.

Gardner was in charge of eight officers, sixty-one enlisted men, and thirteen musicians. The fort, however, was not in the best condition. He and his wife lived comfortably in a home outside the walls. Repair work on the old fortress was under way and proceeded rapidly and efficiently, particularly since the arrival on November 11, 1860, of Capt. John G. Foster of the Corps of Engineers.[2]

The secretary of war, John Floyd, may have believed that an officer with strong ties to the region could defuse the tense situation in Charleston. Married to a Georgia native, Anderson had owned slaves until recently. He had been in uniform since the Black Hawk War, during which he reputedly swore into service a lanky volunteer named Abraham Lincoln. A one-time artillery instructor at West Point, he was now fifty-five years old. Anderson had been posted at Moultrie in 1845 and 1846, and to Floyd it seemed likely that his experience and maturity had prepared him to be more a mediator than an agitator at what had become the most sensitive federal installation in the nation.[3]

Additionally, the major's father, Richard Anderson, was still admired by South Carolinians. In 1780 he had successfully defended Fort Moultrie against British attack and a year later had been imprisoned by his foes. If anyone could pour sufficient oil on the troubled waters of Charleston Harbor, Floyd reasoned, Anderson should be able to do so.[4]

Two days after his arrival on November 21, the new commander sent the first of some one hundred messages to his superiors. Having

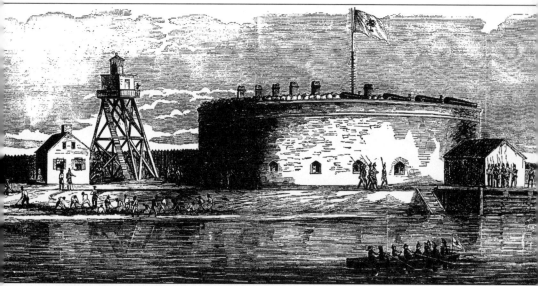

THE SOLDIER IN OUR CIVIL WAR

Castle Pinckney was virtually useless as a defensive post but flew the Palmetto flag after being taken over.

Lewis Cass unsuccessfully urged President James Buchanan to strengthen all southern forts.

inspected the military installations in the harbor, Anderson summarized their condition. He also expressed his determination to "avoid collision with the citizens of South Carolina." That would not be easy, he noted, for he knew that Charlestonians were eager to remove their state from the Union and to occupy the federal forts that protected the city.

"The clouds are threatening," he wrote, "and the storm may break upon us at any moment." Hence he urged immediate reinforcement of his garrison and requested that at least two companies be sent to Charleston to strengthen both Fort Sumter and Castle Pinckney. His first report to Samuel Cooper, adjutant general of the army, ended with a plea for instructions, observing that his position was "rather politico-military than a military one."[5]

PRESIDENT JAMES BUCHANAN, due to leave office in less than four months, avoided dealing with the mounting tensions by deferring to Congress. Over the objections of Secretary of War Floyd, the secretary of state, Lewis Cass, went to the White House and urged that all southern forts be strengthened. When nothing was done, Cass noted that Buchanan was "pale with fear."[6] Soon afterward, Cass, a senior statesman from Michigan, resigned.

While the president refused to act, his subordinates vacillated. The orders urgently requested by Anderson were never issued. Lacking instructions, he warned on November 23, "South Carolina will most assuredly attack us."

Abner Doubleday, Anderson's second in command, kept notes on the developments around Moultrie. Those whom he labeled "the enemy" placed cannon on Sullivan's Island soon after Washington was warned. On December 11 "the enemy began to build batteries at Mount Pleasant" and at other spots bearing upon Fort Moultrie where workmen under Captain Foster did everything possible to strengthen the installation. In the meantime, construction at Fort Sumter was delegated to Lt. G. W. Snyder, who oversaw the work of artisans—mostly local—on that installation.[7]

On December 1 Anderson's Dispatch No. 3 reported that Moultrie was undefensible. Sumter, he noted, was the key to controlling the harbor. South Carolinians were likely to occupy it and then move against Fort Moultrie.[8]

Destined soon to change uniforms, Adjutant General Cooper drafted a reply to a previous dispatch. Secretary of War Floyd, he wrote, had reliable information that Fort Moultrie would not be attacked. Anderson must be careful to avoid initiating "a collision." If he sent additional forces to Charleston, wrote Cooper, they would add to the excitement "and might lead to serious results."[9]

Anderson's Dispatch No. 7 of December 9 described unoccupied Fort Sumter as "a tempting prize, the value of which is well known to the Charlestonians, and once in their possession, with its ammunition and armaments and walls uninjured and garrisoned properly, it would set our Navy at defiance, compel me to abandon this work, and give them the perfect command of this harbor."[10]

Cooper sent Don Carlos Buell, his chief assistant, to Charleston to inspect the forts and confer with Anderson. Wary of putting orders on paper, he made a memorandum of his verbal instructions. Floyd endorsed the memo, which reached the president on December 21, the day after South Carolina adopted an ordinance of secession.[11]

Buell stressed that officers and men must avoid all acts of hostility. Nevertheless, Anderson was directed to hold the full compliment of Charleston's forts. If he was attacked, he was to defend himself "to the last extremity." The command was too small to hold more than one installation, Buell conceded, so he told Anderson to place his men wherever he could best resist. Even so, President Buchanan was angry

Charleston's defenses were formally inspected by Don Carlos Buell.

LOSSING, PICTORIAL FIELD BOOK

at Anderson's subsequent removal to Fort Sumter and said, "It is clear that Major Anderson acted upon his own responsibility, and without authority, unless, indeed, he had 'tangible evidence'" that South Carolina was prepared to take a hostile step.[12]

Lt. R. K. Meade of the Engineer Corps was placed in charge at another Charleston fort, Castle Pinckney. Later resigning to become a Confederate officer, Meade was convinced in December 1860 that "he [Anderson] will be hand in hand with the South as soon as he may be with honor relieved from his position." At the same time, Doubleday criticized his commander for what he saw as an effort both to save the honor of the Union and to save the institution of slavery.[13]

Soon after Buell's departure, Anderson decided to move his men to Fort Sumter, which was larger that Fort Moultrie, far stronger, and a great deal less accessible. The orders that he gave, however, indicated that he expected to go from Moultrie to Fort Johnson; only three subordinates knew that the real objective was Sumter. Initially he planned to use the Christmas Day festivities as cover for his movement, but rain delayed him.[14]

By noon on December 26 forty-five women and children were on two transports stocked with provisions for four months. Lt. Norman J. Hall, post adjutant, moved toward Fort Johnson, knowing that his passengers would not land there. Once he saw two signal guns fired from Fort Moultrie, he altered course and proceeded to Fort Sumter.[15]

Construction at Moultrie continued until roll call was sounded. As the flagpole was cut down, officers and men boarded five barges.

Lt. Jefferson C. Davis, a member of the Federal garrison who later became a general, was not related to the president of the Confederacy.

Anderson, Doubleday, and twenty selected armed men filled the first boat and got under way, leaving Lt. Jefferson C. Davis in charge of the rest of the movement.[16]

Once Anderson reached Sumter, he wrote: "I have the honor to report that I have just completed, by the blessing of God, the removal to this fort of all my garrison, except the surgeon, four non-commissioned officers and seven men. We have one year's supply of hospital stores and about four months' supply of provisions for my command. I left orders to have all the guns at Fort Moultrie spiked, and the carriages of the 32-pounders, which are old, destroyed. The step which I have taken was, in my opinion, necessary to prevent the effusion of blood."[17]

Construction workers at Sumter were more surprised at the developments than were Anderson's men. Ten days earlier they had met and decided to be neutral. As the occupation of the fort signaled that hostilities might begin, many of them left their jobs and returned to Charleston. Some enrolled in South Carolina's militia.[18]

In the city, news of Moultrie's destruction and Sumter's occupation was circulating before 8:00 A.M. on December 27, although many did not believe it. In one account, by noon "the greatest excitement prevailed." Orders to hold themselves in readiness went out to six militia companies and to the cadets at the Citadel military academy. Anderson was denounced as an aggressor who had broken his word. Ordered by Carolina officials to return to Moultrie, he refused.[19]

At about 10:15 the governor sent Col. Johnson Pettigrew and Maj. Ellison Capers to Fort Sumter. Anderson was found in a second-story room within the officers' quarters. Once formal greetings had been exchanged, Pettigrew asked why Anderson had violated the agreement that there would be no change in the status of federal installations in the harbor.

Anderson said that he knew nothing of such an agreement and that he had moved his command to prevent bloodshed. He added that his sympathies were "entirely with the South," but he added that as commander of the harbor, his duty to his government required him to act. Pettigrew then demanded that Anderson and his command return to Fort Moultrie.

"I cannot and will not go back," the major replied.

"Sir," said Pettigrew, "my business is done."[20]

When the Carolina officers withdrew, the men at Sumter were ordered to parade. After a prayer, during which Anderson knelt by the flagstaff, "the band played the National Air, and the flag went to the head of the flag-staff, amid the loud and earnest huzzas of the command."[21]

Throughout the North, newspapers reported the move as having been made by Anderson "on his own responsibility." Many editors stressed that "the [Buchanan] administration is not to blame [for heightened tensions]."[22] The editors of the *Boston Chronicle*, however, exulted that although the president had done nothing, Anderson had acted "to rally the national heart."

Reaction in Washington was mixed. R. W. Barnwell, chairman of a South Carolina commission sent to the capital to purchase Fort Sumter, charged President Buchanan with bad faith. James H. Adams, another commissioner, sent a telegram to Charleston urging the authorities to prepare for war. In turn, Floyd sent Anderson a telegram saying that he did not believe news of the move to Sumter because such a move had not been authorized.

Lincoln's chief secretary, John G. Nicolay, wrote of Anderson's bold action: "This movement filled the Union sentiment of the country with the liveliest exultation. It was a spontaneous, uncalculating act of patriotism which will enshrine the name of Anderson in grateful recollection so long as American history shall be read."[23] Had Anderson and his men heard the accolades in the North, they probably would have replied that ammunition, food, and other essential supplies were more important than praise.

When the garrison had been stationed at Moultrie, meat and vegetables were regularly bought in Charleston; for the Sumter garrison to survive, this practice must continue. There was abundant powder in the installation just occupied, but powder bags were in very short supply. A hasty inventory indicated that there was enough fuel on hand to feed cookstoves for a month, but there were few candles and no soap.[24]

CONSTRUCTION OF FORT SUMTER had begun shortly after the War of 1812, when the national leaders decided to fortify the East Coast. Since Charleston Harbor was large enough to accommodate the largest warships, it needed special protection. Work did not start, however, until 1829, when ships began bringing loads of granite "leavings" from New England. Stone was dumped at a strategic point about one mile from Fort Moultrie and twelve hundred yards from Cummings Point. Over a span of ten years a small artificial island took shape from the granite, costing approximately five hundred thousand dollars.[25]

Once the island was formed and stabilized, work commenced on an immense pentagonal brick fortress. Most walls ranged from twelve to eighteen feet in thickness, and the fortress towered sixty feet over its granite base. Four walls faced the ocean, offering a quartet of opportunities to fire upon belligerents. Since the fifth wall faced the city, it was only **ten** feet thick. Plans called for a garrison of 650 officers and men and 146 guns.[26]

When international tensions abated, Congress was slow to allocate additional funds for the fort's completion. Year after year it sat incomplete and empty. In 1860 lawmakers provided eighty thousand dollars for its completion.[27]

By January 6, 1861, Captain Foster was sure that Sumter's armament was more than a match for any that the South Carolinians could bring to bear. He had twenty-nine guns sitting on the first tier and eleven more on the barbette. Four 8-inch Columbiads were ready to mount, and a few 10-inch Columbiads were to be placed on the parade ground and used as mortars.

"We are determined to defend ourselves to the last extremity," he wrote. Even so, he was in urgent need of at least fifteen thousand dollars to meet his payroll. Food and other essentials were more crucial. There were only two sources of supply: the Carolina mainland and the far North. Thus Anderson's decision to take the best available position did not mean that it would be tenable for long.

The sudden occupation of the fort triggered the immediate seizure of federal installations in all the states that had seceded on the heels of South Carolina: Mississippi, Florida, Alabama, Georgia, Louisiana, and Texas. Aside from Texas, at least twenty-four fortifications and seven arsenals were claimed and occupied as state property. Custom houses, revenue schooners, branch mints, and a marine hospital were soon in secessionist hands across the South.[28]

2

No Foreign Presence

I AM COL. J. J. PETTIGREW of the First Regiment of Rifles, South Carolina
Militia. Whom am I addressing, sir?"

"Lt. R. K. Meade, U.S. Army."

Pettigrew reached the parapet of Castle Pinckney from the
top of a scaling ladder shortly after 4:00 P.M. on December 27,
1860. Pointing toward his party of 150 men wearing winter uniforms and armed with pistols, the secessionist drew himself to his
full height.

"Lieutenant Meade," he snapped, "we are taking possession in
the name of our sovereign state."[1]

Meade protested that the military installation belonged to the
United States, not to South Carolina.

"We know your strength," Pettigrew retorted. "You have Ordnance Sergeant Skillen with his family, three or four mechanics, and
perhaps twenty-five workmen. Resistance will be futile. Behind me
are my men and those of the Meagher Guards and the Carolina
Light Infantry."

The officer in charge of the old half-moon-shaped fort signaled
that no resistance would be offered. He refused, however, to sign a
receipt for "former property of the United States known as Castle
Pinckney in Charleston harbor." Neither would he give his parole not
to engage in hostile action against South Carolina forces.[2]

Although annoyed, Pettigrew did not protest. "Our steamer, the
Nina, brought along a rowboat. You may use it."

Meade gestured for his mechanics to follow him. Soon they were making slow headway toward Fort Sumter, very recently for the first time occupied by a tiny garrison of the U.S. Army.[3]

Pettigrew, later a Confederate brigadier general, ordered an aide to raise the Palmetto flag. Momentarily nonplused when informed that no one had thought to bring a flag along, he pointed toward the steamer that had brought them to the tiny island on which Castle Pinckney stood.

"Haul down the colors of the *Nina*," he directed. "Many a man on shore is watching through a glass. Until our flag is flying, our success will not be known there."

Once Castle Pinckney was in the possession of the state, gangs of workmen were sent to strengthen and extend its defensive walls, and militia units were given garrison duty. To secessionists, ordnance seemed even more important than the site, long fallen into disuse.[4] Since January 1, 1860, Washington had been sending heavy weapons to the fort: four 42-pounders, fourteen 24-pounders, and four 8-inch seacoast howitzers.[5] For the first time, an armed fortress of the United States was surrendered to rebellious citizens who had seized it under orders from Francis Pickens, governor of the Republic of South Carolina. He and others were unwilling to tolerate "the existence of a foreign presence" on their soil.[6]

For years the industrial North and the slave-holding agricultural South had exchanged angry words. Now talk had given way to action. A tiny but bellicose "independent southern nation" challenged the power of the federal government.

News of the exploit reached Washington that night. A few in the capital expressed confidence that President James Buchanan would take quick and decisive action. Most of those who knew him, however, realized that the commander in chief wanted nothing so much as peace. This was soon confirmed; no armed vessel or body of troops was dispatched to Charleston to reclaim the fortress from the hands of secessionists.

Earlier, Governor Pickens had consulted men whom he addressed as members of his cabinet. Without exception, they concurred in his judgment that every potentially hostile presence must be removed from the state.

A few hours after Castle Pinckney had come under the jurisdiction of the state, other bands of militia embarked for Fort Moultrie. More than two hundred members of the German, LaFayette, Marion, and Washington Artilleries were led by Lt. Col. William G. deSaussure. They found a sergeant and ten enlisted men at the fort. Like Meade, the overseer in charge of Moultrie's workmen protested but offered no resistance. In addition to the fort, he surrendered fifty-five pieces of ordnance that included fourteen 32-pounders and ten 8-inch Columbiads.[7]

DeSaussure had been warned to exercise extreme caution, as departing U.S. forces were prepared to destroy the fort, he was told. According to reliable information, "mines had already been sprung, and trains had been laid ready for the application of the match." When the fortress was inspected, however, the story of the mines proved to be false. Soon the Palmetto flag fluttered over Fort Moultrie as it did over Castle Pinckney.

Pickens penned a brief report to D. F. Jamison, president of the convention considering the formation of a southern confederacy. His December 28, 1860, summary stressed that he "considered the evacuation of Fort Moultrie [by Anderson and his men] a direct violation of the distinct understanding between the authorities of the Government at Washington and those who were authorized to act on the part of the state."[8]

On the last day of the year, Col. John Cunningham and the Seventeenth South Carolina Infantry Regiment took over the huge U.S. arsenal in the heart of the city. Ordnance Sgt. F. C. Humphreys, backed by nine enlisted men and six workmen, yielded the installation without a struggle. Along with the sturdy building that occupied an entire city block, Cunningham seized 22,430 pieces of ordnance valued at about four hundred thousand dollars.[9]

On January 2 units of South Carolina militia took over 152-year-old Fort Johnson, which was so dilapidated that federal authorities did not consider garrisoning it.[10] Seizure of this installation rid Charleston of the most visible signs of U.S. power. Perched three miles from the wharfs of the city of fifty thousand, Fort Sumter was the lone hostile presence in the area.

Once begun by bellicose South Carolina, the domino-effect seizure of federal property rippled through the Cotton Belt. Most states withheld action until they had voted to secede, but in some instances seizure preceded secession.

Mississippi declared itself out of the Union on January 9, and Fort Massachusetts and other installations on Ship Island off its coast were surrendered to state forces on January 20. Lt. Frederick E. Prime, who reported the surrender, said that three expeditions were sent against him. Rumor had it that these did not have the governor's sanction.[11]

SKETCH BY A MEMBER OF THE SUMTER GARRISON

Fort Johnson, erected in 1708 and rebuilt in 1793, was described as being in ruins by 1807.

One day behind Mississippi in severing ties with the North, Florida was already in possession of the U.S. arsenal at Apalachicola and Fort Marion at Saint Augustine. During the four days that followed their secession, Floridians appropriated three more U.S. sites. Fort McRee and the naval yard at Pensacola were seized on January 12. An earlier attempt to take Fort Barrancas and its barracks had failed. Lt. Adam J. Slemmer now led his small command to strong but unoccupied Fort Pickens. Floridians hurled their caps into the air and shouted cheers when they took possession of Barrancas on January 13.[12]

Eager Alabamians did not wait for secession of their state on January 11. Five days earlier they appropriated the U.S. arsenal at Mount Vernon. On January 5 state forces seized Mobile's Forts Morgan and Gaines.[13]

Georgia's governor, Joseph E. Brown, contacted Col. Alexander Lawton of the state's First Volunteer Regiment on January 2. In obedience to Brown's directive, Lawton assembled at Savannah the Oglethorpe Light Infantry, the Savannah Volunteer Guards, and the Chatham Artillery. Early the next day they crowded aboard the little steamer *Ida* and soon reached Cockspur Island. Unit flags fluttered in the wind and drummers pounded out a beat as Georgian troops moved on Fort Pulaski, where a civilian caretaker offered no resistance.[14]

Capt. William H. C. Whiting, who was charged with the oversight of unoccupied installations in Georgia and Florida, arrived from Fort Clinch seventy-two hours later. He accepted from Lawton a receipt for the fort and its contents, then discharged the caretaker. Reporting to the U.S. Engineer Office concerning the Florida installation, Whiting stipulated, "It is, perhaps, unnecessary for me to say to the Department that in the present condition of Fort Clinch the idea of arming it either for offense or defense is simply absurd."[15]

Five days after Georgia seceded on January 19, the large Augusta arsenal was surrendered by Capt. Arnold Elzey of the Second Artillery. Two days later there was more frenzied action at Savannah, where Fort Jackson and Oglethorpe Barracks were taken almost simultaneously. Whiting, who made another round trip from Fort Clinch, found both installations swarming with Georgians when he reached Savannah.

Louisiana was next to last among the seven states that seceded soon after Lincoln's election. Louisianians swarmed into the U.S. arsenal and barracks at Baton Rouge on January 10. Maj. A. Haskin, in command, offered no resistance. A demand by Gov. Thomas O. Moore, he noted, was "backed by a very superior force."[16]

Simultaneously, other bands forced Ordnance Sgt. H. Smith to yield strategic Forts Jackson and Saint Philip below New Orleans. A marine hospital and Fort Pike were in state hands before a January 26 announcement that all ties with Washington had been severed. Two weeks later, the quarters of Maj. Albert J. Smith, U.S. Army paymaster

Governor Joseph E. Brown ordered members of the militia to seize Fort Pulaski and other federal installations in Georgia.

Robert E. Lee was briefly stationed at Fort Pulaski; like Sumter, it was pentagonal in shape.

at New Orleans, were "occupied by State officers." His records and funds were retained by the state.[17]

In Arkansas the Little Rock arsenal was surrendered on February 8, three months before secession took place.[18] Four days later a cache of munitions at Napoleon was taken from Maj. Justus McKinstry. During the previous thirty days McKinstry had dispatched eighty-three complete sets of gear for horses, forty thousand .58 elongated-ball percussion cartridges, ten thousand .58 rifle-musket percussion cartridges, twenty thousand Sharp's carbine-ball cartridges, fifty thousand ball cartridges for Colt pistols, and ten thousand blank cartridges for the same weapon. Most or all of these items were seized by agents of the state of Arkansas.[19]

Very early, divisions that could not be healed surfaced in Missouri. At the remote town of Liberty, secessionists seized the U.S. arsenal and triumphantly reported much more than a token victory. Their military booty included three 6-pounder cannon, 180 muskets, 225 rifles, 928 pistols, and more than 400 sabers. Ammunition purchased with federal funds, but now held by insurgents in the state, included 175,000 cartridges and 1,000 rounds of 6-pounder shot.[20]

The arsenal at Liberty was small by comparison to its counterpart at Saint Louis. Repeatedly threatened, this huge installation remained in federal hands through the influence of Francis P. Blair Jr., brother of a member of Lincoln's cabinet.[21]

Stormy confrontations in the West were harbingers of much worse things to come. During the approximately fourteen hundred days of war, only Virginia and Tennessee exceeded Missouri in the number of military events that took place within its borders.[22]

Texas's departure from the Union was stormy in some instances. Early in 1861 Brig. Gen. David E. "Bengal Tiger" Twiggs saw that he was likely to face an irreconcilable conflict. His apprehension about the future led one of the U.S. Army's four general officers to dispatch a January 15 appeal to Lt. Gen. Winfield Scott:

> I am placed in a most embarrassing situation. I am a Southern man, and all these States will secede. What is left will not be the "United States," and I know not what is to become of the troops now in this department. As soon as I know that Georgia has separated from the Union, I must of course follow her. I most respectfully ask to be relieved in the command of this department on or before the 4th of March next.
>
> D. E. Twiggs
> Brevet Major-General, U.S. Army[23]

David E. Twiggs of the U.S. Army surrendered every federal post in Texas at one fell swoop.

Twiggs sent other urgent messages on December 27, 1860, and on January 2, 7, 18, and 23, 1861. He was told that they were received and "duly submitted to the secretary of war." A January 28 order directed him to relinquish command to Col. C. A. Waite of the First Infantry. Sent by mail, it did not reach him until February 15.

An ordinance of secession was adopted by the Texas Convention on February 1. In the immense region over which Twiggs had military jurisdiction, there were twenty forts and camps. With more than two thousand soldiers manning those installations, he commanded about 12 percent of the prewar army.[24]

Washington was thrown into consternation on February 19 by the news from Texas. Instead of relinquishing the Department of Texas to Waite, Twiggs had surrendered his entire command to state officials. Soon one installation after another was listed simply as "abandoned." Buildings and fortifications passed from control of the United States to Texas fairly smoothly. Many field pieces and huge stores of ammunition went the same route. So did miscellaneous property of every variety, including fifty-three camels at Camp Verde that were valued at about two hundred thousand dollars. These animals were relics of an experiment initiated nearly a decade earlier by Jefferson Davis, then secretary of war.[25]

Twiggs expected the Texans would negotiate with his post commanders in planning the orderly sixty-day withdrawal to the coast of all U.S. Army personnel. Vast distances and shortages of wagons and draft animals, however, made it impossible for some units to reach their destinations during this time frame. Many officers accepted an opportunity to pledge their honor in such fashion that they could leave the state, but some were summarily imprisoned. Men "disposed to join the Confederate States Army" were soon sworn into service and promised new uniforms. Many others were to be "held as prisoners of war, at a place judged to be most safe."[26]

The seizure of officers and men as prisoners of war represented a giant step beyond the takeover of arsenals and forts. Far to the west, the movement launched at Charleston reached its zenith. In the Palmetto State federal property was regarded as a potential threat; in the Lone Star State, federal personnel were subject to arrest and imprisonment as soon as the threat of war appeared.

Once enough time had passed to consider the progress of these events, it was not hard to see that the sectional quarrel had undergone dramatic change. U.S. property, whose value in today's dollars would run into a vast sum, was held by seven seceded states. One estimate placed the number of seized weapons at two hundred thousand and the value of property seized at twenty-five million dollars. With more than 150,000 pounds of powder on hand in early May, the Confederacy had enough raw materials to manufacture 1.5 million cartridges.[27]

Seizures occurred on water as well as on land. As was the case with arsenals and forts, records seldom indicate the identity or number of the belligerents and the defenders. South Carolina led again in "cleaning up" the waterways. Five of the twenty-four vessels operated by the U.S. Revenue Service were in Confederate hands before the crisis climaxed at Fort Sumter.

The symbolic importance of revenue cutters was tremendous, for the customs issue was second only to slavery in its divisiveness. Each seizure added to northern fury, while southerners hailed surrenders as though they had made the Confederacy invulnerable. Long before Charlestonians began taking over forts, the U.S. Customs Service and the tariff system had angered the South. Tariffs on imported goods served to protect the industrialized North and boosted the cost of manufactured goods in the agricultural South.

Such sectional differences had surfaced while the United States was still in its infancy. Congress had imposed an 8 percent tariff on imports in 1789, but by 1816 the rate had jumped to 25 percent and continued to rise. A ceiling was reached in 1828 when the so-called tariff of abominations boosted the cost of imported goods 45 percent.[28]

Led by John C. Calhoun, South Carolina protested futilely. The state passed a nullification act, which asserted state sovereignty over the federal government. An injustice such as the tariff ought to be ignored, Calhoun and his followers argued. President Andrew Jackson threatened to collect tariffs by force if necessary, and the southerners backed down. In 1833 the state repealed the nullification act, but the people never forgot. "Our customs service guarantees that the North will get richer and that the South will continue to grow poorer," they grumbled.[29] When the seceded states merged to form the Confederate States of America, most of the southern population believed their cost of living would decline because tariffs would no longer be collected.

With federal property seized across the seven Cotton Belt states, the national presence in that region was now limited to four sites. Three of these were in Florida. Fort Taylor at Key West hardly deserved to be included in a list of fortifications. Although garrisoned, Fort Jefferson in the Dry Tortugas was of little use. Pensacola's Fort Pickens

John C. Calhoun, whose grave is in Charleston, is credited with having framed the doctrine according to which a state could "nullify" federal legislation—a notion revived late in the twentieth century.

CHARLESTON HISTORICAL SOCIETY

was strategically situated, but it lay far from potential sites of major North-South conflict and its garrison was running low on supplies.[30] These circumstances elevated the installation in Charleston Harbor to unique significance.

Today the battle flag of the Confederacy has assumed a highly charged symbolic role. Some persons are ready to fight to keep it flying in prominent places; others are ready to scrap to have it removed. Multiply these groups and the level of their responses many times, and the symbolic importance of Fort Sumter in 1860–61 will be approximated.

As a fortress erected for coastal defense against European warships, Sumter had not been considered worth completing. Yet to millions, it came to symbolize the authority of the federal government. To a majority of southerners it represented the presence of a foreign power. Hence an unfinished and long-deserted fort on an artificial island became pivotal in the increasingly intense confrontation between the North and the South. Confederates expected to get possession of it soon, promising compensation "to the full extent of the money value of the property."[31]

3

Washington Humiliated

ON DECEMBER 27 MANY in Charleston refused to believe that Anderson had moved his troops to Fort Sumter. Others seemed more interested in the condition in which Fort Moultrie had been left. A newspaper writer was allowed to inspect the abandoned installation and learned that shields were being built to protect it from Sumter's guns.[1]

At 8:45 A.M. Anderson sent Lt. G. W. Snyder to Charleston with a request to the state authorities. Police seized his boat and sent him to Governor Pickens. Snyder delivered the message, which asked, "If an attack was to be made upon him, he desired to be informed in time to remove his women, children and non-combatants to a place of safety."

Pickens answered that Anderson was free to send them to Sullivan's Island, where "they would have complete protection." For the present, however, there would be no communication between the garrison and the city except by mail, the governor added. Letters and dispatches would pass freely to "prevent irregular collision or the unnecessary effusion of blood."

Few who were in or near Charleston questioned the possibility of such bloodshed. Newspaper headlines had already goaded readers with demands that "THE FORT MUST BE OURS!"[2] In New York, the *Herald* trumpeted:

IMPORTANT FOREIGN INTELLIGENCE
Major Anderson Abandons Fort Moultrie and Spikes the Guns
MAJOR ANDERSON DISOBEYS HIS ORDERS[3]

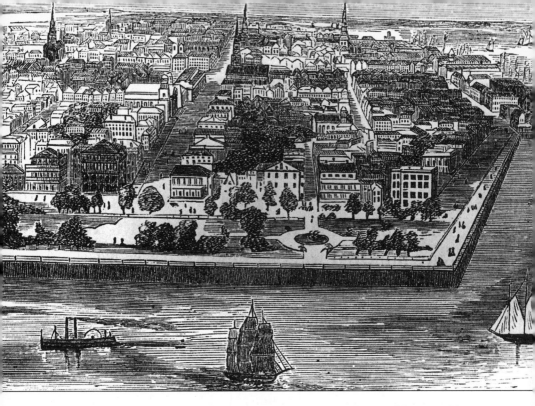

In Charleston, mansions were built very close to the water along the seawall known as "the battery."

As Snyder prepared to return to Sumter, he was permitted to take only his personal baggage. When the next mail boat went to the artificial island, officials removed a shipment of meat from the vessel. At Moultrie, deSaussure allowed the Federals to remove their personal property but claimed everything else, including wood and coal.

In Washington, Winfield Scott send an aide to the Executive Mansion at 3:30 P.M. with a memo informing President Buchanan that Anderson had received "no order, intimation, suggestion, or communication" since he had arrived in Charleston.[4] Scott also withdrew the suggestion that the warship *Brooklyn* be dispatched to Charleston with supplies. A commercial vessel might be less provocative, he believed. It was highly probable, he told the president, that a suitable vessel could be chartered. With Buchanan's approval, Lorenzo Thomas was given the task of finding a ship that could secretly perform the mission of supply and reinforcement.[5]

Anderson received a telegram from the secretary of war demanding to know if the reports of his movement from Moultrie to Sumter were accurate. The beleaguered Anderson replied: "News is correct. I abandoned Fort Moultrie because if attacked my command would have been sacrificed and the garrison would not have surrendered without a fight, and to retain control of the harbor."[6]

Soldiers and civilian laborers worked rapidly to strengthen Fort Sumter's defenses. Special galleries that projected over its walls were built on the parapet so shells and hand grenades could be dropped upon attackers. "Stands of grape and canister carried to the parapet," the surgeon noted. "Barrels of rocks also carried up to the ramparts."

Officers were forbidden to have fires in their bedrooms, so they congregated about a "general fire." Only one fire was permitted in the hospital. The garrison's diet was limited to pork and corned beef, "no milk or liquors."

More telegrams reached Charleston on December 31. Since they warned that a warship would soon be headed to the harbor, cadets at the Citadel accepted the job of erecting a new battery.[7]

In Washington, cabinet members spent hours with the president, who summarized for them the recommendations made by Scott. Having shifted his headquarters from New York to the capital, the general in chief met frequently with Buchanan. Goaded into action, the president proposed to use the heavily armed USS *Brooklyn* to take supplies and soldiers to Sumter.

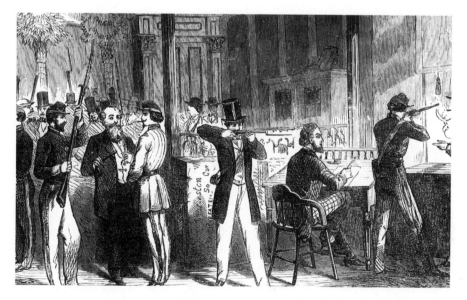

Charleston hotheads began planning to use force if necessary, even before the state seceded.

Scott issued the orders to implement the plan, but he voiced strong objections. The draft of the warship was sixteen feet, he pointed out. Except under ideal conditions, the *Brooklyn* probably could not pass over the Charleston bar. Long before the vessel would have any chance of getting to Fort Sumter, its appearance would be interpreted as a threat.[8]

Hoping to persuade Buchanan to alter the plan, Scott contacted shipping representative A. C. Schultze. One of the Schultze vessels, the merchant ship *Star of the West,* was known to be swift and had a light draft. Since it regularly ran between New York and New Orleans, its appearance was likely to be regarded as routine.

Scott penned an appeal on Sunday, December 30. The weather was bad, his message began, and he was not well enough to go to church, but delay in dealing with matters of the greatest national importance could be disastrous. Begging Buchanan's forgiveness for his zeal, the general in chief requested permission to send the supplies, troops, and weapons to Charleston.[9] The president was also being besieged by commissioners from South Carolina who claimed that they wanted only peace and total control of their state. Finally, Buchanan shed his customary indecision and endorsed Scott's plan without change.

Consequently, on January 2, Thomas was authorized to charter the *Star of the West* to transport two hundred men from New York's Governor's Island to Fort Sumter. The cargo would include ninety days's rations, "ample ammunition, and one hundred extra stand of arms."[10]

Thomas, Scott added, should authorize Anderson to use Sumter's guns if shore batteries should open fire on the vessel. In addition, the sailors and troops aboard the *Star* were required to observe "complete concealment of the presence of the latter when approaching the bay." As a final precaution, Scott dispatched four companies of soldiers aboard the *Brooklyn.* Operating as an escort, the warship would be at hand in case the *Star* "should be shattered or injured."[11]

Thomas was sure the *Star* could make the voyage without arousing suspicion. "No notice will be put in the papers," he stressed, "and persons seeing the ship moving from the dock will suppose she is on her regular trip [to New Orleans]." Two hundred men with three hundred stand of arms and ammunition would be on the wharf "ready to march on board Mr. Schultz's steam-tugs about nightfall."[12] Plans called for these two small vessels to proceed down the bay at low speed. Thomas would "cut off all communication between the island and the

The side-wheel steamer *Star of the West* was central to a futile attempt to resupply Fort Sumter early in 1861.

cities until Tuesday morning," when he expected the *Star* to be "safely moored at Fort Sumter."

WHILE THE EXPEDITION WAS getting under way, the Confederates were converging upon Charleston. On January 5 Lt. C. R. Woods of the U.S. Ninth Infantry was named to command the federal military force, aided by Lts. W. A. Webb and C. W. Thomas. These officers detached two hundred of the "best instructed men at Fort Columbus" to reinforce the garrison at Sumter. Their arrival at the Charleston post would triple its strength.

In his message to Anderson, Thomas said that the *Star* would soon arrive with officers, men, and supplies. Enough beef would be aboard to feed the entire command for three or four days, along with "three months' subsistence for the detachment and six months' desiccated [dried] and fresh vegetables." Anderson was also authorized to use his guns if secessionists fired upon the relief ship. Then came a word of caution coupled with a promise: "You are warned to be upon your guard against all telegrams, as false ones may be attempted to be passed upon you."[13]

In Washington, Scott learned that a battery had been readied at the tip of Morris Island, about one thousand yards from Sumter. Any vessel trying to reach the fort would have to pass under these guns at close range.[14] Reluctantly, he sent new orders to Fort Monroe directing the *Brooklyn* to join the *Star* for its protection.

Capt. John McGowan of the *Star* noted that his vessel had left the wharf on January 5 at 5:00 P.M. After proceeding down the bay, he halted to take on the soldiers, ammunition, and supplies. The carefully coordinated plan appeared to be going as anticipated.

Someone—possibly a member of the ship's crew, a prosecessionist recruit, a clerk in the War Department, or a telegrapher—leaked a detailed account of the expedition and its purpose to the newspapers. New York papers reported the sailing on January 5. Two days later they had the full story, which appeared in Charleston and Savannah the next day, January 8.[15]

When a newspaper account was handed to Anderson, he refused to believe it; he had not yet received word of the mission.[16] Wary of the telegraph service, Thomas had sent his message to Anderson by regular mail, which reached Charleston in three or four days' time and was confiscated. Anderson never received it. Only the Sumter garrison and the men aboard the *Star* were ignorant of the mission already under way. The newspapers gave everyone else the general outline and some details of the plan.[17]

In Washington, the secretary of the interior, Jacob Thompson, submitted his resignation in protest against the expedition. A few hours earlier he had sent to A. N. Kimball of Jackson, Mississippi, a telegram promising, "No troops have been sent to Charleston, nor will be while I am a member of the Cabinet." Other southern officeholders soon learned of the cabinet meeting at which the decision was made to take decisive action. On December 31 Governor Pickens had received an unsigned telegram warning that a warship was en route to Fort Sumter. At about the same time, Floridians were notified that there would be an attempt to strengthen Pensacola's Fort Pickens.[18]

Numerous alerts prompted cadets from the Citadel to work on another battery at a point calculated to command the main channel leading into the harbor. Guard ships were also stationed in the channel to protect the channel the warships would have to use to sweep past Morris Island and approach Sumter. Charleston firemen of the Vigilant Rifles encamped near the south end of Morris Island.[19]

About midnight on January 8, Captain McGowan ordered the lights aboard the *Star* to be extinguished. Moving slowly and cautiously, by 1:30 A.M. he was sure he was close to his destination but was puzzled by the lack of signals from the harbor's lighthouse. Days later he learned that secessionists had smashed its lamp and lenses and had removed the marker buoys from the channel.

Perched on a platform near the bow of the *Star,* the leadsman sounded rapidly until 4:00 A.M. when he saw a light he took to be at Fort Sumter. The vessel turned toward deeper water, found the channel at first light, and moved swiftly to cross the bar while soldiers on the accompanying *Brooklyn* hurried below decks.

Aboard a South Carolina guard ship, Capt. Allen J. Green spotted the intruder two miles out and sent up flares. His signals went up from the deck of the *General Clinch,* named for Anderson's father-in-law. At installations dotted around the harbor, Carolinians knew an invasion of their waters was in progress.

According to a newspaper account, the intruding vessel "rounded the point, took the ship channel inside the bar, and proceeded straight forward until about three-quarters of a mile from the battery."[20] At a masked battery on Morris Island, McGowan saw a flag bearing a white palmetto tree on a red background.

Maj. P. F. Stevens was in charge of forty cadets from the Citadel, the Zouave cadets, and German riflemen. His orders were to fire on any strange vessel attempting to enter the channel. After Stevens sighted a loaded piece, he gave the lanyard to cadet George E. Haynesworth, who was well versed in the use of artillery. At 7:15 A.M.

Charleston's military college, the Citadel, whose cadets turned back the *Star of the West.*

Stevens nodded toward Haynesworth, and the gun roared. Aboard the *Star,* smoke was seen before a 24-pound ball struck the water nearby.[21]

Cpl. H. M. Clarkson was in charge of a 10-inch Columbiad at Fort Moultrie. Designated Gun Number 13, but known to its crew as Edith, the big gun was pressed into action seconds after the first shot had been fired from Morris Island. A third shot by Stevens's cadets crashed through the coal bunker of the *Star,* and a fourth struck close to the leadsman.[22]

William C. Church, a reporter for the *New York Evening Post,* reported that by the time the first shot had passed in front of the bow, McGowan was shouting "Helm out of port!" Church, who had learned that a secret expedition was about to leave the city, had stowed away in the hold of the *Star* until it was too late to send him back ashore. As the first war correspondent of the Civil War, he was the only civilian in the rescue party.[23]

Obedience to McGowan's order caused the rescue vessel to turn to starboard and ride the ebb tide down the channel. About to move beyond the range of the guns that fired a total of seventeen rounds at the *Star,* every officer and man aboard the vessel gave up hope that the weapons at Sumter would silence those of the secessionists.[24]

Some of Anderson's officers urged him to demonstrate his strength as soon as the first shot was fired. Lacking orders to do so, he was unwilling to take a step that might bring on war.

Samuel W. Crawford, a surgeon in the Sumter garrison, later wrote an extensive account of the garrison at Sumter, *The Genesis of the Civil War,* possibly the most detailed record of the occupation, siege, and assault on the fort. In it he noted that Anderson was "excited and uncertain what to do." He refused to use his guns but tried to communicate with the merchant ship. An attempt to use flag signals at the fort failed because the halyards were twisted. Frustrated and isolated from his command, Anderson watched as the *Star* turned swiftly and withdrew.

Some of the officers, among whom Doubleday was most outspoken, never forgave their commander for failing to use Sumter's guns. Even had it been ineffectual, Doubleday argued, firing in the direction of Morris Island "would have encouraged the steamer to keep on its course." Some of Sumter's guns bore on Fort Moultrie, and since that installation was within easy range, Doubleday was sure he could have hit it at once.[25]

McGowan's account justified his hasty flight on grounds that the depth of the water had dropped three feet under a strong ebb tide.

"We proceeded with caution," he reported, noting that they crossed the bar safely at about 8:50 A.M. A steamer from Charleston followed in the wake of the *Star* for three hours, then fell back. After "a boisterous passage," the vessel docked at New York early on the morning of January 12.[26]

The editors of the *Charleston Mercury* exulted that a blow had been struck at the U.S. government. That blow, said the newspaper, "wiped out half a century of scorn and outrage."

Measured by any standard, the belated relief effort was a miserable failure. No one involved in the "secret" expedition could justify the turn of events. Anderson and his men were now effectively on their own, with plenty of artillery and an ample supply of powder, but few powder bags and less food.[27]

Before the *Star of the West* had returned to her starting point, Carolina officials had begun contemplating more drastic action. The South Carolina General Assembly quickly passed a measure critical of Buchanan for his deceptive maneuver.

Anderson submitted a formal complaint to Governor Pickens concerning the firing of South Carolina batteries upon "an unarmed vessel bearing the flag of my Government." Pickens responded that his state would not tolerate "coercion by the armed force of the Government."[28]

Gov. Francis W. Pickens of South Carolina, a former U.S. diplomat.

LIBRARY OF CONGRESS

Anderson then asked that the issue be referred to Washington and that Lt. Theodore Talbot be permitted to serve as his courier. On January 12 Pickens agreed to this proposal and informed Anderson that his own messenger, South Carolina Attorney General I. W. Hayne, would go to the capital at the same time.[29]

Pickens offered to send meat, vegetables, and mail to the fort daily. Anderson indignantly refused this overture but asked that the women "attached to his command" be conveyed to New York along with their children. On January 23 he received permission to get them out of harm's way, but bad weather delayed their departure until February 3.[30]

ALL AROUND CHARLESTON HARBOR—at Fort Sumter and at the installations now under secessionist control—work on building up defenses proceeded rapidly. At Sumter, Foster continued to direct a civilian crew of forty-three men to bring additional guns into serviceable positions. Several of these had to be hoisted into position by means of what the military engineer called gins.

The defensive strength of the fort was boosted by preparation of numerous hand grenades and "explosive shells" (land mines). Old buildings and spare gun carriages were scrapped for wood to be used in essential fires. From his vantage point, Foster saw that by January 14 at least seven hundred workers were busy at Fort Moultrie. Studying the batteries manned by secessionists at eight points, he noted their growing strength. By January 21 he determined that they were manned by two thousand or more men.

In Washington, Joseph Holt filed Anderson's report stating that he "naturally" did nothing to aid the *Star of the West* since he did not know what ship it was nor its mission. A few days later, Sumter's commander learned that there were no new plans for reinforcements.

President Buchanan's use of the *Star* constituted a defensive action only, explained the new secretary of war. "To Congress, and to Congress alone, belongs the power to make war," he insisted. Neither he nor any other federal official anticipated that the incoming president would soon bypass this issue by "seeking to suppress an insurrection" rather than by waging a congressionally sanctioned war.

Anderson's courier, Lieutenant Talbot, returned from his Washington mission with an ambiguous message. The Buchanan administration had full confidence in Anderson, he reported. As a result, he was instructed to use his own judgment.

An inventory of the fort's food supply was made on January 27, and Anderson notified the War Department that he then had on hand "38 barrels pork, 37 barrels flour, 13 barrels hard bread, 2 barrels beans, 1 barrel coffee, ½ barrel sugar, 3 barrels vinegar, 10 pounds candles, 40 pounds soap, and ¾ barrel salt."

Some of Sumter's guns were test fired on February 5, the day on which Carolina troops used T-rails to finish an ironclad defense at Cummins Point. English newspapers, received along with other mail, informed Anderson that three rifled cannon were being shipped from the island kingdom to Charleston.

Anderson glumly realized that these weapons would make Fort Sumter much less secure than he had previously considered. Soon, however, he breathed a trifle easier when Foster reported that forty land mines had been placed around the entrance to the fort. Almost simultaneously, Anderson learned that Secretary of War Holt had promised that no aggressive measures would be initiated in Washington.[31]

Soon afterward, members of Sumter's garrison optimistically noted a lull in military activity on the mainland and on the nearby islands. This change, however, was a sign that their situation was likely to become worse.

It was already known that one of the finest young artillery officers of the U.S. Army, Pierre Gustave Toutant Beauregard of Saint Bernard Parish, Louisiana, had decided to resign his commission and go with his native state. Rumor had it that he might soon be headed for Charleston. Beauregard graduated second in the forty-five-member West Point class of 1838. During the Mexican War he had become acquainted with Gen. Winfield Scott while serving as an engineer on his staff.

Two weeks before the *Star of the West* sailed, the handsome brevet major had been made superintendent of the U.S. Military Academy. His was the shortest tenure on record—just five days—because colleagues confided to Washington that he expressed "strong southern sympathies."[32]

Anderson and his officers knew Beauregard as "the Little Napoleon," a nickname that grew out of his admiration for Napoleon's skill with artillery. To the men cooped up inside Fort Sumter, it was reasonable to believe that the Creole would be given a responsible post in Charleston.

Should that be the case, Abner Doubleday reasoned, Anderson was likely to be confronted by his brilliant former student. That would lead to radical change in the confrontation at Charleston. Until now it was simply one of many sites at which forces of seceded states challenged the authority and might of the United States. Should Beauregard arrive at the port city as a Confederate officer, the Little Napoleon might be placed in command of the recently enhanced batteries. If this happened, the war of words between the Republic of South Carolina and the United States might escalate into something that neither side wished to initiate.

IN SPRINGFIELD, ILLINOIS, President-elect Abraham Lincoln was drafting a short speech to use at whistle stops along the way to his inauguration. He kept abreast of news from the South. He regarded no issue as insoluble, and once he had the reins of government firmly in hand, he expected to end the apparent crisis at Sumter quickly.

President-elect Lincoln, still beardless, framed a course of action designed to quickly end what he called "an insurrection."

ILLUSTRATED LONDON NEWS

4

A New Commander in Chief

FEBRUARY 11, 1861, DAWNED GRAY and windy at Fort Sumter. Watching the activity at Cummings Point, Capt. John G. Foster noted that "appearances indicated that preparations were making for immediate action in case the news from Washington exhibited a coercive policy on the part of the [incoming] administration."

In Springfield, Illinois, townsfolk gathered at the depot for the 7:30 A.M. start of Lincoln's journey to Washington. Mrs. Lincoln remained at home. After a short emotional speech, the president-elect boarded a special train whose route would give him maximum exposure to the citizens eager to know his views on the burning issues of the day.[1]

When Lincoln's special train made its first stop at Indianapolis, Gov. Oliver P. Morton tried to assess the mood of the crowd. "Two thousand Democrats here," he mused. "If hollering meant anything, you'd think them all good Republicans." Packed shoulder-to-shoulder, eager Hoosiers shouted hurrahs as red, white, and blue bunting snapped in the wind.

Looking even taller than his six feet four inches by comparison with Morton, Lincoln stepped to the platform of his railroad car. His stovepipe hat seemed almost to proclaim, "Brand new!" A black necktie drooped below a long and swarthy neck. The sleeves of his black dress coat were two inches short, and his too-short black trousers exposed his elongated feet. A new growth of beard made it hard to distinguish his jaw line.

Springfield, Illinois, residence of attorney Lincoln and his Kentucky-born wife.

Thousands who had waited in bitter cold would be among the first to learn what course the new pilot of the ship of state intended to take. Nodding to Morton, Lincoln thanked the governor "and fellow citizens of the State of Indiana" for their magnificent reception.

Moving to forestall additional criticism of his long-maintained silence, he urged, "It is your business to rise up and preserve the Union. I appeal to you constantly to bear in mind that you, and not with politicians, not with Presidents, not with office-seekers, but with you is the question, 'Shall the Union and shall the liberties of this country be preserved to the latest generations?'"[2]

Lincoln's shrill voice and his gawky stance made him seem ill at ease, yet folk listened when he opened his mouth. He put them under his spell with a few almost-solemn words that somehow conveyed joyous assurance. Secession was not mentioned. It was an effective speech, Morton concluded, not so much because of what was said but in how it was said. After listening to him, one would be inclined to believe the new president was headed to a victory celebration instead of the funeral of the nation, the governor noted.

It had been two months since South Carolina had seceded, and Lincoln had not uttered a word about the tempest brewing in Charleston. For all Lincoln had said, it seemed as if the country needed nothing but a little Fourth-of-July oratory and a parade before breaking out the fried chicken and picnicking.

Pittsburgh, Cleveland, Buffalo, Albany, New York City, Philadelphia, Harrisburg[3]—at every point where Lincoln gave a brief address, the message was the same. "There is no crisis," he assured the listeners repeatedly. Even after learning that Jefferson Davis had been inaugurated as president of the Confederate States of America, the president-elect of the United States did not change his theme.[4]

Many who heard Lincoln as he journeyed to his inauguration failed to realize that he was deeply secretive, prone to say nothing until he was ready to announce a plan of action. A seasoned veteran of fierce courthouse battles, he was adept at hitting an opponent early and hard so that a comeback was difficult. He had made up his mind to employ this tactic with respect to secessionists, but he had no intention of revealing his strategy until he took the oath of office.

Friends and associates who traveled with him attributed his placid and unruffled manner to his frequently expressed confidence in the Unionists of the Cotton Belt. They were there—plenty of them—but

Mary Todd Lincoln tried on her inaugural gown but did not accompany her husband on his trip to Washington.

BRADY STUDIO, LIBRARY OF CONGRESS

James Buchanan rode with Lincoln to the Capitol for the inaugural ceremonies.

having little first-hand knowledge of the South, Lincoln greatly overestimated their power to reverse the positions taken by their states.

In Charleston, as early as the previous November, Anderson had characterized the campaign in which he involuntarily played a key role as being "politico-military" in nature. Few Americans sensed that the political aspect of the complex struggle would soon become dominant.

On Wednesday, February 13, 1861, it was learned that Arkansas state troops had seized the U.S. ordnance store in their state. Addressing lawmakers in Ohio, Lincoln said that he had been criticized for his silence on the issue. He did so, he confided, to gain "a view of the whole field" before voicing his opinions. "It is a good thing that there is no more than anxiety, for there is nothing going wrong," he assured them.[5]

At the urging of detective Allan Pinkerton, unusual precautions were taken to guard the president-elect for his March 4 inauguration. Winfield Scott, aided by marshal Charles P. Stone of the District of Columbia, stationed sharpshooters on rooftops. U.S. Army cavalrymen guarded side-street crossings of Pennsylvania Avenue. Other mounted men moved in double files on both sides of the presidential carriage. The bodies and legs of horses would make it difficult for anyone at ground level to get an easy shot at the incoming chief executive.

Riflemen were stationed at windows in the wings of the Capitol that flanked the inaugural stand. Scott took charge of a battery of flying artillery and led this unit to a slope from which it would be easy to race to the Capitol. At the same point, a second battery was headed by Maj. Gen. John E. Wool, and a third unit was held in reserve at the Treasury Building.

Although the sun was shining, the day was raw and decidedly colder than at Charleston. Shortly after noon, B. B. French led one hundred marshals into position, their horses having blue, orange, and pink trappings. Five hundred prominent Republicans followed them on foot, and behind them thirty-four beautiful girls—symbolizing the thirty-four states—rode in triumphal carriages.[6]

Reaching the unfinished Capitol, the party followed a path along a boarded fence guarded by U.S. Marines. When a door was opened, Lincoln and his attendants moved to a platform beneath which fifty riflemen crouched.

Introduced by Sen. Edward D. Baker of Oregon, the westerner soon to become the sixteenth president of the United States spoke in

Lincoln is quoted as having believed that completion of the Capitol would symbolize the achievement of his primary goal as president—restoration of the Union.

his high-pitched, nasal voice. His sentiments, he emphasized, applied to every citizen of every state. He intended to be president of all the people, not simply those who had supported his campaign.

Lincoln noted that in some southern states there seemed to be apprehension that their peace and security would be in danger under a Republican administration. Such views were without foundation, he insisted. Stressing this position, he said, "I have no purpose, directly or indirectly, to interfere with the institution of slavery in the States where it exists." After a pause he denounced "invasion by armed force of the soil of any State or Territory, no matter under what pretext."[7]

Emphasizing his support of the Fugitive Slave Law, he spoke at length about the importance of the Constitution and the Union, which he characterized as unbroken. Denouncing secession as "the essence of anarchy," Lincoln came to what many considered the heart of his message.

After saying that laws of the Union should be "faithfully executed in all the States," he issued a promise and a warning: "The power confided to me, will be used to hold occupy, and possess the property and places belonging to the government, and to collect the duties and imposts."[8]

He knew that the Revenue Service had only one steam-powered vessel and eighteen smaller wind-powered schooners. Yet the man whose burning passion was the preservation of the Union added a brief but potent clause to his statement of intention: *All the power at his disposal would be used to collect the duties on imports.*[9]

Southerners who read his words knew exactly what he meant. Perhaps secessionists could hold every fort, camp, barracks, arsenal, mint, customs house, and revenue schooner seized during five frantic months. Even if that should be the case, a new fleet of revenue vessels would soon plow through southern waters.

In almost parenthetical fashion, Lincoln commented that if Supreme Court decisions should take instant and irrevocable effect, "the people will have ceased to be their own rulers." Physical separation of states obviously being impossible, his peroration urged: "In your hands, my dissatisfied fellow countrymen, is the momentous issue of civil war. The government will not assail you. You can have no conflict, without being yourselves the aggressors. You have no oath registered in Heaven to destroy the government, while I shall have the most solemn one to 'preserve, protect and defend' it."[10]

In every state and territory the inaugural address evoked emotional responses. Especially in New England, abolitionists raged at lending the influence of the presidency to the enforcement of the Fugitive Slave Law. Throughout the Cotton Belt, the president's emphasis upon taking possession of government property and collecting the tariff was seen as a clear threat of violence to come.

In Charleston, on March 5, Col. Ellison Capers saw Capt. James Conner with a newspaper. "War or no war?" Capers inquired. "War to the knife!" responded his subordinate who was going to Sullivan's Island from Secessionville on James Island.[11]

Also at Charleston, Confederates gave a pass to a man from Nashville to briefly visit Fort Sumter. As the first person inside the fortress who knew something about Lincoln's inaugural message, he was eagerly questioned. Samuel Crawford, an officer of the garrison, summed up the visitor's views as concluding that the new president planned upon "war and coercion."

On the following day Anderson's Dispatch Number 64 noted that Beauregard had taken command on the mainland. When the message was received seventy-two hours later in Washington, the adjutant general, Samuel Cooper, gave lengthy consideration to the major's last sentence: "God grant that our country may be saved from the horrors of a fratricidal war!"[12]

The first thing handed to Lincoln as he entered the Executive Mansion following his inauguration was a letter from Anderson. Provisions were likely to be exhausted before an expedition could be sent to relieve him and his men, he wrote. He estimated that twenty thousand men would be needed to reinforce and hold the fortress.[13] At most, the new president had six weeks' time to chart a course of action concerning Sumter. His anxiety triggered a wave of headaches that sent him to bed several times.[14]

Four days after receiving Anderson's letter, having declined Scott's suggestion that Sumter be evacuated, Lincoln sent his general in chief a letter with questions about supplying and reinforcing Fort Sumter. Simultaneously, a warning went to Charleston from the provisional Confederate capital in Montgomery, Alabama: "Do not permit any attack on Sumter without authority of the Confederates States. This is all important. Inaugural means war. There is strong ground for belief that reenforcements will be speedily sent. Be vigilant."[15]

Another message went from the federal capital to the Confederate secretary of war, L. Pope Walker. Concerning the inaugural address, Virginian Lucius Q. Washington informed Walker, "We [southern gentlemen] agreed that it was Lincoln's purpose at once to attempt the collection of the revenue, to re-enforce and hold Fort Sumter and Pickens, and to retake the other places. He is a man of will and firmness."[16]

On March 6, Jefferson Davis called for one hundred thousand volunteers who would serve for twelve months. As a result, within weeks Confederate forces outnumbered the U.S. Army by a ratio of about three to one.[17]

With General Scott in attendance at a March 15 cabinet meeting, Lincoln posed a question: "Assuming it to be possible to now provision Fort-Sumpter, under all the circumstances, is it wise to attempt it?" He asked for their opinions in writing.[18]

By midnight the president held three sets of replies. Four cabinet members counseled against resupplying Sumter, one was in favor of a relief expedition, and two were ambiguous. For his part, Scott estimated that he would need a fleet of warships and transports capable of carrying five thousand army regulars and twenty thousand volunteers, who would need six to eight months' training.[19]

Lincoln weighed these options for almost three days, drawing up a memorandum on March 18. He listed eight "considerations in favor of withdrawing the Troops from Fort Sumpter." These were followed by two objections to this course of action: Withdrawal would demoralize the Republican Party and would cause the secessionists to claim victory. Thus the president drafted an order establishing a bureau to oversee militia units while in the service of the United States.[20]

Members of the U.S. Senate soon passed a resolution asking Lincoln to provide copies of Anderson's messages. Not yet two weeks into his four-year term, the president refused to do so. Anderson's dispatches would not be made available to the lawmakers, he told them on March 26, because in his opinion such a course of action "would be inexpedient."[21]

By this time most informed persons in the capital knew who would make the key decisions in the new administration. Instead of being a figurehead for the secretary of state, William H. Seward, who had had presidential aspirations of his own, Lincoln was to be chief executive in fact as well as in name. It was also already clear that his role as commander in chief would not be nominal. Military and political decisions would come from him rather than his advisers.

A state dinner for cabinet members and other dignitaries was held on March 28. During the evening Lincoln confided to some of the guests that Scott favored evacuating both Forts Sumter and Pickens, but true to his courthouse practices, he did not divulge his own plans.[22]

Before the following day ended, the president sent duplicate orders to his secretaries of war and the navy. "I desire," he wrote, "that an expedition, to move by sea, be got ready to sail [to Charleston] as early as the 6th. of April next."[23] Regardless of what his cabinet members might prefer to do, Lincoln was almost ready for a confrontation with the secessionists.

His readiness to challenge the South stemmed in part from a personal belief that is sometimes overlooked. Since early manhood, he had believed in what he termed "a doctrine of necessity," by which he meant that people are motivated to act as a result of "some power, over which the mind itself has no control."[24]

This attitude toward life, often called fatalism, was taken very seriously by the sixteenth president. "I have all my life been a fatalist," he admitted, adding, "What is to be will be."[25] Thus it was logical for him to have told some Indianians, "I am but an accidental, temporary instrument."[26] On another occasion he summarized his philosophy of life: "I claim not to have controlled events, but confess plainly that events have controlled me."[27] As a guiding principle for a presidential administration, it is hard to imagine a more comfortable viewpoint. When a man believes that he is not responsible for what he does, he can face difficult situations with equanimity.

Lincoln did just that in relation to the Fort Sumter issue. As he weighed his options, he seems to have thought, *Whatever is destined to occur will take place, and I will be an interested spectator but will not be responsible for the consequences.*

5

He Says We Don't Exist

SOUTHERN LEADERS HAD LAUNCHED a move toward mediation and compromise with Washington while Fort Sumter was unfinished and nearly empty. After the November 1860 election, a delegation of congressmen had conferred with President Buchanan and stressed that Charleston was clearly the focal point of contention.

While Maj. Robert Anderson was begging for help at Fort Moultrie,[1] Buchanan had demanded to know what he could expect from the southern lawmakers if he promised not to reinforce Anderson. The congressmen reputedly had pledged their honor that South Carolina would make no attack on the federal installations so long as negotiations progressed for the eventual transfer of the forts. The president accepted these terms, expecting tensions to be eased soon.

Southerners were less optimistic, however, despite knowing that in a cabinet meeting Buchanan had said he could not order reinforcements to Charleston. Therefore, thirty congressmen from the South endorsed a brief document addressed "To Our Constituents," declaring: "The argument is exhausted. All hope of relief in the Union . . . is exhausted. In our judgment the Republicans are resolute in the purpose to grant nothing that will or ought to satisfy the South." As they saw it, the only hope for the Cotton Belt was the organization of "a Southern confederacy" made up of slave-holding states that had seceded from "hostile States."[2]

Six days later, on December 20, a South Carolina convention passed an ordinance of secession.[3] Three commissioners were named to serve as diplomatic representatives to Washington, and on December 22 a telegram informed the president that R. W. Barnwell, J. H. Adams, and James L. Orr were en route to the capital. They were to "present the Ordinance of Secession to the President," negotiate the purchase of federal installations at Charleston, and seek an apportionment of the public debt in order to foster "the continuance of peace and amity" between the newly independent commonwealth and the federal government.[4]

The South Carolina representatives had planned to reach Washington on Christmas Day, but their train was delayed, and they arrived on Wednesday, December 26. They immediately sent word of their arrival to President Buchanan through W. H. Trescot; the president then consulted with the secretary of state, Jeremiah S. Black, who had assumed his duties nine days earlier. Buchanan notified the commissioners that he would see them at 1:00 P.M. on Thursday, December 27.[5] Matters were proceeding rapidly and smoothly, and the participants in the conference anticipated no major difficulties.

Matters were complicated, however, when word arrived that Anderson had moved his garrison from Fort Moultrie to Fort Sumter. The surprise move was the talk of the capital the next day, which included news that the troops had spiked the guns at Moultrie, destroyed gun carriages, and cut down the flagstaff. Some officials were delighted, but Secretary of War John B. Floyd was thunderstruck. He argued that Anderson had not only acted without orders, but he had occupied Fort Sumter "in the face of orders." According to Floyd, he had been instructed "in case he had to abandon his position to dismantle Fort Sumter, not Fort Moultrie." Only Anderson's immediate withdrawal, he told the president "can prevent bloodshed and civil war."[6]

Sen. Jefferson Davis of Mississippi hurried to the Executive Mansion. There he found the chief executive leaning against a mantelpiece, crushing a cigar in the palm of one hand so that the fragments could be chewed. Davis urged forthright action to defuse the situation in Charleston. Failure to act promptly, he insisted, would result in bloodshed and dishonor on all sides, as South Carolinians would immediately respond to Anderson's move by taking over every other federal installation in Charleston. In Davis's opinion, an attack upon Fort Sumter was likely within a few days unless Anderson and his men were ordered to return to Moultrie.[7]

A hesitant and vacillating man, the president had gone on record as opposing secession while considering himself unable to do anything

Sen. Jefferson Davis of Mississippi, who didn't then dream of becoming president of the Confederate States.

to prevent it. In this crisis he set aside Davis's request for "a return to normalcy" in the forts at Charleston by saying that he must consult his cabinet before sending any order. Then he notified the South Carolina commissioners that their conference would have to be postponed.

The commissioners were received by the president on Friday, December 28, but Buchanan greeted them as private citizens only. Any appeal they might present would have to be brought before Congress, he stipulated. He would, however, serve as an intermediary and transmit to that body any proposals they might care to offer.[8]

Before such an appeal to Congress could be arranged, however, Governor Pickens set in motion the military forces of the Republic of South Carolina. In a matter of hours they seized Fort Moultrie, Castle Pinckney, the arsenal, the post office, and the customs house. Consequently, Buchanan notified the commissioners that he would not order Anderson to withdraw from Sumter. Angry and disappointed, the South Carolina emissaries returned to the Palmetto "Republic."

Meanwhile, Anderson received a stern rebuke from the secretary of war for having acted without authorization. He fired a defiant reply to Floyd and sent an urgent letter to Governor Pickens. "Do all you can to prevent an appeal to arms," he requested, then added, "Why not exhaust diplomacy, as in other matters?"

Soon an agreement was reached. Under its terms, Pickens would send a commissioner to Washington to request the evacuation of Fort Sumter. At the same time, Anderson would send one of his men to give a firsthand report on the condition of the installation.

Isaac W. Hayne, attorney general of South Carolina, was selected as Pickens's agent. He was accompanied by Robert Gourdin, who would serve as his assistant. They were joined by Lt. Norman Hall, Anderson's representative.[9] The three men found the capital in turmoil over major changes in the Buchanan cabinet, precipitated by the Charleston crisis. In addition to having a new secretary of state, the Departments of War, Treasury, and Interior also saw sudden changes.

Jeremiah Black, whose predecessor had resigned over Buchanan's refusal to reinforce Fort Sumter, took a hard line toward the secessionists. He scolded the president for seeming "to acknowledge the right of South Carolina to be represented near this Government by diplomatic officers."[10] Then he insisted that Buchanan refuse to see Hayne. Taking the rebuff in stride, Hayne drafted a proposal for the purchase of Fort Sumter and other federal sites "at a sale price to be determined."

Hoping to avoid hostilities during his remaining forty-seven days in office, Buchanan asked his new secretary of war, Joseph Holt, to

Montgomery, Alabama, was the site of the inaugural ceremonies by which Davis became chief executive of the Rebel states.

Gov. John Forsyth of Alabama was one of three Confederate commissioners sent to Washington.

respond to the South Carolina overture. On January 22 Holt notified Hayne that he could not promise that reinforcements would not be sent to Fort Sumter. The commissioner responded that "continued occupation of Sumter by a foreign garrison could not be tolerated."

Holt's reaction on February 6 greatly limited any hope for a peaceful resolution of the issue. "The President," he wrote, "can no more sell and transfer Fort Sumter to South Carolina than he can sell and convey the Capitol of the United States to Maryland." Hayne returned crestfallen to South Carolina.

THE FORMAL ORGANIZATION of the Confederate States of America led to a third attempt at a peaceful resolution of the Sumter crisis and related issues. Insisting that he must have three of the best men in the South, Jefferson Davis, who had been inaugurated president of the Confederacy on February 22, sent his own commissioners to Washington: Martin J. Crawford of Georgia, John Forsyth of Alabama, and A. B. Roman of Louisiana. They were to meet with the new president, Abraham Lincoln, who was inaugurated on March 4.[11]

Skilled in the art of compromise, the Confederates were warned that Lincoln was not interested. When approached on the subject soon after his election, he had refused to support a Virginia plan for a national conference.

Lincoln's passion was the preservation of the Union, no matter what that required, a senator told Commissioner Crawford. It would be useless to seek a meeting with the new president since he insisted that secession had not taken place. Clearly he would not meet with the commissioners or make any other move that could be construed as recognition of the Confederate States of America.

Having studied Lincoln's inaugural address, the Confederate commissioners decided to work through the new secretary of state, William H. Seward. To their chagrin, although he was publicly committed to a policy of peace, Seward refused to see them. He hinted, however, that he was willing to deal with them through an intermediary.[12]

A telegram to Montgomery dispatched on March 9 conveyed word that "the impression prevails in Administration circles that Fort Sumter will be evacuated within ten days." A few hours later the Sunday issue of the *New York Herald* confirmed that judgment.[13]

On Monday the commissioners enlisted the aid of Virginia Sen. Robert M. Hunter, who agreed to ask Seward if he would consent to "an informal interview." Much to Hunter's surprise, the man widely regarded as the decision maker of the new administration said that he would have to consult with the president. At 11:00 A.M. on Tuesday, Hunter brought them Seward's written refusal to discuss any topic. Angry at facing closed doors, the Confederate representatives sent a formal note to the State Department, asking for an early appointment. Seward responded that he could take no action that would seem to recognize the "Confederate States" as an independent power.[14]

Commissioner Forsyth then turned to John A. Campbell, an associate justice of the U.S. Supreme Court. Although appointed from Alabama, Campbell had gone on record as being opposed to secession. Surely he could persuade Seward to listen to their offers. Campbell consulted Associate Justice Samuel Nelson of New York, who volunteered to warn the secretary of state that the use of force in retaking the forts would constitute "a very serious violation of the Constitution."

Seward talked at length with Justice Campbell. Although still refusing to meet with the Confederate commissioners, he made it clear that he expected Fort Sumter to be evacuated.[15] Yet on April 1 the commissioners learned that there might be another attempt to supply Sumter with provisions, but there was no hint of reinforcements.

In the North a majority of the population strongly favored action to dispel the threat of civil war. Should the fighting go on for twenty years, a Connecticut journal suggested, "The same questions will come up for settlement that we split on." In Cincinnati editors saw the issue simply: "We believe that the right of any member of this Confederacy [the United States] to dissolve its relations with others and assume an independent position is *absolute.*"[16]

Justice Campbell was the only intermediary to transmit an official message from the State Department to the Confederate commissioners. On April 8 he received and forwarded a lengthy memorandum that was accompanied by a copy of Lincoln's inaugural address.[17] "A reference to the address," wrote Seward, would reveal that the secretary of state "is prevented altogether from admitting or assuming that the States referred to by commissioners have, in law or in fact, withdrawn from the Federal Union." Under those circumstances, he continued, he was unable to appoint a day on which he could talk with them and was not at liberty to engage in communication of any sort.

Seward's lengthy document was dated March 15, prompting Campbell to demand an explanation why it had been held for twenty-seven days before being transmitted. Not until long afterward did he learn that Lincoln had polled his cabinet concerning possible relief of Fort Sumter on March 15 only to find his scheme unconditionally supported by no one except the postmaster general. Southerners later decided that "the object of the Federal government in delaying its final answer to the Southern Commissioners was to gain time for the reinforcement of Sumter."[18]

The Confederate commissioners drafted a joint report in which they declared: "When all anxious efforts for peace had been exhausted, it became clear that Mr. Lincoln had determined to appeal to the sword to reduce the people of the Confederate States to the will of the section or party whose President he is."[19]

ON APRIL 4 THE commissioners warned the authorities in Montgomery that they should "strengthen defenses at the mouth of the Mississippi." Having heard rumors that ships were being outfitted in New York, on April 5 they reported, "Statements about sending the armament to S. Domingo may be a ruse."

By April 6 the three were sufficiently sure of what was about to take place to send a telegram warning that Forts Pickens and Sumter were likely to receive reinforcements. So many unverified tales circulated in the capital that on April 7 they reported: "It may be Sumter and the Mississippi; it is almost certainly Pickens and the Texas frontier."

Twenty-four hours later, in Charleston, a carefully crafted challenge was received. Confederates in the port city construed it to mean that they had to move immediately against Fort Sumter or risk the loss of everything for which they had struggled. Ignorant of events in Charleston, on April 9 the Confederate commissioners informed Montgomery, "The public press has announced that the main object of the expedition is the relief of Sumter."

On April 11 the trio of dejected Confederates boarded a southbound train. By then they realized that events in Charleston were out of hand, but they did not know the crisis would climax within the next few hours.

Forsyth hurried to Jefferson Davis's office as soon as he reached Montgomery, remaining with the chief executive of the Confederacy for only a few minutes. "There is little that I can add to letters and telegrams previously dispatched," he said. "We never had a chance to make Lincoln an offer of any kind; you can't negotiate with a man who says you don't exist."

Having erected a barrier that seekers of compromise could not breach, Lincoln planned to act quickly and decisively. Whatever he might do, he must take into account the Western world and not simply the thirty-four American states. In England and Europe strong support of the secession movement was already being voiced. Whatever the new American president did, he had to act carefully to avoid the stigma of being perceived as the aggressor.

6

Keep Your Slaves
and Come Back

SLAVERY WAS THE ROOT cause of the war despite the fact that other issues were also important. States' rights and the tariff were sources of acrimonious debate, but they were much less significant issues than slavery. Anyone who doubts this assertion has only to spend a short time with the writings of rabid secessionists. Less passionate in tone but equally revealing, scores of newspaper editorials place paramount emphasis upon the right of the South to own and use slaves.[1]

At least from early manhood, Abraham Lincoln of Illinois abhorred slavery as an institution, and he was adamantly opposed to the westward extension of the institution. Nevertheless, he was not an abolitionist. If he were to be measured by the standards of the late twentieth century, he would be labeled a racist. Lincoln swore to uphold the Constitution, and that document said nothing about abolition. Hence it was entirely consistent for him to write that fugitive slave statutes "ought to be enforced by a law of Congress."[2]

His views concerning the superiority of whites surface frequently in his well-known election debates with Stephen A. Douglas. Although these references are brief, they are numerous and specific. To grasp the significance of his comments, it is necessary to scan scores of pages; references to a few words or sentences are not adequate.[3]

To Lincoln, the supreme document of American freedom was not the Constitution but the Declaration of Independence. Nowhere else did he refer to it more than in the Gettysburg Address, in which he called for "a new birth of freedom."[4]

Since Lincoln was far more mystical in outlook than is generally recognized, this aspect of his thought must be taken seriously. Part of his famous House Divided speech of 1858 is usually regarded as a thinly veiled threat to the slave-holding South: "A house divided against itself cannot stand. I believe this government cannot endure, permanently half *slave* and half *free*. I do not expect the Union to be *dissolved*—I do not expect the house to *fall*—but I do expect it will cease to be divided."[5] These lines are usually interpreted as "an electrifying challenge to conflict" that "led eventually to the war for the Union,"[6] despite the fact that they are nothing of the sort.

Lincoln believed that the Founding Fathers of the republic failed to mention slavery in the Constitution for a specific reason. He believed that George Washington and his colleagues were confident that slavery would die a natural death; hence they deliberately avoided any reference to it in this document. By engaging in what Lincoln called the "readoption of the Declaration of Independence," his fellow countrymen could wage "the Second American Revolution." When this was done, slavery would vanish.[7]

Lincoln's mystical view of the Declaration of Independence and the Constitution was blended with practical considerations concerning slavery. He believed that the land could be rid of slavery through a three-step process: (1) gradual emancipation with (2) compensation to slave owners and (3) overseas colonization of the freed slaves.

The literature concerning colonization in Liberia and central America is extensive,[8] yet few aspects of Lincoln's thought have been so widely ignored. He persuaded few prominent free blacks, if any. Among his cabinet members, Salmon P. Chase and William H. Seward were openly opposed to colonization. *Harper's Weekly* and the *New York Tribune* blasted the proposal. Some opponents even jeered that freed slaves should be sent to Linconia.[9]

Conversely, Francis P. Blair Jr. of Missouri, Sen. S. C. Pomeroy of Kansas, and a handful of other national leaders became enthusiastic proponents of the president's scheme. The emphasis upon colonization in Lincoln's 1861 annual message to Congress helped persuade lawmakers to make funds available for the project. Although at least seven hundred thousand dollars was appropriated, little of this money was spent.[10]

Efforts were being made to perfect plans for colonization until a few days before the final version of the Emancipation Proclamation was issued in 1863. As a result, some who were scornful of the president's

ILLUSTRATED LONDON NEWS

Speaking in Peoria, Illinois, Lincoln said that his first impulse would be to send all freed slaves to the tiny republic of Liberia.

policies jeered his attitude toward secessionists. It could be summed up in a single sentence, they contended: You can keep your slaves, but you must come back into the Union.

Few if any of his most vocal critics accused the president of failing to seek restoration of the Union. This "last best hope of earth" must not—could not—remain divided, he said,[11] despite the fact that many in the divided nation did not share his dedication to that goal.

Jefferson Davis and Alexander H. Stephens were among the most vocal southern proponents of the argument that secession was a constitutional right. When New Jersey and New York ratified the Constitution in 1787 and 1788, respectively, both states "expressly reserved the right of secession." Although this conclusion can be debated, in New York it was taken seriously during the early decades of the republic. Even Daniel Webster espoused this doctrine during his speeches against the War of 1812.[12] In New York City, Mayor Fernando Wood even urged secession from the state.[13] The New York proposals, however, were not taken seriously and had little impact.

Artist Francis B. Carpenter depicted the first reading of the Emancipation Proclamation to Lincoln's cabinet by the president.

The sectional friction between the North and the South was an entirely different matter by 1860. Proponents of conciliation insisted that any move to coerce a state by military means would be an act of war "tantamount to a dissolution of the Union." Even Jefferson Davis, when he served in the Senate, advocated concessions from the North to forestall secession in the South.[14] Horace Greeley and other respected northern leaders called for "a National Convention to meet at the earliest possible day" to work out a compromise. Henry Villard of the *New York Herald* pointed out that the president-elect was not favorably inclined toward the national peace conference urged by Virginia.[15]

Those who backed the idea of peaceful separation made a great deal of noise. William Lloyd Garrison expressed the hope that "the people of the North, without distinction of party, could see that a time has come for separation from the South." Addressing a mass meeting in Boston, orator Edward Everett thundered, "To hold states in the Union by force is preposterous."

Caleb Cushing of Boston considered it "the duty of the southern states to separate from the northern states." Roger B. Taney, chief justice of the U.S. Supreme Court, labeled peaceful separation as infinitely

better than "union under a military government & a reign of terror."
Sen. Joseph Lane of Oregon delivered an address in which he stressed
the right of secession.[16]

Gen. Winfield Scott considered the division of the United States
into four confederacies "a smaller evil" than a brutal war. Jurist Salmon
P. Chase said that he believed if secession were limited to seven states,
they would soon ask for readmission to the Union. Industrialist Cyrus
H. McCormick of Chicago sponsored a mass meeting whose members
voted for peaceful separation. A Detroit editor thundered, "We must
conquer them, or we must recognize their independence." Many in
New York City were convinced that "no outward pressure of the bayonet" could save the Union. A Wisconsin newspaper pointed out that
the framers of the Constitution expected secession. That was the
reason, it argued, that no clause permitting the use of force against a
seceding state was included in the document.[17]

Similar sentiments were made public in cities as widely separated
as Kenosha, Wisconsin; Albany, New York; Washington, D.C.; Springfield, Massachusetts; Philadelphia; Cincinnati; and Indianapolis.[18]
Greeley, perhaps the nation's most influential newspaper editor, urged
"peace and fraternity," not once, but again and again. Cassius Clay of

Noted abolitionist Edward Everett
protested against the notion of holding
states in the Union against their will.

Kentucky suggested a national referendum to be followed by the independence of states voting for it.[19]

No opinion polls were taken as that method of feeling the public pulse was not yet available. Had northern voters been given an opportunity to register their views, however, a substantial segment would have voiced opposition to any move likely to bring about armed conflict between the sections of the country. Movements designed to effect "peaceable separation" or to hold a mediated conference whose goal was compromise got nowhere. Neither the prominence of the men seeking a way to preserve peace nor the large number of citizens favoring it had vital impact.

From the time of his surprise nomination, Lincoln harbored a vision from which he never wavered. He would quickly restore the Union in its entirety, regardless of the rash actions by secessionists. By effecting this reunion, he would initiate a Second American Revolution by which he would bring to mature fulfillment the glorious promises of the Declaration of Independence. Thus his General Order No. 1, issued January 22, 1862, called for the concerted advance of all armies on or before the symbolic date of February 22, Washington's birthday.[20]

Responding to a famous August 20, 1862, "open letter" in which Horace Greeley called for unconditional abolition, the president made his position clear: "My paramount object in this struggle is to save the Union, and is not either to save or to destroy slavery. If I could save the Union without freeing any slave, I would do it."[21]

Throughout his tenure as chief executive, Lincoln emphasized the primary importance of the Union. His first inaugural address focused not on the divided nation but on "the indivisible Union." To Lincoln, the Union existed before the Declaration of Independence was announced and the Constitution was framed. These documents of freedom nurtured and matured the Union, but they did not create it. Perpetual and indivisible, the mystical Union was a preexistent bond whose nature a few keen-sighted patriots dimly glimpsed when the United States of America was formed.[22]

In adolescence and early manhood, the future president was exposed to few books. One that he read many times may have helped shape his concept of the Union, for in his biography of Washington, Mason Weems stressed the horrors of disunion. A cataclysmic disruption, said Washington through his biographer, was the source of the first president's greatest dread. A schism in the nation's life could "never take place without civil war," said Washington, according to Parson Weems.[23]

From this line of reasoning, it followed that, for Lincoln, the union of the states transcended in importance even the sacred union of man and wife. The ending of the sectional conflict that produced so-called secession would restore the Union in all its unblemished glory. The sixteenth president intended to preserve the national heritage; all that he did was simply a means toward that end.[24]

AN APRIL 1, 1861, memorandum from William H. Seward has generated considerable confusion in the many efforts to extrapolate the events that preceded the crisis at Fort Sumter. Seward had consented to join the Lincoln cabinet because he expected to make the key decisions of the first Republican administration and was subsequently surprised to find that Lincoln alone planned to shape the course of his administration.

That did not deter Seward from offering unsolicited advice to the president. After a month in office, his memorandum noted, the president had shaped neither a domestic nor a foreign policy. As a step toward achieving the former goal, Seward said that Lincoln and his advisers must "change the question before the public from one upon slavery, or about slavery, for a question upon union or disunion."[25] Writing as though he were addressing an uninformed political amateur, the new secretary of state pointed out that the shift in emphasis would change the focal point from "a party question, to one of patriotism or union."

Seward seems to have failed to take into account the fact that the Republican Party (but not Lincoln) was generally known to be committed to abolition. This factor, rather than the president-elect's personal stance, led to the secessions of the southern states prior to Lincoln's inauguration. Because he suggested "changing the question," Seward is sometimes credited with the hard-line position with respect to the Union that was taken by the Lincoln administration.

Some abolitionists in the Northeast were ready to fight to rid the nation of slavery, forming a small but vocal minority. In early official discussions of Fort Sumter and related issues, Lincoln never suggested that slavery was the question of the hour. Instead, he invariably stressed that everything he did was based on the goal of restoring the Union.

Seward's memorandum was not only presumptuous to the point of rudeness, it was factually flawed. No doubt he knew this as well as

Throughout most of the North and the South, the Emancipation Proclamation was mistakenly hailed as primarily motivated by a desire for social justice.

CURRIER & IVES LITHOGRAPH

Lincoln did. The secretary of state seems never to have understood that the president's sole passion was preservation of the Union. Unlike Seward, Lincoln never engaged in surreptitious conversations whose aim was to assure South Carolina that Fort Sumter would be abandoned.[26] So far as Lincoln was concerned, slave owners in the South would not be disturbed in their dealings with their chattels on one condition: They must lead their wayward states back into the fold of the sacred and perpetual Union from which they had strayed.

Part 2

Firestorm at Sumter

A bloodless artillery duel at Charleston, South Carolina, triggered a call for seventy-five thousand militia by Abraham Lincoln.

7

Bread Enough for Five Days

Upon his resignation from the U.S. Senate on January 21, 1861, Jefferson Davis resumed the life of a gentleman farmer at his Mississippi plantation. Within days after reaching Brierfield, he accepted appointment as a major general of the state military forces.

In February a message from Montgomery, Alabama, reached him. According to his wife, Varina, he scanned it, then frowned deeply and remained silent for "what seemed an eternity." Delegates from the seven seceded states had elected him president of the provisional confederation of seceded states.

Davis did not want the post, although he would have welcomed an opportunity to become general in chief of the new nation. Reluctantly, he made his way to Montgomery and was inaugurated. In Richmond on February 22, a day selected because of its links with the American Revolution, he began a six-year term as president of the Confederate States of America.[1]

Before taking charge of the new government, the former U.S. secretary of war had viewed the situation at Charleston with alarm. Fort Sumter would not be relinquished readily, he reasoned, but South Carolina was inflexible in demanding full possession of the island fortress. Hence it was the spot most likely to cause a breakdown in attempts to purchase federal installations within the seceded states.

Davis wasted no time. Aware that P. G. T. Beauregard had resigned his commission in the U.S. Army on February 8, the Confederate

Davis preferred to command secessionist military forces rather than serve as the Confederacy's chief executive.

president on March 1 chose him as his first brigadier general and sent him to take command in Charleston.[2]

The South Carolina governor, Francis Pickens, with whom Davis was in frequent contact, received notice of the impending change. "This Government assumes control of military operations at Charleston," a telegram informed him, "and will make demand of the fort when fully advised. An officer goes tonight to take charge."[3]

Abner Doubleday mistakenly wrote on February 9, "The enemies batteries were completely manned and ready for action." Actually, South Carolina was long on threats but short of gunners and guns capable of reducing Fort Sumter. General Beauregard would soon have more men than he could effectively use—nearly nine thousand members of state forces. Yet they had never experienced combat, and few knew how to aim or to discharge a cannon.[4]

Beauregard knew that a constant stream of commercial vessels came into Charleston Harbor, which had an average width of about two miles. He also knew that Fort Moultrie lay about one mile northeast of Fort Sumter and that Morris Island, southeast of the fortress sheltering a federal garrison, came within about twelve hundred yards of it. During 1863–64, this tiny strip of land would see "many of the awful incidents of the war."[5]

The batteries at Fort Johnson on James Island, southwest of the contested site, were fifteen hundred yards away, and Castle Pinckney was two miles northwest of Sumter, on ground that local residents knew as Shute's Folly.[6] In Montgomery, political leaders boastfully predicted that Fort Sumter would soon sit in the middle of "a ring of fire."

At the isolated federal installation, surgeon Samuel Crawford made regular entries in his diary. "Renewed activity was manifested at every point in the harbor of Charleston," he noted soon after Beauregard assumed command. "New batteries sprang up along the shore, steamers carrying men and materials pass and repass day and night under the guns of Sumter."

On shore, Beauregard promised that soon his guns would span fully one-third of a 360-degree circle. Once all were in place and operable, the handful of men of Fort Sumter's garrison would not have a chance unless aided by powerful guns on federal warships.

Members of the Confederate Congress gave their hearty support when President Davis called for an army of one hundred thousand men to serve for a full year. Provisions were made to establish a corps of engineers, an artillery corps, and regiments of infantry and cavalry as needed. The lawmakers stipulated the monthly pay rates ranging

HARPER'S HISTORY OF THE GREAT REBELLION

Beauregard turned in his U.S. Army commission in order to fight for the Rebel cause.

from enlisted men to brigadier general—$11 to $3,612. They failed, however, to take specific action regarding recruitment. While volunteers from several states hurried to Charleston, the Confederate army began to take form. Within weeks its thirty-five thousand men outnumbered its potential foe.[7]

USING FIELD GLASSES, members of Sumter's garrison scrutinized the freight cars coming into Charleston. The soldiers glumly decided that an entire train of "shot, shell, heavy guns, and mortars" had arrived for possible use against them. Some of the $1.8 million recently appropriated for military purposes by the South Carolina General Assembly had been well spent, they concluded.[8]

Many of Charleston's fifty thousand citizens were enthusiastic about a rifled cannon, secured by Governor Pickens from England, that was likely to prove more powerful and accurate than any weapon in the federal bastion. A report of this weapon's role in a European siege, first published in the London *Times,* was reprinted in one of the city's newspapers.

Close to the tip of Morris Island, Confederate engineers experimented with a so-called iron battery. C. H. Stevens of Charleston directed the placement of heavy wooden beams, forming a framework that was

Gunners at work inside the novel "iron battery" built by Rebels at Charleston.

covered with T-rails made for railroad use. Guns and gunners would be sheltered by the heavy iron. Watching from Sumter, Captain Foster of the corps of engineers managed to sketch the Confederate positions.[9]

Facing a growing number of guns, Major Anderson sent an urgent request to Washington for instructions. Joseph Holt, Buchanan's new secretary of war, had little sympathy for the South. Even so, he urged Anderson to exercise forbearance to avoid "a collision with the forces that surround you."[10]

Other than some officials in the Buchanan administration, few people were confident that the situation at Fort Sumter could be defused without some sense of embarrassment for the North or the South. Readers of the *New York Herald* were told that armed conflict at Charleston was likely.

When he had entered Fort Sumter in December, Sgt. James Chester noted that the structure was crammed with lumber, building stone, unmounted guns that weighed up to fifteen thousand pounds each, flagstones standing on end, gun carriages, derricks, coils of rope, and blocks and tackle. For reasons no one fully understood, huge quantities of powder were also to be found. Thus its magazines were not likely to be empty soon. Powder bags and friction primers, however, were another matter. Soldiers surrendered their flannel shirts, and Anderson gave up several dozen pairs of woolen socks for use by the bag-makers.[11]

Since it was believed that an attacking force would most likely land at the wharf before the main entrance, Captain Doubleday gave special care to defending this point. According to Sergeant Chester, "Two five-gallon demijohns filled with powder were planted as mines, well under the wharf pavement."[12]

These explosive devices that Chester called mines were labeled "infernal machines" by the Charleston newspapers. Soon any weapon of this category was called a "torpedo," a name that persisted throughout the Civil War. Hand grenades were seldom used effectively during the war, but there was a supply on hand at Fort Sumter.

By mid-February the fort's defenders consisted of only ten officers and seventy-five enlisted men, eight of whom were musicians. When workmen of doubtful loyalty were dismissed, fifty-five remained as civilian soldiers.[13] If the March 24, 1861, summary by an officer of engineers was accurate, Sumter's defensive weapons included 61 guns, 225 grenades, and 4 infernal machines.[14] Doubleday, who planned and supervised the distribution of guns and explosives, saw a major problem. The acute shortage of powder bags had not been solved by scavenging all suitable fabric within the fort and using the six needles on hand. The estimated seven hundred powder bags would vanish quickly if an artillery duel should commence. Yet, in spite of the need for powder bags, most of those inside the fort were confident that their adversaries could not quickly force their surrender.

Supplies of food and other essentials were a different matter. For a time the Confederates had permitted the Charleston stores to sell food and fuel to the men of the garrison, but General Beauregard quickly stopped these transactions. As an additional precaution, the Confederate commander secured from New York two large Drummond lights and mounted them inside the bombproofs on Sullivan's and Morris Islands.[15]

On April 3 Anderson ordered a strict inventory. It revealed that, with his men already on half-rations, the bread supply could last no more than five days. Fort Sumter was now totally isolated from shore. Hunger would force him to surrender the installation within a few days unless relief arrived by ship. He was surprised and less than convinced when a message arrived on April 7 from President Lincoln through Secretary of War Cameron, stating that a relief expedition would soon be en route.[16] He did not believe help would arrive before his food supplies were exhausted. Lacking supplies, Anderson was reconciled to either withdrawal or honorable surrender when his command could no longer occupy the fort.[17]

NO ONE IN CHARLESTON and only a handful of his Washington intimates knew that Lincoln was entertaining what he considered an opportunity. Convinced that secessionists permeated the government, the president was wary of any information gained through normal channels. He wanted firsthand reports about Fort Sumter from sources he could trust.

Gustavus V. Fox had presented what seemed to be the most feasible scheme for relief of the installation. It might be well, Lincoln reasoned, to give Fox a look at what he would face if he should be sent to lead the relief of the fort.[18]

Therefore Fox appeared in Charleston on March 21, requesting permission to visit Fort Sumter. Confederate officials approved, and he spent two hours on the little island. During a conference with Anderson, he said nothing about having been sent by Lincoln; members of the garrison assumed that he represented General Scott.[19] Subsequent

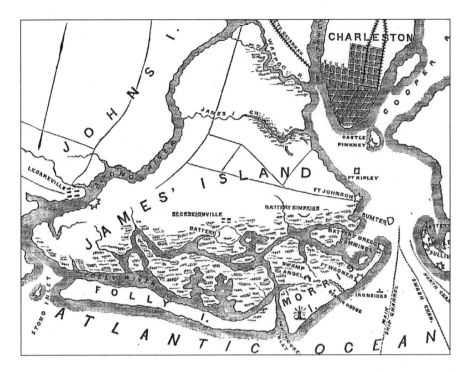

events suggest that the real purpose of his visit was to get a personal look at Charleston Harbor.[20]

Soon after Fox returned to Washington, Anderson received an order to bring away books, drawings, and papers in the event of evacuation. Since evacuation seemed close at hand, he was surprised when another civilian from Washington appeared on March 24.[21]

Virginia-born Ward Hill Lamon, a longtime friend and associate of Lincoln, was the president's second unofficial scout. He met with Governor Pickens and seemed to indicate that he was there to make preliminary arrangements for evacuating the fort.[22] Returning to the capital, Lamon had a private meeting with Lincoln at which no notes were made. Although lacking naval or military experience, Lamon presumably gave his assessment of the physical situation in Charleston Harbor.

At the site of growing tension, Confederate and South Carolina officials expected the fort to be abandoned without a fight. A stream of telegrams reiterated that no efforts would be made to bring food and supplies. These communications did not mention reinforcements; Union leaders earlier had said that they ruled out a military expedition.

Meanwhile, Lincoln took comfort in the fact that he was not bound by the agreements that predated his inauguration. On March 30 Fox left the capital for New York, carrying orders from the president so secret that some cabinet members did not know their nature.[23]

8

An Intolerable Offer

STILL PALLID FROM RUSSIAN winters, Francis W. Pickens moved ponderously through the dimly lighted corridors of the Charleston Hotel. He had no idea what message was being delivered to him by the officers who had just arrived from Washington City. One thing was clear, however. As governor, he would find it as difficult to deal with Abraham Lincoln as he had with Alexander II during his term as U.S. minister to Russia.

Because of the prevalence of smallpox in Columbia, state government offices had been moved from the capital to the coast early in April.[1] Reaching his temporary command post, Pickens provided a gilded chair for Judge Andrew G. Magrath, secretary of state of the newly created republic. David Jamison, South Carolina's secretary of war, would occupy a second ornate chair. Between them, small chairs of heart pine were placed for the men who had reached Charleston on the latest train and who described themselves as "messengers with urgent business."

When the parties assembled and took their positions before the governor's mahogany desk, Pickens recognized Theodore Talbot, who had been stationed earlier at Fort Sumter. The soldier was now a brevet captain serving as assistant adjutant general of the U.S. Army. The thirty-five-year-old Talbot suffered from a lung ailment.[2]

Talbot in turn introduced his companion, Robert S. Chew, who currently served on Secretary of State Seward's staff. Pickens had received numerous communications from Seward's office, and it was

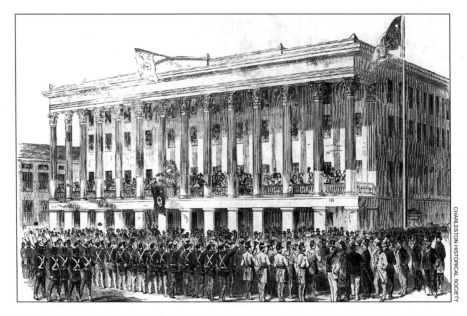

CHARLESTON HISTORICAL SOCIETY

The Charleston Hotel, where Robert Chew delivered Lincoln's message to Pickens, flew the Palmetto flag.

commonly believed that the secretary of state expected that Sumter would be evacuated to avoid a confrontation. Perhaps a formal order relinquishing the installation was about to be delivered.[3]

Instead of delivering the contents of his diplomatic pouch, Chew recited an oral message: "I am directed by the President of the United States to notify you that an attempt will be made to supply Fort Sumter with provisions only; and that, if such attempt be not resisted, no effort to throw in men, arms, or ammunition will be made, without further notice, or in case of an attack upon the fort."[4]

Removing a paper from his pocket, he extended it to the governor. "Here is your copy of the president's directive, sir."

Stunned, Pickens was briefly wordless at its unacceptable alternatives. He immediately sent the message to General Beauregard. Although a Confederate States' army bill had been enacted earlier, most men in and about Charleston were members of South Carolina units with little or no combat experience.[5] Nevertheless, Beauregard was prepared to resist the federal move that hardly anyone had expected. For weeks, Washington officials had used intermediaries to promise that Fort Sumter would be abandoned when the garrison exhausted its supplies. They were now down to little more than three or four days' food and had already begun making plans to leave. Although Beauregard did not know it, on April 11 Gen. Winfield Scott had drafted, but did not send to Major Anderson, an order to evacuate and hire a vessel to take his garrison to New York.[6]

Pickens started to give Chew a message for Lincoln, but he was immediately interrupted. Chew's instructions were specific and detailed, the officer explained. He was not to receive from or convey any communication except Lincoln's ultimatum to a South Carolina official. Hence he and Talbot planned to take a late train back to Washington.

Both men had brought writing materials, so they prepared their reports as the train jolted northward. Chew noted that he and Talbot had reached Charleston about 6:00 P.M. on Monday, April 8. Talbot had arranged the meeting with Governor Pickens, and the president's message was delivered word-for-word orally, then in written form.[7] Talbot reviewed his involvement in the escalating crisis. Assigned to duty at Charleston's Fort Moultrie months ago, he had moved from the run-down installation with the rest of Major Anderson's command on December 26, 1860. Sent to Washington as a courier, he was given a promotion and assigned to a desk job.

Informed on the morning of April 6 that he would accompany Chew to the city he had left ninety days earlier, Talbot was told nothing about the mission. Therefore, he was almost as surprised as was Pickens when he heard Lincoln's challenge. During his weeks in the U.S. capital, Talbot had heard repeatedly from reliable sources that the administration was ready to give up Sumter.[8]

Many in the federal capital knew that the secessionists had been told several times that Fort Sumter would be evacuated, despite the urging of some leaders that the president should strike a vigorous blow at once. German-American Carl Schurz told his friend in the Executive Mansion that as soon as Fort Sumter was reinforced, "Public opinion in the free states will at once rally to your support." Writing from New York, an admirer who signed himself only as "A Republican" warned Lincoln, "Give up Sumter, Sir, & you are as dead politically as John Brown is physically."[9]

Although officials of the new Confederate States of America sent troops to Charleston, they did not expect to use them. Throughout the Confederate Palmetto State, however, the symbolic importance of Sumter overshadowed all other questions relating to the federal government. Blue-uniformed men were holding a military installation

German-born Carl Schurz, who worked
for Lincoln in the election of 1860,
told his friend that Fort Sumter
must be reinforced.

LIBRARY OF CONGRESS

within South Carolina waters. As a result, said Pickens and other leaders, the nation and the world saw the fortress as "affording a standing denial of the sovereignty and independence of South Carolina."

It was imperative, said leaders of the brief-lived self-proclaimed independent nation, that South Carolina gain recognition and respect. That was impossible so long as a foreign power held a military post within its borders. Toleration of a federal garrison at Sumter could only be interpreted as a sign of weakness.

The ultimatum, every word of which was chosen with great care, offered Pickens only two choices, both of which were intolerable. He could disgrace South Carolina and the Confederacy by yielding the fort, or he could take steps to seize it. The latter move would effectively make southerners the aggressors to whom Lincoln had referred in his inaugural address. Regardless of whether Pickens took aggressive action or did nothing, Lincoln and the Union stood to score a huge victory.

As understood in Charleston, the president challenged, "We will not evacuate Sumter under any condition." The "provisions only" clause was interpreted as deliberately deceptive; troops would surely be included in the expedition. Northern newspapers carrying stories about the offer were slanted in their coverage, claiming that the president had only said, "We are bringing food to starving men."

Many of Lincoln's critics in the North had called him "the Illinois baboon," but the uncouth-looking man in the Executive Mansion had outfoxed his opponents. If the rebels yielded, they would relinquish the moral high ground on which they had staked so much. If they fought, they would be labeled the aggressor, and the fragmented North would unite solidly behind Lincoln.

While Talbot analyzed the long-range import of his unexpected journey and Chew wrote his report, Confederate leaders exchanged telegrams. Some favored an immediate reaction to the new challenge from Washington. Roger A. Pryor of Virginia, a recent arrival in Charleston, promised that Washington would soon goad the Old Dominion into secession. Calling his state "an old lady who was a little rheumatic," Pryor cautioned that Virginia was moving slowly in addressing the secession issue. He and his colleagues, however, would "put her in [the Confederacy] if you but strike a blow," he promised.[10]

In Charleston and in Montgomery, some leaders resented what they considered interference with due process. "Delay action and give us time to think things through," they urged President Davis. Their

Secretary of State William H. Seward, an outspoken proponent of peace, seems to have assured secessionists that Fort Sumter would not be resupplied.

plea was partly based on the fact that the U.S. secretary of state, William H. Seward, made no secret of his desire for peace. Along with other presidential advisers, through friends and aides, he had leaked promises that no attempt would be made to resupply Fort Sumter.

During the hours that South Carolina leaders pondered alternatives, the resupply expedition sailed from New York. At the Confederate capital, the southern secretary of war, L. P. Walker, received a telegram from General Beauregard that summarized the Lincoln message brought by Chew. Himself surprised, Walker consulted other officials. One of them pointed out that Lincoln's long inaugural address included a brief threat whose significance was easily overlooked: "The power confided to me, will be used to hold, occupy, and possess the property, and places belonging to the government, and to collect the duties and imposts."[11]

In Washington, Fort Sumter was regarded as federal property. Furthermore, federal duties had been collected in Charleston until secession brought that activity to a halt. Clearly, Lincoln intended for the South to know that seized installations would be repossessed and that revenue cutters would be sent to Charleston and other ports regardless of what happened to Fort Sumter.

A move to collect the revenues would provoke resistance that could quickly turn ugly. One way or another, Lincoln would either humiliate the South or precipitate a fight. If the Sumter issue should be resolved, revenue collection would take its place. That being the case, there seemed no point in waiting; now was as good a time as any for a showdown.

Lincoln's point of view was later expressed in his message to the special session of Congress that convened on July 4, 1861. Speaking of Confederate assailants in Charleston, he told the lawmakers:

> They knew—they were expressly notified—that the giving of bread to the few brave and hungry men of the garrison was all which would on that occasion be attempted, unless themselves, by resisting so much, should provoke more. They knew that this government desired to keep the garrison in the fort, not to assail them, but merely to maintain visible presence, and thus to preserve the Union from actual and immediate dissolution—trusting, as hereinbefore stated, to time, discussion, and the ballot-box for final adjustment.[12]

IN THIS REMARKABLE analysis, the president said nothing about troops sent to Charleston and did not mention his refusal to enter into discussions with South Carolina and Confederate commissioners.

On the mainland, signal guns were fired at the Citadel green in Charleston, and members of the militia quickly responded. From points throughout the city, men hurried toward boats waiting for them at the waterfront site called the Battery. At about 1:15 P.M. three messengers from General Beauregard went to Fort Sumter under a white flag. Col. James Chesnut, recently a U.S. senator, was the senior officer. His wife, Mary Boykin Chesnut, later gained fame as the most widely read Confederate diarist.[13]

Lt. Col. A. R. Chisholm, another aide to Beauregard, sat close to their white flag as they moved across the harbor. Capt. Stephen D. Lee, a West Point graduate distantly related to the Lees of Virginia, was the third member of the official party. Soon he would begin receiving a series of promotions that made him a lieutenant general.

The messengers reached their destination before 2:30, Union Capt. John Foster noted. They immediately conveyed to Anderson a demand for the evacuation of Sumter. Beauregard offered federal personnel "all proper facilities" needed for them to go to any U.S. Army post they might choose. In addition, he informed them that, at the time of hauling down their flag, they could salute it.[14]

Anderson met with his officers, then prepared a written reply to Beauregard's demand. His sense of honor and his obligations to the U.S. government made it impossible for him to comply, he said.[15]

After handing his message to Chesnut, Anderson escorted the Confederate officers to the boat landing. Along with his formal statement he sent an oral message: "If you do not batter the fort to pieces about us, we shall be starved out in a few days."[16] Chesnut requested permission to add Anderson's oral comment to his formal reply. In refusing, the federal commander said that he was simply stating "the fact of the case."

Beauregard's next telegram to Montgomery informed Secretary of War Walker of Anderson's refusal to evacuate. Members of the garrison would soon run out of food, however, he noted. Walker responded by stressing that he wished to avoid "needlessly to bombard Fort Sumter." Beauregard was told to "avoid the effusion of blood" if Anderson would promise not to use his guns first and would indicate a precise time of evacuation.[17]

By 3:00 A.M. on April 12, Morris Island was thronged with gunners waiting to put their batteries into action. At least four thousand men had converged upon Charleston, where regiments were formed to await orders.

According to some estimates, probably inflated, more than eighty-eight hundred Confederates eventually crowded into the city.[18] The newspaper correspondent F. G. Fontaine dispatched a note to Horace Greeley's *Herald,* stating, "Affairs here are culminating." Two civilians were especially eager to become involved—Virginia planter Edmund Ruffin and Louis Wigfall, until recently a U.S. senator from Texas.[19]

Both sides realized it was futile to exchange more polite messages. Barring the sudden appearance of a federal flotilla known to be at sea, the heavy guns would soon begin to roar.

Revised in accordance with instructions from Montgomery, a new proposal reached Anderson from Beauregard after midnight. Again the federal commander called his officers together for consultation. Surgeon Samuel W. Crawford, who took notes at the meeting,

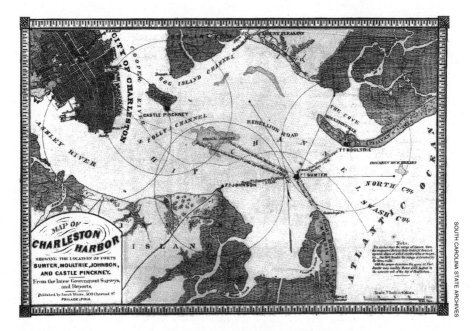

Charleston Harbor as it was mapped in 1861—showing Fort Sumter squarely in the middle of the main channel.

had earlier inventoried the remaining food supplies. His assessment was grim. Provided that the men in the fort were willing to go "three days entirely without food," he estimated they could hold out for five days. Nevertheless, Sumter's commander still refused to say whether his guns would be fired in reply to a Confederate challenge.

Anderson and his men had done everything in their power to get ready. The same could also be said for his former artillery student, P. G. T. Beauregard. The Confederate batteries on the mainland and the nearby islands waited only for a signal.

9

Success in Failure

IN PONDERING HIS OPTIONS regarding the Charleston crisis, Lincoln proved highly receptive to a plan presented by his postmaster general, Montgomery Blair. The plan's author, however, was Blair's brother-in-law, Gustavus V. Fox.

At age thirty-nine, Fox was a veteran of the Mexican War with eighteen years' experience in the navy. He had resigned his commission in 1856 to enter the woolen business but volunteered his services when the Fort Sumter crisis developed.[1] Blair took him to the Executive Mansion on March 13, the same day on which Lincoln had refused to meet with the Confederate commissioners. The president was enthusiastic about the possibility of a Fort Sumter expedition that would serve his ends.[2]

Exuding confidence, the corpulent textile executive explained an intricate scheme he had presented to President Buchanan. It required that he secretly lease two tugboats and a large transport. Noting the lack of action by the navy, he proposed to move reinforcements via the transport, with the holds of the tugs filled with provisions. There was little risk in reaching Fort Sumter, particularly if his small flotilla were given naval protection. Once near the fort, the tugs would ferry the supplies and troops inside, guarded by the fort's guns and the naval vessels.[3]

Lincoln was impressed with the man and his plan, so he met with him again two days later. Everything Fox proposed seemed reasonable and feasible, involving no delay of the sort envisioned by others

Gustavus V. Fox developed a plan for the relief of Fort Sumter but failed to persuade President Buchanan to adopt it.

in outfitting a convoy and training an army. Now the president not only had a goal, he also had what seemed to be a feasible program by which to accomplish it. At his request, Fox drafted a written summary of his ideas that included an estimate of the numbers of ships and men needed to implement them.[4]

No man to waste words, the veteran seaman set forth a succinct plan of operations that read:

> Steamers *Pocahontas* at Norfolk, *Pawnee* at Washington, *Harriet Lane* at New York, to be under sailing orders with stores, etc., for one month. Three hundred men to be kept ready for departure from on board the receiving ships at New York. Supplies for twelve months for one hundred men to be put in portable shape, ready for instant shipping. Two hundred men to be ready to leave Governors Island in New York. A large steamer and three tugs conditionally engaged.[5]

Fox was prepared to shield the tugs with bales of hay or cotton, even though speeding toward Fort Sumter at fourteen knots, they were unlikely to be hit. They could maneuver in waters as shallow as six feet, and Fox was sure that no shoal point in the swash channel was "less than nine feet at high water." Using these special vessels in a variant of his original plan presented to Buchanan, he guaranteed he would reach the fort. To Lincoln, the novel aspect of the Fox proposal was his plan to ferry men and supplies between the fort and the larger vessels.[6]

Brig. Gen. Joseph G. Totten, chief of engineers, analyzed the proposal and argued against it. In his opinion, any attempt to relieve Anderson and his men would "inevitably involve a collision." Winfield Scott maintained that even if the Fox plan should be adopted and should prove successful, it afforded only a few weeks of relief. Positive that abandonment of Fort Sumter was "a sure necessity," Scott continued to insist that the fort be evacuated, "the sooner the more graceful." Naval experts Com. S. H. Stringham and Cmdr. J. H. Ward called the Fox scheme impracticable.

Simon Cameron, the secretary of war, believed that during the weeks given to the cabinet debate over what to do, the difficulty of reinforcing Sumter had "been increased by ten if not twenty fold." Seeing no practical benefit from the venture, he strongly advised against it. The attorney general, Edward Bates, preferred to evacuate Fort Sumter rather than "unwillingly to do anything to start civil war."[7]

These opinions had no influence upon Fox or upon the man he called "Abe" or "Uncle Abe" in letters to his wife. With the steamer

HARPER'S HISTORY OF THE GREAT REBELLION

Winfield Scott, so corpulent he could no longer mount a horse, was called "Old Fuss and Feathers" by some of his subordinates.

HARPER'S HISTORY OF THE GREAT REBELLION

The revenue cutter *Harriet Lane* (right) was among the vessels in the flotilla designed to resupply Fort Sumter.

and tugs already promised to him if needed, he soon received a go-ahead from the commander in chief. An additional tug, the *Freeborn,* was rented, and the cutter *Harriet Lane* was assigned to the flotilla.[8] The success of the Fox expedition, earliest of the Civil War's joint operations, depended upon the cooperation of the navy, the army, and the revenue service.

Even though his department would be intimately involved in the scheme, Gideon Welles, the secretary of the navy, did not know precisely how Lincoln proposed to use these ships. Preliminary orders to the War Department required that two hundred men be made ready but did not reveal why they were likely to be needed.

On March 18 the proposal was adopted, despite the fact that the area Fox specified for the proposed landing would be under direct fire from thirteen guns at Fort Moultrie.[9] On March 30 Fox took command of the expedition to "effect an entrance and place both troops and supplies in Fort Sumter." His vessels were to be "under sailing orders with 300 men kept ready in New York." For his part, Anderson was urged to hold out until relief arrived; however, he could surrender if that became necessary.[10]

Lincoln demonstrated the speed with which he could act once he had made up his mind concerning complex issues. On April 1 he sent a terse directive to Andrew H. Foote at the Brooklyn Navy Yard without consulting the secretary of the navy. Foote was ordered to "fit out the *Powhatan* without delay" and prepare the warship to sail under sealed orders.[11]

William H. Seward, who favored a peaceful solution of the sectional crisis, argued that aid to Florida's Fort Pickens would be less likely to lead to war than aid to Fort Sumter. In addition, insisted the secretary of state, some strategic considerations indicated that the Florida installation was of more importance to the Union than was Fort Sumter.

Ready to act with respect to Charleston Harbor, the president yielded only slightly to Seward's pressure. Perhaps reluctantly, he gave tentative approval to a plan by which Pickens would be resupplied at the same time as Fort Sumter. Thus Lincoln authorized two secret, simultaneous expeditions to southern forts.

Secretary of War Cameron sent a letter of instruction to Anderson at Sumter on April 4. Entrusted to Theodore Talbot, it did not reach its destination because the Confederates halted all mail delivery to the fort. Hence Anderson received no official word that he was urged to hold out for the arrival of relief. During a brief visit to Charleston, Fox unofficially briefed him on the upcoming expedition.[12]

On April 5 Welles ordered Capt. Samuel Mercer to take command of a flotilla consisting of the *Powhatan, Pawnee, Pocahontas,* and *Harriet Lane.* If resistance should be met, the secretary of the navy approved reinforcement of the garrison. Concurrently, Scott authorized the expedition to carry "all artillery implements, fuses, cordage, slow matches, mechanical levers, and guns." Mercer was ordered to leave New York with the *Powhatan* "in time to be off Charleston Bar on the morning of the 11th."[13]

Fox was meticulous in developing and revising his plan, and his enterprise moved ahead almost on schedule. Capt. Montgomery C. Meigs reported to Seward on April 6 that a warship would embark for southern waters at once and by late afternoon the *Atlantic* would follow "with 500 troops, of which one company is sappers and miners, one a mounted battery." Since the ship could not transport all stores that had been gathered, the *Illinois* would follow on Monday with the remainder. Then he warned: "Unless this movement is supported by ample supplies and followed up by the Navy it will be a failure. If you

Montgomery C. Meigs, later a Federal general, helped to assemble the vessels that were led to Charleston by Fox.

NICOLAY AND HAY, *LINCOLN*

call out volunteers you will have no general to command. The general born, not made, is yet to be found who is to govern the great army which is to save the country, if it can be saved."[14]

Lincoln was eager for the Florida expedition to succeed, but his chief concern was South Carolina. Neither he nor the men en route to that point anticipated what occurred.

The element of surprise was lost when the *New York Herald* published a list of "armaments and troops, of the fleet despatched [*sic*] from New York and Washington to Charleston Harbor, for the relief of Fort Sumter." Newspaper readers learned that three vessels had sailed under sealed orders on Saturday, April 6. One of them was the well-known steam-powered sloop-of-war *Pawnee,* under Capt. S. C. Rowan and carrying 10 guns and 200 men. The 2,415-ton *Powhatan* rode low in the water with 11 guns and 275 men aboard.

10

A Continuous Bombardment

NEITHER ROBERT S. CHEW nor Theodore Talbot had any idea how the Confederates would react to the message they delivered in Charleston. On their return trip to Washington they carried neither promises nor threats.[1]

In Montgomery, Secretary of State Robert Toombs was a minority voice. Learning about Lincoln's message, he was dismayed at the notion of using force against Fort Sumter. "The firing upon that fort will inaugurate a civil war greater than any the world has yet seen," he warned.[2]

At the point of potential conflict, it was assumed that from a distance of more than four hundred miles, Montgomery would authorize direct action. Nevertheless, a vocal minority disagreed with the sentiment expressed in a local newspaper: "The gage is thrown down and we must accept the challenge. We will meet the invader, and God and Battle must decide the issue between the hirelings of Abolition hate plus Northern tyranny, and the people of South Carolina defending their freedom and their homes."[3]

R. W. Gibbes, surgeon general of South Carolina, hurriedly spent $8,871 on hospital supplies. The shelves at Fort Moultrie and on Sullivan's Island were soon filled, so most of the money was devoted to stocking an improvised one-hundred-bed hospital.

Charles K. Prioleau, an investor in the Liverpool branch of Charleston's John Frazer and Company, was thumped on the back. A splendid English-made Blakely gun, the first to arrive in America, was

Robert Toombs, Confederate secretary
of state, opposed the use of force at
Fort Sumter.

aboard a vessel standing off the harbor. Prioleau's gift was believed capable of reducing the time needed to convince the Yankees infesting Fort Sumter to surrender.[4]

From the provisional Confederate capital, the secretary of war, H. P. Walker, sent an urgent message to Governor Pickens. Letters went simultaneously to the governors of Alabama, Florida, Georgia, Louisiana, Mississippi, and Texas, informing them that a large force was likely to be needed "to resist the coercive measure of the Washington administration." Each governor was urged to call "at once for three thousand volunteers, to be drilled, equipped, and held in instant readiness."[5] At the same time, Walker authorized Beauregard to open fire on Fort Sumter.

Almost all the participants in the crisis in Charleston Harbor recorded their experiences up to and including the bombardment of Sumter. Both sides are largely in agreement as to what happened. Thus, collectively, they provide a detailed story of the cannonade that initiated the war.

AT 6:30 A.M. ON April 11, the Sumter garrison and the remaining workmen assembled in response to a drumbeat. Eight musicians were included in the group, and Charleston lore says that a hospital matron, Ann Amelia Weitfieldt, remained in the fort when the other women left.[6]

With shattered glass having been removed from the last supplies of rice, a few pints of this South Carolina staple remained. Breakfast consisted of a spoonful of stale grains, cracker crumbs, and a strip of almost rancid salt pork. When they had eaten, the men moved their belongings into the lower casemates where they hoped to sleep that night in safety.[7]

CAPT. JOHN FAUNCE'S *Harriet Lane* was heavily loaded with 96 men and two 21-pounders. The *New York Herald* added that three steam transports were also headed south. When the *Atlantic* sailed on April 7, it had 358 men aboard, and the *Illinois* carried 300 soldiers.[8]

Greeley's paper noted that the steam tugs *Yankee* and *Uncle Ben* departed New York on April 8 and 9. The article also pointed out that the flotilla carried approximately thirty launches that would be "most useful in effecting a landing of troops over shoal water, and for attacking a discharging battery when covered with sand and gunny bags." Fox, who had anticipated a news leak, attributed it to "somebody's influence," but he suspected Seward had let the news out to prevent the implementation of the plan.[9]

On April 12 the Charleston newspapers reported that the tug *Uncle Ben* and the warship *Pawnee* had sailed south under sealed orders a few days earlier. News that an expedition was under way was published simultaneously in Savannah. Throughout the seceded states it was well known that a showdown of some sort was likely to take place soon in South Carolina waters. Whatever the expedition might accomplish, it would not be done in secret.

A second blow to Fox's plans was the loss of the powerful *Powhatan,* which carried howitzers and launches needed for the Charleston operation. In obedience to Lincoln's orders this vessel had been fitted out without revealing to the Navy Department what was being planned. Telegrams of instruction went to the ship's commander from both the president and Seward, which confused him. He left New York on April 6 and headed toward Pensacola rather than Charleston.

A third disappointment came in the form of inclement weather. The ships were delayed and the tugboats were blown off course. Of the flotilla, only the *Baltic* managed to reach the designated rendezvous

OFFICIAL RECORDS OF THE UNION AND CONFEDERATE NAVIES

The USS *Pawnee* was one of the few steam-powered vessels of the U.S. Navy in waters north of Mexico.

point near Charleston at about 3:00 on April 12. The *Pawnee* arrived later and dropped anchor, futilely waiting for the *Powhatan,* which maintained its course to Florida.

Throughout the night of April 12 and the following morning, the wind "blew strong, with a heavy sea." Moving about in search of the *Powhatan,* the *Baltic* was briefly grounded in Rattlesnake Shoal. Not having the three hundred men promised to him, Fox thought it foolish to do more than try "to get in a few days' provisions to last the fort until the *Powhatan*'s arrival."

11

The Heroes of Fort Sumter

FIRED FROM JAMES ISLAND at 4:30 A.M. on April 12, the shell that announced the beginning of the Civil War burst harmlessly about one hundred feet over its target. Edmund Ruffin boasted that he had been permitted to pull the lanyard, but South Carolina fighting men denied his claim.[1] Jefferson Davis later denounced the chain of events that led to the first shot as being a product of "unscrupulous cunning [on the part of Lincoln]."[2]

All Confederate batteries were in action by 4:45, but Fort Sumter remained dark and silent. In Charleston, Mary Boykin Chesnut opened her diary at 5:15 and confided to it that she was full of hope, but she did not say why she hoped.

Ruffin mistakenly decided that the federal commander relied so greatly upon casemates now housing his men that he did not plan ever to fire. Had that been the case, he later wrote, "It would have cheapened our conquest." Unknown to the Confederates or to Sumter's garrison, federal ships were close to a rendezvous point twelve miles off the Charleston bar. Hours later, visibility improved enough for signals to be exchanged between the fort and the relief expedition.

At 7:30 A.M. on April 13, a gun commanded by Abner Doubleday roared for the first time. The shot missed its target, the iron battery on Morris Island. The federals fired on Fort Moultrie and then focused on the tip of Sullivan's Island, sheltering a floating battery

Edmund Ruffin, a civilian, is widely but incorrectly credited with having fired the first shot at Fort Sumter.

and holding both an enfilade and a Dahlgren battery. The fort's defenders laid on a steady fire.[3]

According to Beauregard, once the exchange of fire got under way, "a steady and almost continuous fire was kept up throughout the day." Stephen Lee characterized the rain of lead from Fort Sumter as being "rather wild," but he considered that of the Confederates to be "tolerable good."

On the mainland it had been expected that casualties would be numerous. Anticipating the need for beds, civilians sent offers to South Carolina's surgeon general. Many of them said they were ready to take into their homes two to fifteen wounded or exhausted men. In several instances women also offered to serve as nurses.[4]

With the coming of twilight, fire spitting from the mouths of guns became more vivid. Soon the rooftops of houses close to the waterfront were crowded with spectators. Each dramatic demonstration by Confederate forces evoked applause from the assembled ladies and gentlemen.[5]

Fire from the fort slackened during the evening. Beauregard did not know that Anderson had decided to use only his casemate guns. To the Confederate commander, the slow pace of federal fire implied that the relief expedition was probably close to Sumter.

The Confederates resumed a brisk fire at 4:00 A.M. on April 13 and maintained it until 7:00. During a one-hour lull, furnaces at Moultrie were put to work, and forty 32-pound balls were heated until they were red hot. One or more hot shot hit Fort Sumter's wooden quarters, starting a raging fire.[6] About this time some of the Federal ships lying off the harbor were identified by the Confederates.[7]

Since his supply of powder bags would soon be exhausted, at 9:15 Anderson silenced most of his guns. From this time forward, only those bearing upon a Fort Moultrie battery were fired at intervals of about ten minutes. At 12:45 a shot from a Confederate battery clipped the flagstaff at Sumter. Beauregard, who had seen a column of smoke over fort, took the absence of the national emblem to be a signal. Hence he directed Lee and three other officers to go there under a flag of truce.

Chesnut's wife, the former Mary Boykin, wrote one of the most widely read Civil War diaries.

VALENTINE MUSEUM

Fort Sumter ablaze, as depicted by a Northern artist whose sketch was prepared in New York City.

Arriving before 2:00 P.M. they were met by Anderson, to whom they offered to help fight the fire. He declined, saying that the fires were out. Then he gave the messengers some startling news. Louis Wigfall had reached Sumter about 3:30 A.M., Anderson said, intimating that he had come straight from Beauregard's headquarters. The terms of that commander's initial offer would still be honored, said the former Texas senator, if Anderson would raise a white flag.[8]

While Captain Lee and the federal commander discussed Wigfall's unauthorized visit, Maj. David R. Jones arrived from Confederate headquarters. He detailed specific terms for the evacuation, to which Anderson reminded them Beauregard had promised they would be permitted to salute their flag. Although fire had gutted the living quarters, he noted that the walls of the fort had suffered little damage.[9]

According to a semiofficial estimate, forty-eight guns were used at Fort Sumter and forty-seven were employed by the Confederates. No defender of the fort died during the bombardment, and Anderson claimed that his gunners fired only at the surrounding batteries—

never at civilian property. Their aim was poor, however, and seventeen homes near Fort Moultrie were destroyed or damaged.[10]

When the Confederate messengers arrived, the U.S. flag was flying from an improvised staff, and it was clear that the fight was nearly over. A fire engine from Charleston arrived too late to be of use.[11] At 7:30 P.M. Beauregard's subordinates stressed that every detail of the terms offered on April 11 would be honored, and Anderson accepted the conditions.

No one made a record of when the last shot was fired, but a bombardment of more than thirty-three hours was over. During the artillery duel, Confederates fired at least three thousand shells, and Federal guns threw almost seven hundred without the loss of a single life.[12]

Inspection of the fort by Beauregard's aides revealed that its walls were badly damaged. Iron cisterns were ruptured beyond repair, and the stairway was burned so badly that it could not be used. The engineer Foster measured holes made by projectiles from the 8-inch Columbiad at Cummings Point. They had penetrated approximately twelve inches of masonry, having about the same effect as the light

Wigfall, standing, was incorrectly depicted as holding a discussion with Anderson while outside the fort instead of inside it.

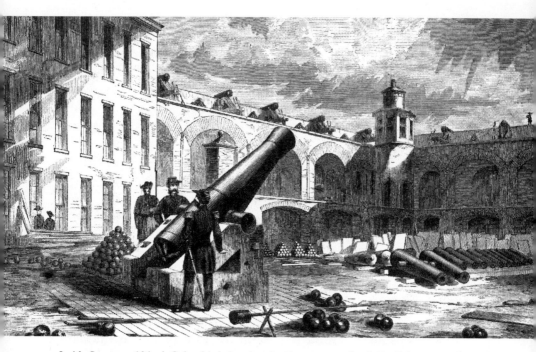

Inside Sumter, a 10-inch Columbiad aimed at the city was never fired; Confederates used an 8-inch weapon of the same design against the fort.

"12-pound bolt from the Blakely gun." Most of the mines prepared under Foster's direction had sustained hits that caused them to detonate.

Fort Sumter's walls were visibly scarred, and the pungent odor of charred wood was almost overpowering, yet the damage could readily be repaired. South Carolina had gained an immense installation that would be usable soon after the surrender ceremonies were completed.

Before 8:00 A.M. on Sunday, April 14, both Anderson and Beauregard recorded their satisfaction regarding casualties. During the bombardment soldiers inside the fort had suffered only three minor contusions. Injuries sustained by Confederate gunners were so minor that a report concerning them was never compiled.

In order to give the U.S. flag the promised one-hundred-gun salute, scraps of blankets were sewn together to make powder bags, and some pieces of papers were formed into pouches. Because high tides delayed embarkation, members of the garrison did not assemble at 1:00 P.M.

Foster, the only absentee, was preparing a summary of events. After noting that evacuation was taking place on the Sabbath, he wrote:

"The want of provisions would soon have caused the surrender of the fort, but with plenty of cartridges the men would have cheerfully fought five or six days, and if necessary much longer, on pork alone, of which we had a sufficient supply."[13]

Doubleday, who was in charge of the salute to the flag, later wrote that it was obviously a dangerous undertaking. Sparks flew everywhere, he said, and there was no secure place to store blank ammunition. As he saw it, the forty-eighth or forty-ninth shot went awry and all hell broke loose. A gun went off prematurely, causing sparks or flaming scraps of powder bags to fall into a pile of cartridges. Gunner Daniel Hough died almost instantly, and the five men injured in the explosion were consigned to the care of Dr. Crawford. He arranged for Pvts. George Fielding and Edward Galloway to be taken to a Charleston hospital, where Galloway died after five days. Wounds sustained by Pvts. John Irwin, John Pritchard, and James Harp were not life-threatening.

The surrender ceremonies, reported by Anderson as having consisted of fifty guns, came to a halt when the powder exploded. Men

Federal surrender ceremonies, interrupted by an explosion, caused the only deaths in the struggle for Fort Sumter.

HARPER'S HISTORY OF THE GREAT REBELLION

were quickly formed on parade, and the musicians were directed to play. "With colors flying and drums beating" to the tune of "Yankee Doodle," Anderson recorded, he evacuated and took away "company and private property."

When he walked out of Fort Sumter, Anderson carried under his arm the tattered flag that had flown during the bombardment. He and his men boarded the *Isabel* at 4:00 P.M., April 14, to go to the nearby USS *Baltic*. Their departure was delayed by the tragic powder explosion and caused their ship to miss the tide.[14] After a cold and dreary night, they steamed past Morris Island and reached New York shortly after 11:00 A.M. on April 18. Anderson's report, written that day, stressed the damage suffered during the thirty-four hours of bombardment. He made no mention of the casualties incurred during the salute to the flag.[15] New York artists, who had a large number of engravings and woodcuts on hand, adapted them and claimed to give their newspaper readers a detailed look at the engagement in Charleston.

The news reached Lincoln on April 13 via the Magnetic Telegraph Company. At Savannah, a man named H. W. Denslow wired him that "Fort Sumter has surrendered there is nobody Hurt." From the Charleston office of the same telegraph company, Isaac W. Hoyle notified the president of the unconditional surrender.

Northern newspapers called the garrison "the heroes of Fort Sumter." Before they reached their destination, artisans were already working on the Sumter medal commissioned by the New York Chamber of Commerce for presentation to Anderson. At a parade on April 20, thousands thronged the streets to take an excited part in what was described as "America's most gigantic tribute." Throughout the North, guns roared salutes to Anderson and his men. At Reading, Pennsylvania, thirty guns were fired, and at the Boston ceremony one hundred shots boomed over the city. Horace Greeley had mixed emotions. "Sumter is lost," he mourned before rejoicing, "Freedom is saved!"

Nevertheless, in nearly every Northern state, a minority of voices joined in protest or despair. At Saint Clairsville, Ohio, editors of the *Gazette and Citizen* hoped that Congress would soon impeach Lincoln and give him "the reward of a traitor." A New Hampshire newspaper editorialized, "The administration might have saved the country from this great calamity." At Newburyport, Massachusetts, the *Daily Herald* asserted that there was blame enough to be distributed to all principals. Both "mad disunionists of the South" and "mad fanatics of the North" were castigated as having "lost all reason and common sense."

Editors bewailed failure to see evidence of "moderation and an attempt at conciliation on either or both sides."

Expressions such as these represented minority views in the North. They were not voiced in the South, for in the Confederacy the seizure of the fort had effects called "galvanizing and electrifying." Charleston went wild with excitement. Grimy gunners boasted, "The sacred soil of South Carolina is free! We have thrown out the invaders from the North."

Officials in Montgomery were less exuberant, although to a man they agreed that "the business at Sumter" would lead to federal action that might bring wavering Virginia into the Confederacy. Other states that had hesitated would be influenced by what Washington did to retaliate for the loss of the fortress, they believed.

Regarded in the South as lawful and legitimate, secession was considered by many to have been vindicated. With U.S. forces removed from Charleston, said optimists, the peace movement would gain strength. Perhaps the new president of the United States would now consent to submit the issue to the Supreme Court. Even if that body should render an adverse ruling, a divided North would hardly risk war with a unified South!

In the Union capital the desk of the commander in chief was piled with stacks of paper bristling with legal opinions. Having pored over them, he and only he knew what he was about to do in response to the seizure of a fortress that had sat incomplete and empty a year earlier.

A single artillery shell had signaled that neither of Lincoln's alternatives was acceptable. The president's intolerable message led to the action he foresaw as a strong possibility when he framed it, and that action was expected to persuade the hesitant North to explode with anger at a flagrant insult to national honor.[16]

12

Point of No Return

It BECAME EVIDENT TO the Fox expedition that Anderson and his men had surrendered Sumter. Soon it was also learned that the *Powhatan* would not be arriving. Fox flew into a rage and inserted a vigorous protest into his official report: "I was permitted to sail on the 9th, the *Pawnee* on the 9th, and the *Pocahontas* on the 10th, without any intimation that the main portion—the fighting portion—of our expedition was taken away."[1]

Lincoln assumed responsibility for the fiasco by which the ship upon which Fox depended most was sent to Florida rather than to South Carolina. On May 1 he sent Fox an apology for "an accident, for which you were in no wise responsible, and possibly I to some extent was."[2] Soon Lincoln created the office of assistant secretary of the navy and named Fox to fill it.

Fox and his officers initially felt their expedition was a fiasco, and their verdict was echoed by Abner Doubleday and many others.[3] Some members of the public, and at least one Federal official, denied that the Fox-led effort ended in failure. Several Northern newspapers suggested that Lincoln's actions were designed to evoke the chain of events that followed. In Pittsburgh it was said that Jefferson Davis and his subordinates "ran blindly into the trap" set by the first Republican president, that "Lincoln used Fort Sumter to draw their fire."[4]

Sen. Orville Browning of Illinois, a longtime adviser to the president, maintained that the Fox expedition achieved success in failure. A few days after Fort Sumter fell, Browning told his friend, "I am not

Abner Doubleday, a member of the Sumter garrison, led the first Federal force that invaded Confederate soil.

NATIONAL ARCHIVES

sure you expected or desired any other result." Two months later he heard Lincoln comment, "The plan of sending supplies succeeded. They attacked Fort Sumter—it fell, and thus did more service than it otherwise could."[5]

Presidential secretaries John G. Nicolay and John Hay concurred in saying that when Chew was sent to Charleston, Lincoln "expected resistance and hostility." He showed his genius, they felt, by devising a plan by means of which "the rebellion should be put in the wrong."[6]

Two weeks after Fox returned to New York, Lincoln wrote to him. A final sentence in the presidential document of May 1 stressed that success of a special sort was attained by members of the Fort Sumter expedition. In almost confidential style, the letter, signed "Very truly, your friend," assured Fox: "You and I both anticipated that the cause of the country would be advanced by making the attempt to provision Fort Sumpter [*sic*] even if it should fail, and it is no small consolation now to feel that our anticipation is justified by the result."[7]

Lincoln's view is widely shared, even by some who hold that he had little or no part in starting the conflict.[8] Surviving documents give no suggestion that Lincoln ever wavered from his conviction that the Confederates started the war. Addressing Evangelical Lutherans on May 13, 1862, he spoke of "the sword forced into our hands."

As late as Lincoln's brief but carefully crafted second inaugural address, he noted that four years earlier "all thoughts were anxiously directed to an impending civil war." In almost self-righteous fashion, he laid blame for the long and bloody war squarely upon the shoulders of the secessionists at Charleston to whom he had given two unacceptable choices: "Both parties deprecated war, but one of them would make war rather than let the nation survive, and the other would accept war rather than let it perish."[9]

LONG BEFORE HE TOOK the oath of office, Lincoln had pondered his options. Discussion with secessionists that could lead to mediation and delay or compromise was out of the question. Persuasion might be tried, but it seemed unlikely to sway the diehards of the Cotton Belt. Brief and limited military action—or the threat of it—was the only viable choice.

John G. Nicolay, seated at left, was Lincoln's private secretary and later his biographer.

Without having voiced his views, Lincoln stood to assume the reins of power in Washington on March 4, 1861. Ignoring the emotion-charged issues of states' rights and the sectionally biased tariff, he held that slavery was "the only substantial dispute." Since he was willing to make major concessions here, he hoped that he would not be forced to chastise the "erring brethren of the South."

This notion lasted only a few hours after he reached Washington at 6:00 A.M. on February 23. Political insiders of the capital had little in common with the villagers of the western frontier. On the banks of the Potomac, the reality of secession was accepted, and few from either the North or the South believed the schism could be healed easily.

Victory at the polls meant that a multitude of federal positions had to be filled. They ranged from membership in the president's cabinet to the management of post offices at remote crossroads around the country. Lincoln's first signature as chief executive was affixed to a document naming John G. Nicolay of Illinois as "Private Secretary to the President of the United States."[10]

Visited by delegations from California, Illinois, Massachusetts, Michigan, Minnesota, New York, Ohio, Oregon, Pennsylvania, Rhode Island, Vermont, and Wisconsin, Lincoln spoke briefly to each. He made many appointments and persuaded William H. Seward "to take charge of the State Department." A youthful friend from Illinois, Elmer Ellsworth, was nominated for a post Lincoln wanted to create for him—chief clerk of the War Department.[11]

After attending to the necessary personnel matters of his new administration, on his fifth day in office Lincoln sent a series of questions about "the Sumpter issue" to Winfield Scott. In a separate memorandum, he urged his general in chief "to exercise all possible vigilance for the maintenance of all the places within the military department of the United States."[12]

There is no evidence that Lincoln ever considered yielding at Charleston. He knew that to regain possession of nearly one hundred seized federal properties, it would be necessary to win a military victory. He felt confident that once a little blood was drawn, secessionists would come to their senses.

Pondering the best way to take decisive action, he concluded that the U.S. armed forces were inadequate for his purposes, which were not yet clearly defined. Perhaps the Revenue Service might be more effective than widely scattered units of the army. So he addressed a question to his secretary of the treasury, but he already knew the answer.

Asking whether any goods were being imported without payment of duty, he wanted to know where such infractions of the law were taking place. Salmon P. Chase replied that he had no customs officers south of North Carolina, Tennessee, and Arkansas. That meant he was receiving no reports from seceded states. Having confirmed what he was sure to be the case, the president turned to his secretary of the navy with another question: what amount of naval force could be put at the disposal of the Revenue Service?[13]

Gideon Welles could give no firm figures, so Lincoln felt that he no alternative except to turn to individual state militias. As a result, on his fourteenth full day as commander in chief, he drafted a proposal to establish a national militia bureau. Before the day ended, however, Attorney General Edward Bates ruled that creation of such a bureau would require congressional action.[14]

Lincoln mulled over this rebuff, and by April 1 he had settled on a strategy concerning Fort Sumter. During the days of waiting to see what the expedition led by Gustavus Fox would accomplish, the president returned to the issue of military manpower.

He was already familiar with Pennsylvania's famous Whiskey Rebellion of 1794. A protest against a liquor tax was staged by several distillers of rye whiskey and grew into an organized movement backed by thousands of armed men. Congress hastily passed legislation authorizing George Washington to put down this insurrection by drafting the militia from the states adjoining Pennsylvania. Washington ordered the protesters to disperse, then briefly led the militia units that quickly put an end to the four-county "rebellion." A few leaders were sentenced to hang, but Washington commuted their sentences.[15]

Some advisers had wanted President Buchanan to call for troops to subdue the secessionists, turning to the legislation of 1794 as a precedent for his authority. He considered the matter but decided that the old statute was inapplicable to the secession issue.[16] Lincoln, who seldom agreed with a decision made by his predecessor, took a different view of the matter. Not only was he determined to react strongly to the threat toward Fort Sumter, he was also gravely concerned about the safety of the capital.

Long-standing policies required federal officials to disburse arms to state militia units under a quota system. In addition, state officials could purchase weapons from the U.S. government at bargain prices. During 1860, Alabama, Arkansas, Louisiana, Mississippi, and Virginia had bought muskets in quantity from the War Department at $2.50

per weapon. No northern state made a purchase during this period.[17]
To Lincoln, the stockpiling of muskets by the southern states meant
that an army was likely soon to try to conquer the District of Columbia. Rumors of plots to seize the district began surfacing soon after
the *Star of the West* fiasco.[18]

On April 1 the president requested General Scott to begin sending each day a summary of matters he considered significant. These
memoranda emphasized the danger of "machinations against the Government and this capital" while detailing the ineffectiveness of protection by the U.S. Army.

Scott's April 5 report showed the strength of the U.S. Army to be
17,113 officers and men. This total, however, existed on paper only.
Those effectively ready to take to the field numbered perhaps 11,000,
but they were scattered through five widely separated departments.
Governors of Indiana, Maine, Ohio, and Pennsylvania conferred with
the president on the following day. Except for Maine, each state represented could field forces several times larger than the regular army.[19]

By April 9 the aging general in chief was calling for companies of
militia, or uniformed volunteers. They were needed, he said, "to aid
in the defense of the public buildings and other public property of
the Capital against an invasion or insurrection." Numerous members
of the militia refused to take the required oaths of allegiance, perhaps
out of fear that they would be sent to fight in the South. Men who pro-
fessed loyalty to the Union were assigned to guard public buildings of
the capital.[20]

No prominent secessionist had done more than engage in empty
threats about "taking the U.S. flag from the dome of the Capitol." Yet
Washington was believed to be in grave danger. Veteran fighting men
of the U.S. Army were seen as too few to match the growing military
strength of the Confederates. If the army could not protect the capital, it was obviously incapable of taking action to restore the Union's
honor if Fort Sumter should fall.[21]

To get sufficient men to protect the capital and also to teach
secessionists a quick lesson, the president turned to state militias. His
decision was made easier by the arrival of unsolicited offers of fighting
men from Iowa, Kansas, Massachusetts, Minnesota, and Pennsylvania.[22]

Lincoln knew of only one statute that could be construed as
authorizing him to make a call for men serving in state militia units.
In this situation he decided that legislation enacted to quell the
Whiskey Rebellion was adequate for his purposes. He also knew that

the service of volunteers was limited to thirty days after the beginning of a congressional session.

When he told the lawmakers why they had not been called into special session earlier, he explained that he was afraid the rebellion might prevent their assembling.[23] Records fail to indicate when he began drafting a proclamation, calling them to the capital, but it was in final or semifinal form by the time the Fox expedition sailed.

On the evening of Sunday, April 14, the commander in chief brought his cabinet together.[24] He read a proposed proclamation, which included a call for a special session of Congress to convene on July 4. William A. Stoddard, an assistant secretary, said that there were "dark circles under his deep-set eyes," and he seemed "to be gazing at something far away, or in the future."[25]

When his advisers signified approval of the document that would be made public on Monday, Lincoln's long fingers wrapped around a quill pen and moved toward an ink well. Seconds later he signed a second document and in doing so passed the point of no return. With soldiers due to converge upon the capital soon, civil war was now a reality instead of a possibility.[26]

Lincoln's rather lame excuse for delaying the start of a special session of Congress was a fear that the lawmakers would not be able to reach the capital.

Democratic presidential candidate
Stephen A. Douglas thought Lincoln
should have called out many more men.

Having promised to say nothing, members of the group that met on Sunday evening revealed no details to the press. Even Seward, who earlier had leaked assurances that Sumter would be abandoned without a fight, maintained his silence. "Wait until tomorrow," he is said to have told an insistent correspondent. "You will get the biggest story of your life then—and so will the rest of our divided nation!"

Stephen A. Douglas, in earlier years the president's most prominent political rival, visited the Executive Mansion during the fateful Sabbath. He stayed with Lincoln for two hours—long after the cabinet members had gone home—and he pledged his support for any move calculated to save the Union.

Sharing widespread concern for the safety of the capital, Douglas had only one criticism of the still-private proclamation. He suggested that Lincoln should call for at least three times as many men as the proclamation specified.[27]

13

The Call

With a south carolina flag fluttering over still-smoldering Fort Sumter and Anderson's men in New York, Lincoln turned his legal-trained mind to the congressional act that had authorized Washington's use of state militias to quell the Whiskey Rebellion. He then turned to the first president's proclamation.[1] Lincoln's document, here condensed, was adapted from Washington's of August 7, 1794:

> Whereas the laws of the United States have been for some time past and now are opposed and the execution thereof obstructed . . . by combinations too powerful to be suppressed by the ordinary course of judicial proceedings or by the powers vested in the marshals by law: Now, therefore, I, Abraham Lincoln, President of the United States . . . hereby do call forth the militia of the several States of the Union, to the aggregate number of 75,000, in order to suppress said combinations and to cause the laws to be duly executed. . . . And I hereby command the persons comprising the combinations aforesaid to disperse and retire peaceably to their respective abodes within twenty days from date.[2]

The 1795 congressional act authorized the chief executive to call out the militia only if Congress was not in session. In addition, use of the militia was limited to thirty days after the beginning of the next session of Congress.[3]

Lincoln was not dealing with a group of angry farmers such as gathered in Pennsylvania in 1794; he was concerned about states that called themselves independent. So his order "to disperse and retire" did not fit the situation he confronted. Of greater significance, the legislation on which he depended also tied his hands. Should Congress be immediately called into special session, the militia would have to be discharged before July 1.

This factor, the unpredictable nature of Congress, and his eagerness to see Kentucky hold special elections led the chief executive to delay calling the lawmakers back to the capital. In his proclamation, issued on April 15, two days after the surrender of Sumter, he specified noon on July 4 as the starting time of the special session of Congress.[4] Perhaps because he depended upon authorization framed for a different situation, Lincoln's proclamation did not mention defending the capital. As a result, secessionists and patriots alike interpreted the call for men to indicate that an invasion of the Confederacy was likely.

Two days earlier the president had said that he did not intend to make such a move but would use all of his power to hold "the property and places belonging to the Government." Except to attain that end, he promised, "there will be no invasion—no using of force against, or among the people anywhere."[5]

Lincoln spoke to a delegation of three Virginians only, so these emphases were not made public. Even if his solemn promise had appeared on the front pages of newspapers across the country, few in the Confederacy would have believed him.

Some in the North were ready for military action, mainly ardent abolitionists eager to fight to end slavery, not to restore the Union as Lincoln expected. Because the honor and pride of the North were besmirched at Fort Sumter, many governors received the telegraphed proclamation enthusiastically. In each instance, it was accompanied by an explanation and a table of quotas drawn up by Simon Cameron, the secretary of war.[6]

Twelve states accepted their quotas within a few hours after receiving them. Gov. John A. Andrew of Massachusetts offered money and credit in addition to men. Gov. William Dennison said that Ohioans would fill as many regiments as needed and was disappointed when instructed to send only thirteen regiments.

Gov. Thomas H. Hicks of Maryland was hesitant to make a commitment because thousands of his constituents were Southern sympathizers.[7] In New Jersey, the quartermaster general of militia reported that his men were "poorly provided with serviceable arms and accouterments." His reply concerning the state's quota was

Gov. John A. Andrew of Massachusetts
was an ardent supporter of the Lincoln
policy when the call for militia was
issued.

deferred until he could find out whether or not the U.S. government
could furnish these.

Conditional replies such as that from New Jersey were rare. In
Pennsylvania the Ringgold Artillerists of Reading were already on the
way to Washington when Lincoln's call was issued. Iowa also responded
early. Before receiving the telegram from Washington, Gov. Samuel J.
Kirkwood had informed the secretary of war that "fifteen to twenty volunteer companies have already tendered their services." Soon he dispatched an urgent new message to the capital: "For God's sake send us
arms! We have the men."[8]

Replies from the governors of those Southern states that had not
seceded were exact opposites of those of the Northern governors. John
W. Ellis of North Carolina was incredulous. Responding to Cameron,
he doubted the authenticity of the extraordinary dispatch. Any call for
troops for Federal service, he said, could only be "for the purpose of
subjugating the States of the South in violation of the Constitution."

Gov. Beriah Magoffin of Kentucky—a large state that Lincoln
considered crucial—replied to Cameron that his state "will furnish no
troops for the wicked purpose of subduing her sister Southern States."
Gov. John Letcher of Virginia refused to send troops and added a
warning: "You have chosen to inaugurate civil war, and having done
so, we will meet it in a spirit as determined as the Administration has
exhibited toward the South."

Gov. John Letcher of Virginia interpreted the call for troops as meaning that Washington had started a civil war.

Gov. Isham G. Harris of Tennessee responded that his state would not provide a single man "for purpose of coercion, but 50,000 if necessary, for the defense of our rights and those of our Southern brothers." From Jefferson City, Gov. Claiborne F. Jackson of Missouri castigated Lincoln's requisition of troops as "illegal, unconstitutional, and revolutionary in its object, inhuman and diabolical."[9]

The reactions of citizens, North and South, were as vigorous and diverse as those of their governors. Horace Greeley rejoiced that the widespread view that the president needed the consent of Congress "to call out troops and to initiate war" was erroneous. Initially apathetic, New Yorkers soon staged a massive parade in support of Lincoln's proclamation. Citizens of Philadelphia notified Scott, "It is enough for us to know that the beloved and glorious flag of our Federal Union has been assailed [at Fort Sumter], and we ask no further questions."[10]

The president of the University of Michigan, Henry P. Tappan, said, "The 700 young men committed to my charge are ready to march in a body if need be, & I am ready to march at their head." In Madison, Wisconsin, a Democratic newspaper announced, "The South having taken up the sword against the Government, let the rebellious spirit be subdued by the sword."[11]

Newspaper editors in Philadelphia did not agree with one another. At the *Press,* one month was considered time enough to quell the rebellion, but at the *Public Ledger* the editors believed that the call for arms would bring an end to sectional strife.[12]

An informal poll in Baltimore suggested that Lincoln was insane. In Saint Louis the president was castigated for having assumed "an authority to levy war without the consent of Congress." Several Southern editors suggested, "Mr. Lincoln needs no Congress." Confederate Vice President Alexander H. Stephens said that the call for "men to defend the Government" was wholly unconstitutional." Jefferson Davis accurately labeled the proclamation as a presidential declaration of war.[13]

One of the most unusual responses appeared in Mobile, Alabama. Twenty-four hours after Lincoln's call was issued, the local newspaper carried in one of its business columns a display advertisement that read:

> 75,000 COFFINS WANTED
> Proposals will be received to supply the Confederacy with 75,000
> black coffins.—No proposal will be entertained
> coming north of Mason and Dixon's line.
> Direct to
> Jeff Davis, Montgomery, Alabama[14]

Editor Horace Greeley of the *New York Herald* wrote that the president had full authority to call out troops without consulting Congress or the people.

IN NEW ORLEANS, SOMEONE familiar with the 1794 Whiskey Rebellion denounced the presidential document as insolent, taking "the form of proclamation [used] against a disorderly mob [rather than sovereign states].[15]

Lincoln biographer Carl Sandburg concluded that the president's decision to call for the militia grew out of his preference for a brief "immediate war" rather than "many smaller wars to follow." If that verdict is accurate, it indicates that Lincoln failed to understand the South. Not simply in the seceded states, but in others north of the Cotton Belt, he was generally considered to have been the aggressor at Fort Sumter. When the call for troops came immediately after the Charleston struggle, the rank-and-file Southerners quickly reconciled to the idea of war.[16]

Many in the North shared the president's view that the South would be vanquished in a few weeks, with little loss of life. As a result, some states offered so many men that a number of their regiments were refused. A total of 91,816 men were reported as having responded to the call for 75,000. Of these, approximately 80,000 were mustered into Federal service for ninety days.[17]

On May 15 Lincoln made public his confidence in the strength of perhaps one hundred regiments of state militia. Although many had little training and carried nearly obsolete weapons, the president was sure they could bring the wayward states back into the Union in less than three months.

At least four nonmilitary factors were basic to the complex national situation. Lincoln assessed one of them correctly but failed to gauge the significance of the other three.

(1) *In resources the twenty-seven loyal states vastly exceeded those of the seven seceded states.* The president's unbounded optimism reflected that of the North in general. An editorial in the April 17 issue of the *New York Times,* here greatly condensed, analyzed several aspects of sectional resources:

> Money is equivalent to numerical superiority in men, in ships, in means of locomotion and subsistence, and in their perfection and completion of instruments of destruction. We may concede personal courage to our opponents, fully equal to our own, and still leave them in hopeless inferiority as to their ability to maintain anything like an equal fight. The Confederate states contain a white population of about 2,500,000, or about one-eighth the population of the northern states.

In the seceding states there is neither a powder mill nor a foundry for the casting of cannon, nor an establishment for the manufacture of arms. The seceding states cannot manufacture a yard of clothing fit for a soldier's wear, nor raise the food for his rations. The North has an immeasurable advantage in its command of the sea. All the southern produce must float upon it to market.[18]

Although oversimplified, this summary is an index to the outlook of the North in general and the president in particular.

(2) *Unionists, both prominent and obscure, could be found throughout the South.* Jefferson Davis, Alexander H. Stephens, Robert E. Lee, and scores of other men destined to lead the Confederacy were in principle opposed to secession.

Western Virginia and Eastern Tennessee were wholeheartedly on the side of the Union. Fifteen counties in Texas and one in Mississippi voted down the concept of secession. In North Carolina an early attempt to hold a secession convention was suppressed by Unionists. When Arkansas held a state convention in March, secession was defeated by a vote of thirty-nine to thirty-five.

Lincoln knew of these matters and many more, so he expected that a show of force on his part would enable Unionists to triumph in state after state. He was right in recognizing the importance of these persons but wrong in thinking them capable of seizing the reins of state government throughout the Cotton Belt.[19]

(3) *Especially, but not exclusively in the South, primary loyalty came to focus on the state rather than on the nation.* This attitude was a holdover from colonial times during which thirteen sets of pride developed. When the league of states was formed under the Articles of Confederation, geographically based pride was conspicuous. New Yorkers were so state-oriented that ratification of the U.S. Constitution nearly failed among them. Most early threats of secession centered in what is now the Northeast.[20]

Skilled as Lincoln was as a statesman, his background on the western frontier lacked any sensitivity to the attitudes in the South and the East. When he called for troops, he did not realize that even among many of his volunteers, their primary loyalty was to their state rather than to the nation. State loyalty led many West Point graduates opposed to secession to resign their commissions and accept appointment in the Confederate military. Union armies never ceased to struggle with problems rooted in the selection of lower-level officers by their own states rather than by the nation for which they were fighting.

Alexander H. Stephens, vice president of the Confederate States, made empty threats concerning the magnitude of the manpower pool within the seceded states.

LIBRARY OF CONGRESS

(4) *Lincoln's call for seventy-five thousand men gave secessionists a clear signal that they must fight to defend their homelands from invasion.* Lincoln failed to understand this long-range implication, although warnings were voiced, such as this from a Louisville newspaper: "Only by the utter annihilation of the whole population of Seceding States, only by the transformation of the entire South into a red and reeking desert, could the laws of the United States be enforced there; and they could not be enforced even then, for there would be none upon whom they could operate."[21]

Scoffing at the notion that seventy-five thousand men could put an end to sectional strife, Alexander H. Stephens said, "We [in the Confederacy] can call out a million of people, if need be, and when they are cut down, we can call out another, and still another, until the last man of the South finds a bloody grave."[22] Quoting Jefferson Davis, P. G. T. Beauregard declared that he fought "to save our homes and firesides from Northern invaders, and to maintain our freedom and independence as a nation."

Lincoln expected too much of Unionists in the South, failed to grasp the depth of state pride in the South and East, and did not dream that secessionists would fight so fiercely for "homes and firesides." Although met promptly, his call for men did not signal the quick capitulation by his foes. Instead it started a fast-moving series of increasingly severe strikes and counterstrikes.

14

War on the Water

In MONTGOMERY, ALABAMA, Jefferson Davis paced nervously as events unfolded in rapid fashion following the surrender of Fort Sumter. He knew that Lincoln would respond, but he did not expect a call for militia would come so quickly.

To be ready to react to whatever news might come from Washington, the Confederate commander in chief had devised a plan, confident that it would allow the South to strike at the most vulnerable part of the Northern economy: its seaborne commerce. On April 17 he made public a proclamation offering to issue letters of marque and reprisal. Such documents would authorize ships to become privateers, preying upon Union vessels and taking them as prizes of war.[1]

In Charleston, news of the Confederate policy was hailed with delight. Newspaper editors were confident that Federal commerce "will fall an easy prey to our bold privateers; and California gold will pay all little expenses on our part."

Soon detailed regulations were issued, linked with a formal declaration of war by the Confederate States of America, which regarded Lincoln's call for troops as equivalent to a declaration of war by the United States. The appearance of these documents in Northern ports threw some ship owners into panic. Most of them were aware that the U.S. Navy was powerless to protect more than a tiny fraction of the oceangoing vessels sailing from the major cities along the East Coast.[2]

There was no other way for Davis to take the conflict to the water, as the Confederacy had no warships. Also, using privateers was a

When chasing prey, the privateer *Savannah* flew only the Stars and Bars until within gunshot of its target.

time-honored practice. They had participated in every previous war in which the United States was involved. For centuries, such vessels had supplemented the fleets of Great Britain and other European countries.

Just as Lincoln had done advance research on the Whiskey Rebellion legislation, so Davis had prepared to launch privateers as early as the start of the artillery duel between Beauregard and Anderson. Had this not been the case, it would have been impossible for a band of twelve Charleston ship owners to receive letters of marque dated April 18. In one of these documents, Davis wrote: "By virtue of the power vested in me by law I have commissioned and do hereby commission the schooner or vessel called the *Savannah* . . . to act as a private armed vessel in the service of the Confederate States on the high seas against the United States of America, their ships, vessels, goods and effects."[3]

News of the *Savannah*'s commissioning as a privateer did not reach Washington until May, but Lincoln had the text of Davis's proclamation in hand only a few hours after it was issued. The next day, April 19, only four days after having called for the militia, Lincoln issued another proclamation. The insurrection under way in seven states, he said in two introductory paragraphs, made it impossible to collect revenues there. Also, the insurrectionists "have threatened to grant pretended letters of marque" authorizing assaults against U.S.

commerce. Then two paragraphs, here condensed, proclaimed that until Congress met and deliberated the president deemed it "advisable to set on foot a blockade of the ports within the [insurgent] States aforesaid, in pursuance of the laws of the United States, and of the law of Nations. [A]ny person [who] shall molest a vessel of the United States will be held amenable to the laws of the United States for the prevention and punishment of piracy."[4]

Although his last sentence soon came back to haunt him because of international laws, the president was confident that his blockade would bring a halt to commerce in every Confederate state. Eight days later he extended the blockade to Virginia and North Carolina, although neither state had yet seceded. Thus the U.S. Navy was required to take control of a thirty-five-hundred-mile coastline.[5]

Many Southerners laughed, boasting that the privateers being outfitted in New Orleans, Charleston, Savannah, and Wilmington would soon be more numerous than Federal warships.[6] Officers and seamen of the U.S. Navy were astounded. Incredulity was the prevailing mood in France and England. In the British House of Lords, the earl of Darby challenged the legality of the blockade on May 16. The editors of the French newspaper *La Patrie* pointed out that the Federal fleet consisted of "86 vessels, on paper."[7]

The French information was erroneous; the U.S. Navy had forty-two vessels in commission. Many warships, however, were on foreign duty, and most of the ships at home were laid up for repairs. On March 10 naval personnel in Atlantic Coast ports and receiving ships numbered 207, but that number had begun to increase before the firing upon Fort Sumter.[8]

Reacting in much the same way as did the editors of foreign newspapers, Lt. William H. Anderson of the U.S. Navy said, "We threw down our gauntlet to the world on the strength of a few decrepit and superannuated hulks." Observers later noted that Lincoln did not wait for the Confederates to fire to begin getting ready for war on the water.

Presidential secretaries Nicolay and Hay reported that when the blockade was announced, "The Navy Department had only three steam-vessels at its immediate disposal in home ports." Sen. Charles Sumner, who knew only a little about the condition of the U.S. Navy, strongly objected to use of the word *blockade* in the president's proclamation. As he saw it, this term "vindicated" the Confederate claim of a state of belligerency, not insurrection.[9]

Well before Confederates fired upon Fort Sumter, activity at the Brooklyn Navy Yard suddenly accelerated, although no one would tell newspaper reporters why this activity took place. Schedules for refitting the *Minnesota, Mississippi, Colorado,* and *Bainbridge* were drastically reduced. Two ocean steamers of the Collins line, the *Baltic* and the *Atlantic,* were suddenly "appropriated to Government service."

During the decade between 1851 and 1860 the U.S. Navy rarely acquired half a dozen vessels during any twelve-month period. With Congress not in session to appropriate funds, thirty-seven vessels were somehow chartered, purchased, or transferred from the army and the revenue service between April and June 1861. Twenty-two more were acquired in July.[10]

Looking back on what took place so quickly and quietly that few citizens knew what was happening, newspaper editors concluded that "the man from Illinois didn't wait for Confederates to fire before putting things in motion for war on the water."

If Union naval readiness was greater than it seemed at first glance, legal preparation for a blockade was not. Under international law, a nation could declare a blockade only when fighting against another nation. Thus some of Lincoln's advisers warned that the blockade gave implicit recognition to the Confederate States of America, which Lincoln was adamantly withholding. Also, international law recognized a blockade only if it were enforced. A "paper blockade" had no legal standing among maritime nations.

Congressman Thaddeus Stevens of Pennsylvania, head of the House Ways and Means Committee, made a special trip to Washington to challenge the proclamation of a blockade. Tradition has it that the president listened politely to an exposition concerning international law, then responded, "I see what you are driving at, but I don't know much about the laws of nations, and I don't think they apply to this situation."

Nearly impotent to enforce the blockade at the time it was announced, the U.S. Navy gained rapidly in size and power. Soon the reality of the blockade at Charleston was acknowledged.[11] By year's end the register showed that 136 vessels had been bought, 34 had been repaired, and 52 were under construction. By 1865 the ranks of the Federal navy included 51,500 men. From its $12 million budget in 1861, it jumped to annual expenditures of $123 million. Assessed from a distance, Lincoln's blockade proved to be among the most effective of Federal war measures.

During the spring and summer of 1861, however, many Federal officials wished they had never heard of the president's warning linking the letters of marque and piracy. On June 3, the privateer *Savannah* was captured by the USS *Perry* and taken to New York.[12] Since the officers and members of the crew were considered pirates, they were treated as criminals rather than as prisoners of war.

Clapped in irons, the seamen from the South were taken to Philadelphia for a trial that gained great publicity.[13] A sister vessel, the privateer *Jeff Davis,* sailed into the spotlight almost as soon as it was captured, and its crew members were also tried for the crimes of treason and piracy.[14]

As soon as the Confederates learned that some of their seamen were facing the death penalty, President Davis sent a special agent to Washington. Lincoln refused to receive the Confederate, whose message included a threat: "Painful as will be the necessity, this Government will deal out to prisoners held by it the same treatment and the

Libby Prison in Richmond was reserved for captured Union officers; enlisted men went to Belle Isle in the same city.

Libby Prison inmate Alfred Ely, congressman from New York.

NATIONAL ARCHIVES

same fate as shall be experienced by those captured [on the *Savannah* and the *Jeff Davis*]."[15]

Receiving no reply from Lincoln, Davis ordered that Federal officers held as prisoners should be selected as hostages for the safety of the Confederate seamen. When lots were drawn at Richmond's Libby Prison, Alfred Ely of New York, captured at Manassas as a civilian, was "selected to do the honors" for men whose lives were to be laid on the line. The first man chosen to die in retaliation for the execution of the "pirates" was Col. Michael Corcoran of the Sixty-ninth New York Infantry. Soon he and other hostages were sent to Charleston, where they were imprisoned in Castle Pinckney. The charges of piracy were quietly dropped, and the seamen and hostages were eventually exchanged.[16]

The piracy charge, one of the most inflammatory of the war, was of minor importance when compared with another issue that revolved about captured ships. In his May 18, 1861, proclamation concerning letters of marque, Davis recognized the existence of a state of war. His verdict was supported by the Confederate Congress on May 6. Lincoln, however, branded the conflict as an insurrection, holding that war can be waged only between independent nations. This remained the official Federal stance as late as 1863.[17]

Eventually the question of whether or not the capture of enemy ships was legal reached the U.S. Supreme Court. Confederate owners of four small vessels sued the nation, claiming that a blockade could not be imposed until war was declared. With three new Lincoln appointees having joined the court, evidence was heard concerning the ships *Amy Warwick, Crenshaw, Hiawatha,* and *Brilliante.*

In a five-to-four decision, the Court upheld the legality of the blockade and the four early captures. So in spite of the fact that Lincoln's blockade was illegal under international law, the date of his proclamation, April 19, became recognized as the start of the war he persisted in calling an insurrection.[18]

Records fail to indicate how many additional privateers were built after twenty had been commissioned by November 1861. Many Confederate documents were destroyed, and the only Federal list is far from complete. No letters of marque were issued by the Lincoln administration, but vessels privately owned or chartered were put into Federal service.[19]

It was Davis's threat to use small and obscure privately owned ships that evoked Lincoln's angry proclamation of a blockade. Many months later, a rapid-fire exchange of challenges between the presidents who took the war to the water went to the U.S. Supreme Court. The decision of the high court eventually gave legality to the by-then awful conflict.

Col. Michael Corcoran, imprisoned for months, spent part of the time at Castle Pinckney in Charleston Harbor.

U.S. ARMY MILITARY HISTORY INSTITUTE

15

Citizen Rights Suspended

Dabbing his rheumy eyes with a handkerchief, Lt. Gen. Winfield Scott bellowed for an aide. Handing over a sheet of foolscap that had come from the Executive Mansion, he indicated that he wished it read to him. Signed by Lincoln and dated April 27, 1861, it said: "You are engaged in suppressing an insurrection against the laws of the United States. If at any point on or in the vicinity of the military line which is now used between the City of Philadelphia and the City of Washington . . . you find resistance which renders it necessary to suspend the writ of Habeas Corpus for the public safety, you . . . are authorized to suspend that writ."[1]

Dismissing his aide, Scott retrieved a document in the president's handwriting that had been transmitted two days earlier. It noted that the Maryland legislature would assemble on April 26 and that it appeared likely that the lawmakers would "arm the people of that State against the United States." If they proceeded to arm their citizens, the president continued, Scott was authorized "to adopt the most prompt, and efficient measures to counteract their actions, even if necessary, to the bombardment of their cities—and in the extremist necessity, the suspension of the writ of habeas corpus."[2]

The general was surprised at the president's second order concerning habeas corpus. If it became necessary to take a bridge burner into custody, officers of the U.S. Army were not to release him if some judge who sympathized with secessionists issued a writ of habeas corpus.

After moving his headquarters to Washington, Gen. Winfield Scott visited the Executive Mansion daily.

During this period in which the capital was in isolation, the president's mood in the Executive Mansion alternated between fear and rage. According to his secretaries, he paced the floor for long periods, wondering when militia units from the Northern states would arrive and whether secessionists would dare to launch an attack before then. It was imperative, he insisted, that Union forces keep control of the railroad link between Baltimore and Washington; without it, defensive forces could not reach their destination.[3]

Anticipating even worse trouble in Maryland than had already been experienced, Lincoln pondered his options. He knew that the time-honored writ of habeas corpus took precedence over military tribunals, even during the Aaron Burr conspiracy.[4] Yet it would be futile to have hostile citizens arrested if they could be turned loose by a few strokes of a judge's pen.

After having called for seventy-five thousand volunteers, the president asked Attorney General Bates to prepare an opinion on the legality of bypassing the Fifth Amendment to establish martial law, if needed. Bates turned Lincoln's request over to an assistant, Titian J. Coffee, whose report reached the chief executive on the morning of April 20. It pointed out that habeas corpus is the only law concerning personal liberties that is mentioned in the body of the U.S. Constitution. The Founding Fathers initially voted that it should not be suspended under any circumstances. At the insistence of Gouverneur Morris, they agreed that it might be temporarily suspended when the public safety was endangered. Coffee's summary suggested that Lincoln did not have authority to suspend the writ.[5]

An opinion rendered earlier by Associate Justice Joseph Story of the U.S. Supreme Court stipulated that only Congress had the power to suspend habeas corpus. Legal experts and many ordinary citizens had adopted this position long before the Coffee brief was prepared.[6]

Lincoln, however, considered the language of Article 1, Section 9, to be ambiguous. Therefore, with the existence of the nation at stake, he drafted the directive that reached Scott on April 27. Since the military order was not made public, there was no outcry.

Soon the president took another giant step. On May 10 a proclamation suspending habeas corpus along the Florida coast and on the adjoining islands authorized military authorities "to remove from the vicinity of the United States fortresses all dangerous or suspected persons."[7]

Two days before the 1861 special session of Congress was scheduled to begin on July 4, suspension of the long-cherished process aimed at preserving personal liberty was extended to New York. Ninety days

HARPER'S HISTORY OF THE GREAT REBELLION

George P. Kane of Baltimore made no secret of his readiness to support secessionists.

In divided Maryland, Gov. Thomas H. Hicks was a strong supporter of Lincoln's moves aimed at bringing an early end to "the insurrection."

HARPER'S HISTORY OF THE GREAT REBELLION

later the directive was enlarged again and extended to Bangor, Maine. Another proclamation applied only to the District of Columbia.[8]

Temporarily the hot spot of trouble outside the states that had seceded, Baltimore soon felt the full impact of Lincoln's presidential wrath. Suspected of disloyalty, police marshal George P. Kane and mayor George W. Brown were imprisoned late in June. With the Maryland legislature due to convene on September 17, it was feared that secession might be voted. So beginning on September 12, a series of raids sent numerous lawmakers and the chief clerk of the state senate to jail.[9] Because Gov. Thomas H. Hicks was an outspoken Unionist, he was not arrested. Lincoln's public justification of his actions with regard to civil liberties took the form of a question: "Are all the laws, but one, to go unexecuted, and the government itself go to pieces, lest that one be violated?"[10]

In July 1861 the Thirty-seventh Congress began considering the habeas corpus issue, which by then was being debated throughout the North. Two years later, lawmakers would bypass the question of whether or not Lincoln acted within his authority, but during the closing hours of the short session in 1861, by voice vote Congress authorized the president to suspend the writ "whenever, in his judgment, the public safety may require it."

Before this legislation was enacted, suspension had been extended to the entire Union. Persons trying to evade military service or seeking to stir up trouble were as likely to be targets as were outspoken friends of secession. Many in the North were arrested for expressing opposition to the draft. Some went to jail in 1864 because they opposed Lincoln's reelection.[11]

By September 1863, the once-uncertain chief executive was ready for the most sweeping edict of all. In a brief proclamation, he repeated the national suspension and stipulated that it "will continue throughout the duration of the rebellion, or until this proclamation shall be modified or revoked by a subsequent one issued by the President of the United States."[12]

As conducted under the regime of Secretary of War Edwin M. Stanton, the working formula used by military leaders was: Seize suspects and jail them without trial or explanation! Statutes were fuzzy; record keeping was casual and often sporadic. As a result, no one found out how many citizens were locked up on charges that were often vague.

In 1925 U.S. Adjutant General Robert C. Davis admitted that he saw no hope of reaching "an approximately definite estimate of the total number" of persons imprisoned for political reasons during the Civil War. A count made in the record and pension office

Secretary of War Edwin M. Stanton was merciless in putting suspects into jail without trial.

of the War Department listed 13,535 citizens "arrested and confined in military prisons from February, 1862, to the end of the war." This total does not include military arrests that were not reported to the commissary general of prisoners.[13]

Challenges by legal authorities had no more impact than did cries of indignation from members of the general public. With freedom for slaves added as a military goal, the initial drive to preserve the Union became an unyielding demand for the unconditional surrender of the Rebels. In this climate, civil rights meant little. Once Lincoln's letter was delivered to Scott on April 27, 1861, there was no stopping the drive to stamp out opposition of every kind. Late in the conflict there was a move to refer the habeas corpus issue again to the U.S. Supreme Court. Yet when the president died on April 15, 1865, edicts that denied constitutional rights to citizens everywhere remained in effect.[14]

Lincoln justified his disregard for civil rights by saying that in order to save the entire Constitution, it was sometimes necessary to violate a small part of it. In a letter to a Kentucky editor he argued that "measures, otherwise unconstitutional, might become lawful, by becoming indispensable to the preservation of the constitution, through the preservation of the nation."[15]

Initially reluctant to try to gain their freedom, slaves began flocking to Union lines in large numbers after they learned that emanicipation had become a war goal.

Habeas corpus was suspended in the Confederacy also, but there Congress rather than the president was in control. The Confederate Congress gave Davis limited discretionary power on February 27, 1862, and on March 1 he suspended the writ in Richmond.[16] Davis could act only when cities or regions were considered to be in danger of invasion, and he exercised this power less frequently than he wished. Some analysts believe they see a link between the "turning of the tide against the Confederacy" and its congressional refusal to give the president a free hand to establish martial law and suspend habeas corpus.[17]

With the issue of states' rights still a touchy subject, suspension of habeas corpus was widely denounced as "usurpation from Richmond." In Georgia the legislature ordered that any judge who refused to issue a writ should forfeit twenty-five hundred dollars to the aggrieved party. North Carolina's governor denounced "suspension of the civil authorities" as establishing a dangerous precedent.[18]

Records concerning arbitrary arrests in the South are even less complete than are those of the North. John Minor Botts, a Unionist living in Virginia, was among the most prominent Southerners to be imprisoned on vague charges. A financial analyst, J. B. D. DeBow, was imprisoned for writing, "Cotton has failed us; the negro has failed or will fail us." Slaves, who constituted about 40 percent of the population of seceded states, never enjoyed the protection of the writ and were not involved in Southern debate about it.[19]

Another of Lincoln's measures was ignored in the South but created turmoil in the North. On May 3, 1861, he ordered the size of the U.S. Army increased by 22,714 officers and men. At the same time, he directed the U.S. Navy to accept 18,000 volunteers. A congressional attempt to reduce the size of the army to that of July 1861 "within six months after the rebellion should be put down" was easily defeated.[20]

Throughout the North, many people questioned Lincoln's authority to take extraordinary measures without congressional approval. As a result, a special resolution was introduced in the Senate on July 7, 1861. Its preamble listed six moves taken by Lincoln that had been challenged: (1) his call for seventy-five thousand militia, (2) his April 19 proclamation of a blockade, (3) his April 27 extension of the blockade to Virginia and North Carolina, (4) his first suspension of the writ of habeas corpus, (5) his enlargement of armed forces without congressional approval, and (6) his suspension of habeas corpus in Florida.

This legislative measure ended with a paragraph stipulating that each of the president's "extraordinary acts, proclamations and orders" was in every respect "legal and valid." Although the act failed to pass, Lincoln took its introduction as his personal vindication. During the closing hours of the session, Sen. Henry Wilson of Massachusetts drew up an amendment that legalized Lincoln's use of war powers. Attached to a military pay bill, the measure passed without opposition.[21]

The turbulent days after the fall of Fort Sumter led to changes seldom clearly seen at the time. When Lincoln became the sixteenth president, he was chief executive of twenty-seven loosely linked and largely independent states and—he insisted—seven states claiming to have seceded.

By the time Congress approved what he had done without legal action, the nation was looming into larger significance. The power of the states was beginning to wane, and the United States as we know it was beginning to take shape.[22] In Charleston, neither Robert Anderson nor P. G. T. Beauregard realized that their artillery duel would have such far-reaching effects in so short a time.

Part 3

The President Loses Control

Self-taught Abraham Lincoln towered above nearly all of his contemporaries, mentally as well as physically.

16

The Loss of a General

W EARY FROM TRAVEL, LT. COL. Robert E. Lee reached Arlington on March 1, 1861.[1] Family members soon learned that he had packed his gear hurriedly, knowing that he might never return to Texas. His ambulance had been ready on the evening of February 12, so he had left his post the following day.[2]

Orders from Maj. Gen. David E. Twiggs had reached Lee at Fort Mason a few days earlier. According to the dispatch relayed to him by the commander of the Department of Texas, Lee was relieved of duty "by direct order of the War Department" and was ordered to report in person to Lt. Gen. Winfield Scott no later than April 1.[3]

According to the recollections of Lt. R. W. Johnson, Lee was deeply troubled upon receiving these orders. Although he had not been promoted during the last five years, a jump in rank would hardly call for a personal visit to the office of the general in chief. With sectional strife becoming increasingly likely since Lincoln's November 1860 election, almost anything could happen. Earlier, Scott had made no attempt to conceal his affection for the officer of the Second Cavalry. Was it possible that Scott would now ask him to fill a post in his headquarters staff? That seemed improbable since Lee earlier had declined the opportunity to become Scott's military secretary.

As Lee climbed into his ambulance at Fort Mason, Johnson waved his hand for the vehicle to wait. Dashing to it, he tossed an eager question: "Colonel, which way will you go—North or South?"

Having already wrestled with the possibility of having to make such a decision, Lee responded without hesitation: "I shall never bear arms against the Union—but circumstances may force me to carry a musket in defense of Virginia."[4]

Lee reached San Antonio's Read House early on the afternoon of February 16, and he soon found himself surrounded by a crowd of people curious to hear what an army officer would have to say. Puzzled, he asked a few questions and was thunderstruck to learn that earlier that day members of the Texas state forces had seized the federal installations in the city.[5]

Wanting nothing to do with quarrels in Texas, he headed for Indianola in hope of finding a steamer that would take him to New Orleans. When Lt. R. M. Potter, who had served under him, came to tell him good-bye, he saw that Lee was distraught. According to Potter's recollections, his former commander told him that he did not believe in secession as a constitutional right, but he feared that Virginia might secede. "When I get there," Lee said, "the country is likely to have one soldier less; I think I may resign and go to planting corn."[6]

It took two weeks to reach New Orleans but then only four days to travel to Alexandria. From the depot, Lee went directly to Arlington. Inherited by his wife, a great-granddaughter of Martha Washington, it sat within sight of the Capitol in now-divided Washington.

Reporting to the War Department after an arduous journey that spanned almost half the continent, Lee spent nearly three hours with General Scott. Neither man left a record of their conversation. Almost certainly, however, Scott informed his protégé that a promotion to full colonel was in process.[7]

According to Lincoln's personal secretaries, the president had asked Francis P. Blair Sr. "to ascertain Lee's feelings and intentions."[8] During months spent in Saint Louis as an engineer in charge of construction of a controversial dike, Lee had become well acquainted with Francis Blair's son, Montgomery, a rising civic leader. Six years younger than Lee, Montgomery Blair was now postmaster general in Lincoln's cabinet.

Francis Blair, now seventy years old, had been brought to Washington in 1830 by Andrew Jackson. While editor of the *Globe* newspaper, he became acquainted with the men of influence in all the political parties. As a delegate to the Chicago convention at which Lincoln was nominated, the elder Blair helped to persuade delegates from the western states to back the candidate from Illinois. That was

DICTIONARY OF AMERICAN PORTRAITS

At age seventy, journalist-politician Francis Blair Sr. wielded great power.

enough to give him a close relationship with the first Republican to occupy the Executive Mansion. Although he offered advice to the point of annoyance, he was among Lincoln's inner circle of advisers. Hence it was natural for the president to use him in delicate matters.

On April 18 the newly promoted Colonel Lee made his way to Blair's yellow mansion at 1651 Pennsylvania Avenue, where Lincoln's confidant wasted little time with formalities.[9] It was known, he remarked, that the president's militia call of April 15 would soon cause troops to converge upon the capital. With the approval of both the president and the secretary of war, Simon Cameron, the elder statesman wanted to know whether or not Lee would take field command of the armies of the United States.

Lee was as direct as his host. According to his account of the interview, he told Blair that "though opposed to secession and deprecating war," he could under no circumstances participate in "an invasion of the Southern States."[10] Although the offer to Lee is sometimes described as "having probably been made," Secretary of War Cameron attested to its authenticity.[11]

From the residence later known as Blair House, Lee went to Winfield Scott's office. Before he reported to the portly commanding general about his session with Blair, Scott sensed what the outcome had been. He listened to Lee's account, heaved a great sigh, ponderously drew himself to his full six feet four and one-half inches in height, and delivered a verdict obviously prepared in advance: "There are times when every officer in the United States' service should decide upon the course he will pursue, and frankly state what it will be. No one should continue to be employed by the government who will not actively do his job. If you purpose to resign, it is proper that you should do so immediately; your present position is equivocal."[12] Scott's warning was not needed, for Lee knew that if he refused to follow an order to take action against secessionists, he would be stripped of his uniform and good name.[13]

No one was more keenly aware than Lee that his experience in field command was extremely limited. Once, for six weeks in 1856, he had led a scouting expedition that included four squadrons of horse soldiers. He had never commanded in battle.[14] Other men in uniform outranked him. Fellow West Pointer Joseph E. Johnston, with a staff rank of brigadier general, had been quartermaster general of the U.S.

Joseph E. Johnston, shown surrendering to Sherman, would have been a logical choice for field commander of Union forces.

Numerous Civil War generals gained their first combat experience at Cerro Gordo and other battles of the Mexican War.

Army for nearly a year.[15] Why was the offer of top command not made to him?

Why not another Johnston—Albert Sidney? Two years ahead of Lee at West Point, he had been secretary of war in the Republic of Texas and had led the First Texas Rifles during the Mexican War. Back in the regular army, he became colonel of the famous Second Cavalry in 1855. After serving in the 1857 campaign against the Mormons in Utah, he was breveted a brigadier general. Why was Lee, rather than Albert Sidney Johnston—or some other seasoned combat leader— offered the key post?

Could it be that Lincoln hoped Virginia would remain in the Union if the Federal forces in the field were headed by a native son? Perhaps. Yet Joseph E. Johnston was also a Virginian, and Albert Johnston, like Lincoln, was a native of the crucial border state of Kentucky.

Lee may have arrived at a satisfactory answer to the question, "Why me?" If so, he never revealed what it was. Forty-eight hours after having returned to Arlington from his Washington visit of April 18, he penned a letter so terse that from the perspective of generations it seems almost curt:

Arlington, Virginia (Washington City P.O.)
20 April 1861

Honble Simon Cameron
Secty of War
Sir:

I have the honor to tender the resignation of my commission as Colonel of the 1st Regt. of Cavalry.

Very resp'y Your Obedient Servant.
R. E. Lee
Col 1st Cav'y[16]

A much longer communication, almost apologetic in tone, was directed to Scott. In it Lee offered an explanation of this momentous change in his life: "Save in defence of my native State, I never desire again to draw my sword."[17]

When that memorable sentence was framed, Lee may have hoped for the life of a gentleman farmer to which he had alluded upon leaving Texas. He was perhaps disappointed as well as surprised to receive on April 20 a letter from Judge John Robertson of Richmond. Happening to be in Alexandria, the writer explained, he begged the favor of an interview.[18]

Dressed as a civilian, Lee attended services at Christ Church, then found that Robertson had been called to Washington. That evening a courier brought an apologetic letter that urged him immediately to go to the Virginia capital for a conference with Gov. John Letcher. Such a communication could mean only one thing. Virginia needed the services of the man who still did not know why he had been offered field command of all Federal forces. Official acceptance of his resignation did not reach him until April 25.[19]

Out of the U.S. Army barely forty-eight hours, Lee would soon exchange his civilian attire for a uniform identifying him as an officer of Virginia state troops. He had no idea what Letcher might expect him to do, but he knew that Virginia held vital military posts that were manned by Federal forces.

Lee's resignation was the most significant of many, but it was far from the first. P. G. T. Beauregard, second in the forty-five-member West Point class of 1838, had relinquished his commission on February 8 and was removed from rolls on February 20. Lt. R. K. Meade, who helped to defend Fort Sumter against Beauregard's artillery, resigned to become a Confederate officer. Gunners who fired at the

Known to intimates as "Seminole," E. Kirby-Smith changed uniforms without a moment's hesitation.

LIBRARY OF CONGRESS

fort from shore included Lt. Wade Hampton Gibbes, enrolled at West Point until recently.[20]

In addition to Lee and Beauregard, officers who changed uniforms included Albert S. Johnston, Joseph E. Johnston, E. Kirby-Smith, Franklin Buchanan, Matthew F. Maury, and Samuel E. Cooper. Some of these men kept their emotions to themselves, but Joe Johnston did not. With the secession of Virginia regarded as a certainty, he told Secretary Cameron, "To leave the service is a hard necessity, but I must go [with my native state]."[21]

At the outbreak of the Civil War, the U.S. Army included 1,098 officers, of whom 286 resigned and accepted Confederate commissions. Two-thirds of these professional soldiers were graduates of West Point. Resignations from the U.S. Navy were in approximately the same ratio.[22]

Much of Maj. Robert Anderson's anguish at Charleston stemmed from his sense of duty that forced him to make war against the South in which he had been born. Most of the resignations "that left U.S. armed forces leaking like sieves" stemmed from placing loyalty to a man's state of birth or state of adoption above loyalty to the Union. Perhaps because he was a son of the frontier, this factor was never understood by Lincoln. As a result, he vastly underestimated the emotional fervor of those born and reared in long-established states.

17

Four More States Are Lost

Two DAYS AFTER ANDERSON surrendered Fort Sumter to South Carolina, the editors of the *New York Times* observed:

> The reverberations from Charleston Harbor have brought about what months of logic would have been impotent to effect—the rapid condensation of public sentiment in the Free states.
>
> The North is now a unit. Party lines have shriveled, as landmarks disappear before the outpouring of volcanic lava. The crucial test of this is New York City—the spot most tainted by the Southern poison . . . [of] life-long Democrats.
>
> There will be no "fraternal blood" shed unless it be the blood of men who are willfully and persistently in the position of traitors.[1]

Later that day the president announced his call for seventy-five thousand troops from twenty-seven states. Forty-eight hours later, the governor of Virginia affixed his signature with a flourish to a document that ended: "In witness whereof, I have hereunto set my hand and caused the seal of the commonwealth to be affixed, this 17th day of April, 1861, *and in the eighty-fifth year of the commonwealth*" (emphasis added).[2]

The significance of the final phrase lies in its emphasis upon the continuity of the commonwealth. Likewise, Lincoln's April 15 call for troops was fixed in time as taking place "in the year of our Lord One thousand eight hundred and Sixty-one, *and of the Independence of the United States the eighty-fifth*" (emphasis added).[3]

In the Virginia capital the *Richmond Dispatch* reassured its readers: "The announcement that the Convention of Virginia has passed an Ordinance of Secession was received with the most universal and profound satisfaction. There are no longer in Virginia two parties. The Union men and the Secessionists are arrayed in a solid band of brotherhood under the flag of Virginia."[4]

That statement fell considerably short of accuracy. Unionists in the mountainous western sections of the state were already talking of secession from Virginia to form a new state, despite the fact that the ordinance of secession would not be final unless ratified by the popular vote in May.[5]

Gov. John Letcher was among those who did not want to see Virginia leave the Union. He and many others were not positive that the seven seceded states would form a lasting confederation or that all of them would remain out of the Union. Partly because Virginians formed anything but "a solid band of brotherhood," it took months for secessionists to get the upper hand. Once Letcher fell into the secessionist camp, however, he was eager for action against the Federal installations in his state.[6]

Sen. John J. Crittenden of Kentucky drafted a compromise that bears his name and presided over a special Committee of Thirteen that rejected it.

NATIONAL ARCHIVES

[Special Despatch to the Morning News.]

IMPORTANT FROM WASHINGTON!

Address of Senator Toombs to the People of Georgia.

PROPOSITIONS FOR NEW GURAN- TEES REJECTED!

THE SOUTH TREATED WITH DERISION AND CONTEMPT!

Senator Crittenden's Amendments Unani- mously Voted Down!

Secession the last and only Resort!

Washington, Dec. 23.—Senator Toombs telegraphs this morning the following, addressed to the people of Georgia:

Fellow-Citizens of Georgia:—I came here to secure your constitutional rights, or to demonstrate to you that you can get no guarantees for these rights from the Northern confederates.

The whole subject was referred to a Committee of thirteen in the Senate yesterday. I was appointed on the Committee and accepted the trust. I submitted propositions, which so far from receiving decided sup- port from a single member of the Republican party on the Committee, they were all treated with either derision or contempt. The vote was then taken in Committee on the amendments to the Constitution proposed by Hon. J. J. Crittenden, of Kentucky, AND EACH AND ALL OF THEM WERE VOTED AGAINST UNANIMOUSLY BY THE BLACK REPUBLI- CAN MEMBERS OF THE COMMITTEE.

Robert Toombs sent a special dispatch to Georgia when the Crittenden Compromise failed.

At the instigation of Virginia's legislature, delegates from both North and South had met for a peace conference on February 4, 27, 1861, in Washington, D.C. Unfortunately, a spirit of compromise was lacking. Some delegates were labeled "visionaries," and others became belligerent. The proposals drafted by the convention were submitted to Congress three days before its recess. They were rejected, as the president-elect had predicted.

Unionists predominated when Virginia's convention initially voted upon the secession issue and won by a majority of eighty-nine to forty-five.[7] L. Q. Washington, a veteran political leader who favored withdrawal from the Union, thought he knew why the delegates rejected secession. They were under the delusion, he said, that the compromise proposed by Sen. John J. Crittenden of Kentucky would be accepted. Crittenden's December 1860 proposals aimed at averting secession and war failed to gain the support of President-elect Lincoln and were rejected after strenuous debate. Washington believed that had the Crittenden Compromise been approved, the North would have quickly ratified it and made it a part of the Constitution. He was personally convinced that "Lincoln's own feeling and theories of duty all run on the side of coercion [at Charleston]."[8]

Lincoln reportedly had not yet reached a firm decision concerning Fort Sumter, hence he offered to make a deal. Under its terms the president is said to have tentatively suggested that he would let Confederates force Anderson from Fort Sumter by starvation, provided he could be assured that Virginia would not secede.[9] "A fort for a state is not a bad swap," the president is quoted as having told Virginia Unionist John B. Baldwin on April 4.[10] Baldwin seems to have had good intentions but lacked authority to give the required promise. As a result, within hours after Baldwin left the Executive Mansion, the president authorized the Fox expedition to get under way.[11]

Not knowing that the president had triggered an artillery duel at Charleston by stating that he had authorized the resupply of Anderson at Sumter, three Virginia commissioners were received at the Executive Mansion on April 12 or 13. Lincoln stressed that he was seeing William B. Preston, Alexander H. H. Stuart, and George W. Randolph unofficially. Before they left, he gave them a message of some length whose central emphasis was, "I shall, to the best of my ability, repel force by force."[12]

Partly because Lincoln was widely regarded in the South as having taken the offensive at Charleston, some Virginians began making overtures to Montgomery. Should seventy-five thousand men respond to the president's call, they pointed out, they would have to pass through Virginia to reach the Deep South. Hence they urged Montgomery to send Alabama and Georgia troops to the Old Dominion. A month passed, however, before Jefferson Davis and his advisers agreed to send "2,500 well-armed men."[13]

Earlier, Virginia had been given an eight-gun salute at Montgomery when delegates to the state convention voted for secession on April 17. On the same day the secretary of state, Robert Toombs, made the vice president, Alexander H. Stephens, "special commissioner to the Government of the Commonwealth of Virginia."[14]

The influence of Stephens had little or no impact upon the citizens of the commonwealth. Complaining that they preferred talk to war, he may have failed to grasp the extent of anti-Washington sentiment. A majority of the one hundred thousand voting on April 25 cast their ballots in favor of secession, so the ordinance adopted earlier by the convention became official. It was not until May 7, however, that Virginia was formally admitted to the Confederacy as its eighth state.[15]

By that time two more states had passed ordinances of secession, and another was poised to take the same step. Arkansas went out on

May 6, and Tennessee followed the next day, but North Carolina waited to act until May 20.[16]

Other divided states faced internal dissension as least as great as that in Virginia. Swift action by Union soldiers under the command of Maj. Gen. Benjamin F. Butler effectively ended the strong secession movement in Maryland. With Baltimore firmly under the army's control and most city and state officials imprisoned on political grounds, Maryland remained in the Union.

In Kentucky and in Missouri, dual governments were formed, with the Confederates claiming both states before they were securely in hand. Union manpower, weapons, and money eventually prevailed in both of these border states. Since stars representing them had already been added to the Confederate battle flag, they remained in place even though the Confederate States of America never included more than eleven states.

Delaware, by far the smallest of the sixteen states in which slavery was legal, was several times entered by Federal troops. Never seriously interested in secession, citizens of the state rejected Lincoln's plan for compensated emancipation and kept their slaves until the Thirteenth Amendment was ratified.

Thus the four border states—Delaware, Kentucky, Maryland, and Missouri—in which slavery was legal remained in the Union either by sentiment or by force of arms. Yet the domino effect initiated by

Gen. Benjamin F. Butler arrested prominent secessionists of Maryland and clapped them into jail.

J.C. BUTTRE ENGRAVING.

Virginia's secession added four states to the Confederacy in less than five weeks—Arkansas, North Carolina, Tennessee, and Virginia.

Virginia alone was believed to have 2,547 cavalrymen, 820 artillerymen, and 7,180 infantry—more men than were readily available to Washington from the U.S. Army. Each of the other three states that followed Virginia's lead had numerous organized militia units.[17]

The available military manpower of the newly seceded states was not nearly so important as were other factors. As the most northern of Southern states, Virginia lay midway between Florida and Vermont. Her sixty-five thousand square miles—before the separation of West Virginia—made the Old Dominion one of the nation's largest states. Its location was such that it was sure to bear the brunt of whatever battles might be fought in the war.

The population of the seven states that had seceded prior to Lincoln's call to arms was just over 5 million, while that of the four states that joined them later was 4.1 million. Unlike most cities of the South, Richmond was an important manufacturing center. Its Tredegar Iron Works, the largest of its kind in the Confederacy, was equipped to manufacture heavy cannon and railroad iron. Thus the 80 percent increase in population, coupled with new manufacturing and financial resources, meant that the eleven-state Confederacy was far more formidable than the previous seven-state confederation.

In his message to the special session of Congress that began on July 4, Lincoln wrote at length about the attack upon Fort Sumter and the loss of Virginia to the Union. He said nothing, however, about the effect his call for men had upon the Old Dominion. Like many of his followers, he may have believed that the guns that battered Sumter swept Virginia into the Confederacy.

Widespread as it was, this verdict was wrong. The guns that battered Sumter prompted the president to launch a course of action that had been carefully planned. Lincoln's demand for troops was the match that ignited an explosion of pro-Confederate sentiment. With the call for seventy-five thousand troops, support for the Union was described as having "all but vanished in the Gulf States."

Disclaiming charges of placing war guilt upon Lincoln, the constitutional scholar James G. Randall summed up the dynamic response to Lincoln's call for militia by saying: "At one stroke the Washington government lost four important and strategically situated commonwealths whose preference for the historic relationship under the old roof had held them within the Union."[18]

ALEXANDER GARDNER PHOTOGRAPH, LIBRARY OF CONGRESS

Some observers said that Lincoln seemed to age almost overnight when four more states seceded after his call for militia was issued.

On April 17 Lincoln was agonizingly conscious of having lost these states. To many Virginians, one sentence of his address to Congress suggested that the worst was yet to come. "The people of Virginia have allowed this giant insurrection to make its nest within her borders, and this government has no choice left but to deal with it [insurrection] where it finds it." Acknowledging that some of the things he did were of questionable constitutionality, the president nevertheless told the assembled lawmakers: "It is now recommended that you give the legal means for making this contest a short and decisive one; that you place at the control of the government, for the work, at least four hundred thousand men and four hundred millions of dollars."[19]

18

The Loss of an Armory
and a Naval Base

POISED FOR SECESSION OF their state, Virginians were eager to take possession of all Federal installations within their borders. Fort Monroe, however, was judged to be too strong for immediate attack. It had been regularly enlarged and reinforced from Washington, and it was the only major Federal fort on Confederate soil that would never be captured. Harpers Ferry and the Gosport Navy Yard were correctly gauged to be much more easily taken.

Henry A. Wise, a former governor who had no military experience, urged that Robert E. Lee be immediately placed in command of state forces. While waiting for him to take charge, Wise urged that it was imperative to strike a decisive blow at what was now the enemy. Believed to have been acting for Gov. John Letcher, Wise directed trusted men to meet at Richmond's Exchange Hotel after 7:00 P.M. on April 16. A military move of paramount importance would be considered, he told them.[1]

When his men assembled, the former governor wasted no time. He quickly presented Alfred M. Barbour, widely known for his work at the Harpers Ferry Arsenal. Barbour, explained Wise, knew every detail about the layout of the 1,669-acre installation that dated from 1796. In the United States it had no counterpart except in Springfield, Massachusetts.[2]

With a called session of the state convention expected to vote for secession on the following day, every Virginia military unit would need weapons. At Harpers Ferry, the inventory sometimes showed as many

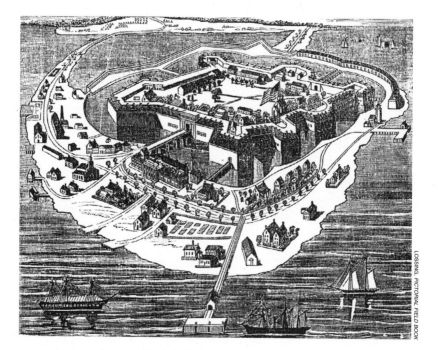

Fort Monroe, at the tip of a Virginia peninsula, was the only large U.S. installation on Confederate soil that was never seized by the Rebels.

as ninety thousand muskets on hand. It was this cache of weapons that had led the abolitionist John Brown to select the armory in 1859 as the target of his famous raid.[3]

Confiding in "loyal Virginians," Wise informed them that Letcher had sent agents to the North to buy whatever guns and ammunition they could find. No matter what purchases might be made, however, Virginia and every other state in the Confederacy would be woefully short of weapons if a Federal invasion should be launched.

Wise informed his listeners that the armory he wanted for Virginia was believed to hold twenty thousand or more muskets that had been altered so that percussion caps could be used with them. The men in the room knew why they had been called together; it was necessary to move against the place before additional Federal troops arrived to protect it.[4]

Wise did not know the size of the present defense force. When Barbour resigned, however, it was briefly guarded by a detachment of only sixty or so men who were headed by Maj. Henry J. Hunt. Hunt was known to have been reassigned, and there were reasons to believe that since then the size of the force had been somewhat reduced.

Capt. Ashby Turner of Fauquier County spoke up and explained that the arsenal was situated "in the bottom of a cup" that was the lowest point in the state. Surrounded by mountain ridges, it was all but impossible to defend. The men under his command would be sufficient to capture it, he believed.

Wise responded by pointing out that the taking of the arsenal would constitute a first step only. To make it truly valuable, it must have a garrison strong enough to hold it against counterattack. He did not know that Abraham Lincoln and Winfield Scott had conferred at length that very day about the arsenal and the Gosport Navy Yard.[5]

By midnight, the conspirators had perfected most details of their plan. Railroad presidents earlier contacted by Wise had offered their advice. Handed a list of military companies expected to be under arms and ready for action, the governor agreed to send telegrams calling them into service as soon as secession became a reality. Because government agents were likely to be watching telegraph offices, it was decided to conceal the real objective by telling units to be ready to march against the navy yard at Portsmouth.

When Capt. John D. Imboden of the Virginia militia led his mean into Staunton, about 4:00 P.M. on April 18, he found thousands of people milling around the depot. Having no horses, the men making up his Staunton Artillery prepared to "run guns forward by hand." That would permit them to fortify Bolivar Heights, a site from which the entire Federal installation at Harpers Ferry could be shelled.[6]

Since their commander had planned a predawn assault, the men were assembled and about ready to move when a vedette gave a warning cry. A brilliant flash of light followed by the muffled sounds of an explosion came from the general direction of their objective. Some officers immediately realized what had happened; the Federals had fired the arsenal to prevent its capture.[7]

Situated about fifty miles northwest of Washington in a narrow gorge at the confluence of the Shenandoah and Potomac Rivers, Harpers Ferry lay on the vital Baltimore and Ohio Railroad and was the site of the only Federal installation of its sort in the South. Maj. Henry H. Jackson had tried earlier to prepare it "for defense or destruction," then left Lt. Roger Jones of the Mounted Rifles in charge of a defensive force that had shrunk to forty-five men.[8]

Barbour reached the village dwarfed by the Federal buildings about noon on April 18, then called groups of workers aside and told them that the ownership of the facility was about to change. For the sake of Virginia and their jobs, he urged them to do all they could to thwart any Federal plans to destroy the installation.

Having been uneasy for days, Lieutenant Jones sensed trouble as soon as he learned that Barbour had returned. During the afternoon the Federal officer received a report that state troops were in Charles Town and had reason to believe that more were expected soon at Hall-town. About 9:00 P.M. he drafted a report to Washington. After citing his reasons to believe that the arsenal was under imminent danger, he noted: "I have taken steps which ought to insure my receiving early intelligence of the advance of any forces, and my determination is to *destroy* what I cannot defend." If faced by an overwhelming number of attackers, he continued, he would retreat into Pennsylvania. As he ended his report, a courier dashed in to say that state troops had indeed reached Halltown, twenty minutes away.[9]

Earlier, soldiers had laid trains of powder throughout the Federal buildings, but they did not know that the workmen had dampened many spots. Soon after he received the warning from Halltown, Jones ordered his men to apply the torch. In three minutes or less, according to his estimate, the arsenal buildings, carpenter's shop, and machine shops "were in a complete blaze."[10]

Hurriedly crossing the Potomac into Maryland, the fleeing Federals turned north. They reached Carlisle Barracks, Pennsylvania, about 2:30 P.M. the following day. Meanwhile, the Virginians occupied the armory without any loss of life. When the triumph by the secessionists was reported, it was incorrectly stated that "15,000 stand of arms were destroyed."[11]

According to an estimate prepared shortly before Virginia seceded, Harpers Ferry land and the arsenal, forges, rolling mills, machine shops, and their contents represented an investment of about $2.3 million. Jones was confident that everything of value had been destroyed and for this feat received a congratulatory letter from the secretary of war. Letcher, who soon learned that much could be salvaged, overestimated the value of the arsenal and its contents.[12]

The Virginians who occupied the facility immediately after the flight of the garrison were chagrined that they had not arrived a few hours earlier. To their delight, however, they found that the subtle sabotage of the powder trains by the civilian workers had saved the

A handful of Federal soldiers believed, mistakenly, that they had rendered the Harpers Ferry Arsenal totally useless.

machine shops and their valuable contents. Barrels and locks of twenty thousand muskets and rifles were pulled from the ashes and sent south to be reworked. In Richmond; Columbia, South Carolina; and Fayetteville, North Carolina, the majority were made functional. At least some of them saw service in most Civil War battles.[13]

Wearing the uniform of the Virginia Military Institute, easily mistaken for Federal blue, Col. Thomas Jonathan Jackson—not yet known as Stonewall—took command of Harpers Ferry during the first week of May. Soon the garrison swelled to an estimated six thousand men.

When news of what had taken place reached Washington on April 19, it was clear to Lincoln and his aides that the secession of Virginia was proving more costly than had been estimated. Col. Charles P. Stone, in charge of the defense of the capital, brought the grim news to Scott. He listened, then responded: "They are closing their coils around us, sir."[14]

ALTHOUGH ELATED AT THE bloodless coup at Harpers Ferry, Governor Letcher considered the Gosport Navy Yard to be even more important. Hence he called leaders together to reveal a plan of action against the military site across the Elizabeth River from Norfolk.

Thomas J. "Stonewall" Jackson, soon to become a general, briefly commanded at Harpers Ferry during May 1861.

VIRGINIA STATE LIBRARY

Having been in touch with Jefferson Davis, the governor reported that the Confederate president had agreed that Gosport must not remain in Federal hands. Responding to a call from Montgomery, two thousand men from North Carolina and Georgia were headed for Richmond to help seize the navy yard.[15]

Robert E. Lee was scheduled to take command of the state's forces. With fifteen hundred Virginians holding Harpers Ferry, however, it would be folly to wait for his leadership, Letcher believed. Therefore he directed Gen. Alexander G. Taliaferro of the militia to lead the assault. Since state troops had no guns heavier than 6-pounders, the governor decided to wait for reinforcements before setting his forces in motion against a facility dotted with superior Dahlgren guns.[16]

A MEETING IN RICHMOND on Thursday, April 18—the day after Virginia's secession—turned out to be a briefing session. Some who were there doubted the wisdom of attempting to seize the largest and most modern facility of its sort on the continent. At least five thousand men would be needed, they believed. Others listened attentively, then applauded the governor's recommendations.[17]

Three-quarters of a mile in length, Gosport Navy Yard was the base of the Home Squadron and was big enough to accommodate an entire road of fleets. Machine and boiler shops were crowded together, along with sawmills and carpenter shops. Since most steam-driven wooden vessels also depended upon sails, the yard included a rope walk and lofts for sails, spars, and rigging.[18]

Capt. Charles S. McCauley, base commander, was a career navy man who had been in uniform since 1809. The probability of trouble from Virginia aside, he correctly believed that most of his 1,028 civilian workmen were Southern sympathizers. Several times he had requested Washington to boost the size of his 176-man defense force, but he received only a promise of action "in the event it becomes necessary." Some of his apprehension eased when the mighty USS *Cumberland,* with a battery of heavy guns and a crew of 300, arrived from the Gulf of Mexico late in March.[19]

In Washington, Lincoln had resisted urging by Secretary of the Navy Gideon Welles that every available man be sent to Norfolk at once. Such a course of action, the president said, would be construed as belligerent. With Virginia teetering in the balance, nothing should be done that might tip the scales toward secession. Far better to take a calculated risk at Norfolk than play into the hands of men eager to take the Old Dominion out of the Union, he insisted.

The mood at the Executive Mansion changed on April 18 when news came of Virginia's secession. Winfield Scott selected Capt. H. G. Wright of the Corps of Engineers to design and execute a plan of defense at the base. Capt. Hiram Paulding, who had spent half a century aboard warships, was detailed to command the party so it would appear to be an expedition of the navy rather than the army.[20]

Early on the morning of April 19, officers and men went aboard the USS *Pawnee* and headed toward Norfolk by way of Fort Monroe. There Wright was loaned 370 volunteers from Massachusetts. As a precaution, the hold of the warship was partly filled with combustibles: cotton waste, gunpowder, and turpentine. The men aboard the *Pawnee* cheered when Norfolk was sighted soon after dark.[21]

Their elation was soon found to be premature. Acting on advice of subordinates, many of whom subsequently went into the Confederate Navy, base commander McCauley refused to let the *Merrimac* depart. Fearing the loss of the vessels in his custody, he had scuttled most of them: the twenty-two-gun sloops *Plymouth* and *Dolphin,* the forty-gun steam frigate *Merrimac,* and a four-gun brig. The upper works of the *Merrimac* were destroyed, but there was little damage to the vessel's engines, boilers, and hull. Soon raised and plated with iron, the ship became the clumsy but powerful CSS *Virginia*.[22]

Astonished and furious at what he considered to be premature destruction, Paulding saw there was nothing to do but complete what had been started. Early Sunday morning he gave orders "to finish the destruction of scuttled ships, then burn and otherwise destroy as far as practicable, the property in the yard."[23]

One of the most valuable properties was an immense and nearly new dry dock built of granite. Wright, along with navy Capt. John Rodgers, was given a detail of forty men and told to demolish the structure. They spent much of the day building a huge floating platform and loading it with twenty-six barrels of powder. After dark they "established a train of powder to the outside and connected with it four slow matches."[24]

A tug pulled the *Cumberland* into nearby Hampton Roads and from its deck a rocket signaled that the fires should be started. Squads of soldiers and sailors hurried from ship to ship, throwing chunks of lint on the decks and preparing torches with which to set the fires. Ashore, teams made the machine shops and other buildings ready for destruction. A special unit tried to complete the work of disabling hundreds of Dahlgren cannon earlier spiked by McCauley's small force. Even eighteen-pound sledge hammers failed to break the weight-bearing trunnions, so this effort was abandoned.

Leaving behind Wright, Rodgers, and the men detailed to start other fires, the *Cumberland* was towed out of the yard after midnight, followed by the *Pawnee*. At 4:20 A.M. on Monday, the waiting squads saw their signal.[25]

When torches were thrown aboard the scuttled ships, flames raced along their decks and climbed the rigging before the barrels of gunpowder exploded. On the *Pennsylvania* flames belched from every porthole so that in Norfolk the inferno "seemed like the day of judgment." For hundreds of yards "the light was bright enough easily to read a copy of the *Washington Globe*."[26]

Then the demolition crew ignited their slow matches and ran for the boat landing. Flames from the burning buildings prevented their reaching it. Turning aside, they raced through a blazing gateway and found a small boat in which they took to the river. After rowing a short distance they were spotted from shore and fired upon. Wright reported, "We concluded to land on the Norfolk side and deliver ourselves up to the commanding general of the Virginia forces."

Fires set at the Gosport Navy Yard could be seen for miles around.

There General Taliaferro received the captured officers with courtesy, then sent them to Richmond. They remained on parole until April 24, when they were released and returned to Washington.[27]

Taliaferro's bloodless victory evoked from him a stream of abuse. Federal actions designed to destroy the yard and its contents, he raged, constituted "one of the most cowardly and disgraceful acts, ever, on the part of the government of a civilized people."

His anger cooled faster than the ashes of the buildings deliberately burned. An initial survey showed that the work of Wright and Rodgers had been in vain. No one learned why their explosives failed to detonate, but the granite dry dock was virtually undamaged. So were two thousand naval guns that were quickly distributed throughout the Confederate states. Even the fires designed to destroy the ships had failed to do their work. The *Merrimac*, which required a crew of six hundred, was hardly damaged below the water line.[28]

In Richmond, Vice President Alexander H. Stephens exultantly telegraphed Jefferson Davis: "GOSPORT NAVY YARD BURNED AND EVACUATED; 2,500 GUNS, ARTILLERY AND ORDNANCE SAVED, AND 3,000 BARRELS OF POWDER." A few days later in Atlanta he said that "priceless war material and naval facilities without equal" were saved for the Confederacy "by direct interposition of Providence."[29]

Like the artillery duel at Charleston and the occupation of Harpers Ferry, the Gosport Navy Yard fell into Confederate hands without the loss of a single life. On both sides a few men reported bruises and minor injuries, but nothing more. As professional military men saw the matter, there was only one casualty: McCauley's reputation.

McCauley had given up the finest facility of the U.S. Navy without a fight, yet he was not subjected to a court-martial or even a session before a board of inquiry. He requested his retirement, received it, then remained on the retired list until he was promoted to the grade of commodore. The editors of the *New York Herald* found consolation in their certainty that before the captured facility could be of use to the Confederates, "this war will be ended."

Leaders in Washington did not fare as well as McCauley. Frightened, they called a hasty conference to plan their defenses if the Confederates should make the capital their next target. Tossing sleeplessly for night after night, Lincoln realized that he could have afforded to give up Fort Sumter and much more to avoid the actions that had caused the rebellion to spread like wildfire.

19

Many Lives Are Lost
in Baltimore

Gov. JOHN A. ANDREW of Massachusetts, ardent abolitionist and a vocal admirer of John Brown, became eloquent every time he faced an audience after the secession of South Carolina. Having been chairman of his state's delegation at the convention that nominated Lincoln, he had a close relationship with the president. By January 1861 he told everyone who would listen that "Lincoln is girding up his loins for the battle that is almost upon us."

He repeatedly said, "War is around the corner, just as surely as the sun will rise tomorrow. Let it come—the sooner the better! When the Rebels have received a few good old-fashioned New England spankings, they will be happy to crawl back into their holes!"

Andrew's preparation for conflict caused Massachusetts units to be drilled, disciplined, and provided with weapons and gear long before the Confederates fired upon Fort Sumter. In February he had estimated to a colleague that if necessary the state could field thirteen thousand troops in a matter of days. His elite Sixth Regiment of eight hundred young men was ready for action two days after Lincoln issued his call for troops.[1]

Commanded by Col. Edward F. Jones, the unit pulled out of Boston on the day Virginia seceded. In New York on the following day, the exuberant peacetime soldiers were given a tumultuous send-off. Masses of folk assured them that their role in "the show of strength by Lincoln" would put out the fires of secession in a matter of weeks.[2]

After spending the night of April 28 in Philadelphia, the men of the Sixth marched to the rail yard before dawn and filled ten coaches to capacity. About one thousand members of the city's Washington Brigade had made arrangements to depart at the same time. Hence, firemen were hard pressed to keep enough steam in the boilers to pull the train of thirty-five cars to Washington by way of Baltimore.[3]

Many easterners did not realize that Baltimore was one of the most bitterly divided cities in the nation. Led by Maryland governor Thomas H. Hicks, Unionists in the state considered themselves to have a precarious upper hand. Hicks had warned Lincoln that "the consequence of a rash step will be fearful."[4]

Great numbers of citizens, not always in full sympathy with secession, were strong supporters of the South. Men wore Confederate cockades, and a few women incorporated the Stars and Bars into dresses and gowns. Having tried to feel the pulse of the public, the *Baltimore Sun* denied that the state had any quarrel with the Union. Still, the editors condemned the Lincoln administration as "a vast consolidated despotism" and called for peaceful recognition of Southern rights.[5]

No state or city official was notified that a large body of troops would pass through Baltimore about noon on April 19. The soldiers from Massachusetts and Philadelphia reached the President Street depot without incident about 11:00 A.M. To proceed to the nation's capital, it was necessary for them to walk a distance of about one mile to the Camden station, whose line ran to Washington.[6]

Having been warned about the divided sentiment in Baltimore as they left Philadelphia, Colonel Jones took steps to avert trouble but said that he wanted to be prepared for it should it come. Soon after their train had departed Philadelphia, he distributed ammunition to his troops and told them to load their weapons. According to his report filed a few days later, he issued just one order: "The regiment will march through Baltimore in a column. Prepare to be insulted and even assaulted, but pay no attention whatever and march with your faces square to the front. If you are fired upon and anyone is hit, your officers will order you to fire. Do not fire into any promiscuous crowds, but select any man you may see aiming at you, and be sure you drop him."[7]

When their train pulled into the station, Jones faced an unexpected decision. Soldiers could ride the horse cars to the Baltimore and Ohio Railroad station instead of going on foot. He decided that his men would prefer not to march the mile across cobblestoned streets.[8]

Mayor George W. Brown had learned at about 10:00 A.M. that troops were on the way. Hoping to avoid trouble, he took a carriage to the Baltimore and Ohio (Camden Street) station, and his chief of police led fifty men to the potential trouble spot.[9]

The soldiers who piled into the horse cars traveled through the city on a route that took them through busy but narrow Pratt Street. Near a bridge on the thoroughfare, a mob gathered to mock and jeer. Nine horse cars passed without incident other than a torrent of verbal abuse from people who later insisted that they wanted nothing to do with any war waged by the North or the South.

Brake failure caused the tenth car to stop; it had barely halted before the mob began throwing stones. When glass from shattered windows cut a few of his passengers, the frightened driver raced his team to the rear of the car. He then hurried back to the depot of the Philadelphia, Washington, and Baltimore Railroad, from which they had just come.[10]

Some members of the mob pursued this car and continued to pelt it with stones. Many had gathered up cobblestones from the road and threw up a barricade. They soon tore up fifty yards of the street-car line's tracks, using the rails to fortify their position. Eight heavy anchors from a nearby wharf were used to top the barrier. With Pratt Street blocked and the hostile mob growing larger by the minute, officers of companies not yet in motion reverted to Jones's original plan for the men to march to Camden station.[11]

While descending from the streetcar and getting into double file, the soldiers were faced by threats no more serious than jeers and hoots. According to an eyewitness account by Frederic Emory, a band of about one hundred civilians suddenly dashed toward the men. At their head, an unidentified man shouted and waved a Confederate flag. As the soldiers began moving toward the Baltimore and Ohio depot, the man carrying the flag raced in front of the columns in an attempt to force the soldiers to march behind the emblem of rebellion.[12]

Union sympathizers, who may have been in the majority, taunted their fellow citizens before scurrying into the ranks of the soldiers for protection. Infuriated, antiwar demonstrators and Southern sympathizers began hurling cobblestones. Knocked to the ground by one or more of these missiles, William Patch of Lowell, Massachusetts, fell on his face. As soon as he hit the ground, the demonstrators seized his musket and began beating him with it. With the crowd now grown to an estimated eight thousand and occupying the whole of the narrow

HARPER'S WEEKLY

Men of the Sixth Massachusetts Regiment took careful aim upon civilians, then fired.

street, the soldiers were forced to halt. As soon as they did so, a shower of stones fell upon them.[13]

His military experience having been limited to weekend encampments, thirty-two-year-old Jones could think of nothing except extreme measures. In a voice that Emory claimed "was heard even above the yells of the mob," he shouted, "Fire!" According to later accounts, troops fired randomly until their ammunition was exhausted. They then fell upon the mob with bayonets and managed to push enough people aside to force their way over the barricade. With fierce fighting continuing all the way to the Camden Street station, most of the men of the Sixth Massachusetts boarded thirteen railroad cars and continued their journey to Washington.[14]

Some officers knew that dead and injured soldiers had been left in the streets, but not until they were nearly half an hour out of Baltimore did anyone realize that several members of their regimental band had been left behind at the President Street depot. The band members took a train back to Philadelphia and proceeded to Washington by a circuitous route that bypassed Baltimore.[15]

In the riot-torn city, Mayor Brown discovered that about 130 men of the Sixth had been left behind. He collected and sheltered them in police stations, under guard, before sending them back to Philadelphia by train. Kane, head of the Baltimore police, reported that his men discovered the bodies of four soldiers and twenty-two civilians in the streets. No list of wounded citizens was compiled; according to most estimates, at least thirty-six suffered wounds that ranged from superficial to critical. Merchant Robert W. Davis, an innocent bystander, had been killed by a single shot from a soldier.[16]

Although unarmed and not in uniform, the one thousand Pennsylvanians had been recognized as soldiers when they reached Baltimore. During a two-hour brawl with civilians, Lt. Albert B. Rowland, George Leisenring, Peter Rogers, John Greaves, and "a German" were killed or mortally wounded. Newspaper reports did not indicate how many nonfatal casualties were suffered or how many civilians were wounded in the second clash between soldiers and civilians. Abandoning plans to reach Washington immediately, members of Philadelphia's Washington Brigade returned home to regroup. Mayor Brown warned President Lincoln that "it is not possible for more soldiers to pass through Baltimore unless they fight their way at every step."[17]

Late that night, Baltimore police chief Kane drafted a summary of the day's events. He noted with sadness and anger that the clash came on the anniversary of the Revolutionary battle of Lexington, fought to win freedom from England. "Cobblestones soaked with blood of Marylanders who wanted no part in civil war," said Kane, would forever mark the spot where the first hand-to-hand engagement of the war was fought.

In Washington, Lieutenant Jones was given quarters for his men in the Hall of Representatives of the Capitol. His report, filed a few days later, stated that his regiment suffered forty-three casualties. Three men were already dead and forty were wounded, some critically. Since his list of those killed was later found to be erroneous, Jones's count of wounded soldiers suggests that more than one hundred civilians must have been injured in the melee with the Massachusetts militia who were answering Lincoln's call.[18] More angry than he had ever been in his life, Governor Andrew dispatched a telegram to

Artist Franck Schell showed civilians in action in Baltimore (left half of sketch).

Baltimore: "Have bodies of hero-martyrs preserved in ice and tenderly sent forward."[19]

Rage may have been the prevailing mood in Boston, but fear permeated Washington. Reacting to what seemed an imminent threat to Washington City, the authorities took over Potomac River boats and put them on guard duty. Many men stored their possessions and sent women and children to points they considered safe. Bridges over the river from Virginia were hastily secured. Numerous business establishments were shut down, barricades were erected in front of government buildings, and theaters were closed. A newspaper report attributed these moves to the "dreadful work at the [Baltimore] depot."

In the Executive Mansion, Lincoln paced the floor. Thinking of the seventy-five thousand men for whom a call had been issued, he repeatedly asked, "When, oh, when will they come?" At least once, he sighed in dismay, "I don't believe there is any North." Edwin M. Stanton summarized the situation, noting, "No description can convey . . . the panic that prevailed [in the capital], partly because reports of the trepidation of Lincoln were circulated through the streets."[20] As legal adviser to Simon Cameron and destined to succeed him as secretary of war, Stanton was already deeply concerned about the safety of the capital.

To prevent a repetition of Friday's violence, Baltimore authorities decided that the only way to avert another calamity caused by passage of troops through the city was to burn the bridges. Probably with the approval of the governor, volunteers set out about midnight on Friday. By dawn, rail connections with the North were severed, with bridges being destroyed at Melvale, Relay House, Cockeysville, Harris Creek, Bush River, and Gunpowder River. On April 21 a Washington-

Washington was so unprepared to receive militia units that men of the Eighth Massachusetts Regiment were bivouacked in the rotunda of the Capitol.

Men of the Eighth Massachusetts Regiment were put to work repairing burned bridges on the railroad linking Annapolis with Washington.

bound regiment from Pennsylvania was halted by one of the burned bridges, possibly forestalling another violent clash.[21]

Pondering the unexpected chain of events, presidential secretary John Nicolay noted that at noon Kane was risking his life to protect soldiers and twelve hours later he was burning bridges. Actions of the Baltimore official, he concluded, "sufficiently show the over-mastering outbreak of revolutionary madness." That madness, he mused, leaves no one unaffected. Civilians of Maryland and soldiers of two states were dead. Soon women, children, and infants might find themselves as vulnerable as frontline troops heading into battle.[22]

Lincoln's secretary did not know that the *New York Herald* failed to see organic ties between the struggle in Charleston, the president's call for seventy-five thousand men, and the Baltimore riot. As a result, the nation's most influential newspaper regarded the Baltimore clash as decisive and proclaimed: "Civil war has commenced."[23]

20

Personal Safety Is Lost in Saint Louis

WHEN HE JUDGED ARMED conflict between the North and South to be inevitable, Ohio-born William Tecumseh Sherman resigned as head of a southern military academy that later became Louisiana State University. Bringing his family to Saint Louis, the largest city on the upper Mississippi River, he took a job as head of a streetcar company at a salary of twenty-five hundred dollars per year.[1]

During his first week on the job, the man known to relatives and friends as Cump discovered that tensions were running far higher in Missouri than in Louisiana. As in Maryland and Kentucky, sentiment in the border state west of the big river was divided and remained so for the duration of the war. Advocates of secession, led by Gov. Claiborne Jackson, were in control at the capital, Jefferson City. In Saint Louis, however, Unionists seemed to be in a majority, partly because tens of thousands of Germans wanted nothing to do with anything that smacked of rebellion.[2]

Leaders representing both sides of the issue kept their eyes on the fifty-six-acre federal arsenal that adjoined the Mississippi River. According to the War Department's most recently published inventory, the sprawling installation was stocked with 33,015 muskets and 719 rifles. Estimates of the powder stored there ranged as high as ninety thousand pounds. Unionists lived in dread that this huge cache, casually guarded, could fall into rebel hands. Some secessionists saw the Saint Louis Arsenal as both offering an immense supply of badly needed weapons and as a symbol of hated federal authority.[3]

A major river port, Saint Louis built a street railway system well before the war began.

MISSOURI HISTORICAL SOCIETY

Francis P. Blair Jr., a congressman who led the Unionist faction, was so well known that even newly arrived immigrants who spoke little or no English knew something about him. His brother, Montgomery, was a member of Lincoln's cabinet, and his father was the best-known politician in the state. Although wary of elective office himself, Francis P. Blair Sr. had presided over the first Republican national convention in 1856 and had helped to nominate and elect Lincoln in 1860.[4]

Before Sherman and his family left Louisiana, young Blair took steps to hold his state in the Union. Bypassing the mayor of Saint Louis and other elected officials of whose loyalty he was in doubt, the congressman set up a Committee of Public Safety and established a home guard. Supported by several units of state militia, his committee ruled Saint Louis by the time secessionists fired upon Fort Sumter. Germans who backed Blair's organization used their Turners' Hall as a place to rendezvous and exchange information.[5]

Although the city seemed secure, the arsenal was a tempting plum that to secessionists seemed ripe for the picking. On many nights they held secret meetings in the Bethold Mansion that belonged to one of the wealthiest French families in the state. If they should decide to move on the arsenal, it would be difficult or impossible to stop them.[6]

Blair did not try to hide his contempt for sixty-one-year-old Brig. Gen. William S. Harney, commander of the federal forces in the Department of the West. Using his influence in Washington, he succeeded in having Harney recalled "for consultation."[7] Once Harney was out of the city, the power vacuum he left behind was filled by Capt. Nathaniel Lyon. Head of an infantry company made up of U.S. Army regulars, he became Blair's right-hand man despite the fact that his own ambitions proved troublesome.[8]

Lyon took charge of the arsenal in early April. Through Blair he obtained permission from Lincoln to proclaim martial law, if necessary. At the same time, the red-haired captain was authorized to recruit and arm volunteers. By April 15 he was in command of forty-eight hundred men.[9]

Matters took a sudden and unexpected turn early in May. Governor Jackson decided to exercise an 1858 law under which he ordered militia members to assemble in camps for six days of training. On May 6 hundreds of them converged upon Lindell Grove, not far from Saint Louis. Once there, they dubbed the place Camp Jackson in honor of the secessionist governor.

Their coming together, Sherman explained to his wife and son, was legal in every respect. Also, a large U.S. flag flew over the camp.

Less imposing in appearance than its counterpart in Charleston, the Saint Louis Arsenal was crammed with weapons.

Upon taking command in the West, William W. Harney issued a proclamation to the general public.

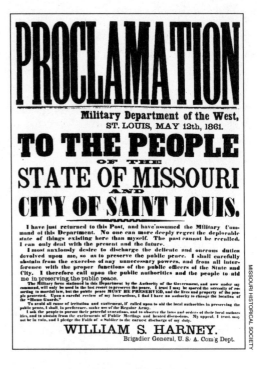

PROCLAMATION

Military Department of the West,
ST. LOUIS, MAY 12th, 1861.

TO THE PEOPLE
OF THE
STATE OF MISSOURI
AND
CITY OF SAINT LOUIS.

I have just returned to this Post, and have assumed the Military Command of this Department. No one can more deeply regret the deplorable state of things existing here than myself. The post cannot be recalled. I can only deal with the present and the future.

I most anxiously desire to discharge the delicate and onerous duties devolved upon me, so as to preserve the public peace. I shall carefully abstain from the exercise of any unnecessary powers, and from all interference with the proper functions of the public officers of the State and City. I therefore call upon the public authorities and the people to aid me in preserving the public peace.

The Military force stationed in this Department by the Authority of the Government, and now under my command, will only be used in the last resort to preserve the peace. I trust I may be spared the necessity of resorting to martial law, but the public peace MUST BE PRESERVED, and the lives and property of the people protected. Upon a careful review of my instructions, I find I have no authority to change the location of the "Home Guards."

To avoid all cause of irritation and excitement, if called upon to aid the local authorities in preserving the public peace, I shall, in preference, make use of the Regular Army. I ask the people to pursue their peaceful avocations, and to observe the laws and orders of their local authorities, and to abstain from the excitements of Public Meetings and heated discussions. My appeal, I trust, may not be in vain, and I pledge the Faith of a Soldier to the earnest discharge of my duty.

WILLIAM S. HARNEY.
Brigadier General, U. S. A. Com'g Dept.

Although it seemed likely that many of these six-day soldiers were prosecession, there was no firm evidence to support this view.

Had Harney been in the city, he would have ignored the nearby gathering. He was in Washington, however, and Lyon doubted the loyalty of the man in command at Camp Jackson. Dan M. Frost, a native of New York who had graduated fourth in his West Point class of 1844, was rumored to cheer sometimes when "Dixie" was played.[10]

With the Shermans sitting at the supper table on May 9, Cump relayed the humorous news of the day to his wife, Ellen, the daughter of a U.S. senator and mother to seven-year-old Willie. A shipment consigned to Camp Jackson from Baton Rouge marked "marble" was believed to contain howitzers and siege guns. Captain Lyon had decided that the only way to find out what was taking place in the camp was to make a personal inspection. Knowing that sentries would not let him pass, he went in disguise.

Lyon borrowed a black bombazine gown from Blair's mother-in-law. Donning the dress, a sun bonnet, and a heavy veil, he drove in a barouche with a black coachman to the camp. Calling himself "Mrs. Alexander," he pretended to ask for news about a grandson. Inside the secessionist camp, he failed to see a mounted cannon, but he found that makeshift streets were named for Davis and Beauregard. When news of his exploit became public, so much laughter echoed in the city that May 9, 1861, was a day Saint Louis residents did not expect soon to forget.[11]

Within the next forty-eight hours other events pushed Lyon's expedition to Camp Jackson into the background. Whatever he may have learned on his scouting expedition, the federal officer remained convinced that secessionists in the camp posed a threat. He arranged for many of the weapons in the arsenal to be moved to Illinois under cover of darkness, but the general public did not know of his actions. Secessionists thought the arsenal was filled with military hardware, he reasoned, and with time on their hands they might decide to attack at any minute.

To forestall action by Missouri state units whose members had broken no law, Lyon assembled his troops during the morning of May 10. Detailing several companies to guard the arsenal, he then marched on Camp Jackson with six regiments. Following Lyon's orders, Col. Franz Sigel of the state volunteers placed six artillery pieces on knolls near the encampment.

Around noon, Lyon sent in a message by a courier who carried a white flag. When Frost read the demand for surrender, he scribbled a

NICOLAY AND HAY, *LINCOLN*

Although only a captain, in February 1862 Nathaniel Lyon was in command of forty-eight hundred men.

According to a Northern artist, civilians started the fight in Saint Louis.

hasty note that ended, "Having no choice, I am forced to comply with your demand."[12] Lyon had hardly finished reading the memorandum of capitulation when a horse belonging to another officer kicked him squarely in the stomach. Still not having fully recovered after an hour, he decided to move on the enemy. At his signal, ranks opened to admit an estimated six hundred to eight hundred prisoners who were ordered to march to the armory.[13]

By the time the hollow phalanx began moving slowly away from Camp Jackson, it was almost surrounded by hordes of civilians. Many of them were angry; others were simply curious. Then someone shouted at the top of his voice, "To hell with the Dutch!"

That expression of contempt for Lyon's German troops triggered a splattering of mud and stones from prosecessionists. Before the last clod had fallen, a civilian who was never identified reportedly fired a single shot. Polish-born Capt. Constantin Blandowski fell, mortally wounded but having enough strength to call to his men, "Fire at will!"[14]

Other accounts say that several members of a German company fired a volley from the rear ranks while civilians used shotguns and rifles against them. Accompanied by Willie and a brother-in-law, Sherman watched from a little open square. When he saw that violence was about to erupt, he pulled his son to the ground and lay on him, later estimating that at least one hundred bullets whizzed over them.[15]

"Men who a moment earlier had been in the prime of life lay gasping for breath," a Saint Louis newspaper reported of the clash. "Children of tender years became as pale and motionless as if they had been asleep under the trees. Lying in her mother's arms, a baby's brains were blown out by a direct hit."

No accurate roster of casualties suffered on May 10 was compiled. Various accounts say that fifteen to thirty civilians and two soldiers were killed and that many were injured. Lyon issued a formal statement in which he lamented the sad results of the clash. Branding "the killing of innocent men, women, and children" as deplorable, he stoutly defended the actions of his men. The troops, he insisted, displayed every forbearance "and discharged their guns simply obeying the impulse natural to us all in self defense."[16]

Hordes of people who were neither fire-eating Unionists nor zealous secessionists condemned what residents of the region still call the Saint Louis Massacre. In what appears to have been revenge upon Lyon's forces, three Germans were murdered in the streets during the night.

With tempers still at the boiling point on Saturday, May 11, Lyon sent the Fifth Reserve Regiment on a special mission. As it reached the corner of Fifth and Walnut Streets, members of a mob began shouting obscenities and abuse. Soon the verbal attacks were followed by stones and brickbats. A contemporary account reported:

> The firing of revolvers from the crowd, and soldiers becoming exasperated, began an indiscriminate firing into the mob.
>
> So completely bewildered by excitement and passion were many of the troops that they fired wildly, some shooting into the air, others into the eaves of the surrounding buildings, and some in opposite directions from their assailants.
>
> The crowd fled panic-stricken; and the soldiers, after considerable efforts of their officers, were restored to their places in line, and marched to their destination.
>
> The result of this ruffianly attack was the killing of seven persons and the wounding of several others. This second attack upon German troops aroused the whole German population, and as they were armed and organized, they began themselves to threaten that they would retaliate.[17]

Fortunately, the threatened retaliation never took place. Nevertheless, casualties from violent clashes between soldiers and civilians in Saint Louis reached or exceeded the total in Baltimore.

No one had yet died on a battlefield, but ordinary citizens were learning how costly the coming conflict could be to those who stood on the sidelines. Soon the man whose rash actions precipitated the first slaughter west of the Mississippi River received a promotion. On May 12 Captain Lyon of the U.S. Army became Brigadier General Lyon of the Missouri State Volunteers.[18]

Not until long afterward was it generally known that a future military leader experienced a baptism of fire on May 10. Many civilians tried to take cover when Lyon's troopers turned upon them. One of them was an old acquaintance of Sherman, a former U.S. Army officer presently working as a clerk in a family-owned leather store and briefly living in a tiny house in Saint Louis. Returning to Galena, Illinois, after having visited his wife's family in Missouri, Ulysses S. Grant was in Saint Louis on that fateful day.[19]

According to Grant's *Memoirs,* "Union men became rampant, aggressive, and, if you will, intolerant," as soon as they learned that Camp Jackson had fallen. He watched as a group of them ripped the rebel flag from a Pine Street building. Wishing to see the return of troops with their prisoners, the Illinois visitor considered heading toward the site of the camp but decided instead to take one of Sherman's streetcars to the arsenal.

At that site he was impressed by the anti-Union sentiment of "a dapper little fellow who might be called a dude." Challenging the vocal secessionist, Sherman's old army friend waited until the prisoners arrived to see them herded into the arsenal. Early the next morning he left for Illinois.[20] When he wrote his memoirs, Grant vividly described his brush with the "dude," yet he said not a word about the slaughter in the streets that took place about the same time he was busy trimming a vocal secessionist down to size.

Multiple deaths failed to bring peace to Saint Louis or to Baltimore. In the Maryland city, so many citizens harbored secessionist views that Federal leaders agreed something must be done. Should the city "go southern," Maryland might secede, causing the danger to Washington City to be multiplied. This factor led to wholesale arrests of city and state officials, preventing the legislature from meeting and perhaps voting to secede.

Some of the intense anger felt by many Southerners in Saint Louis stemmed from Lincoln's call for militia. Governor Jackson angrily labeled it "illegal, unconstitutional, and revolutionary . . . inhuman and diabolical."[21]

The constitutionality of the president's prepared response to the fall of Fort Sumter did not receive serious consideration in the North. Regardless of how the justices of the U.S. Supreme Court might have ruled had they been consulted, the call soon became recognized as revolutionary in all its consequences.

21

Lincoln Loses His Reins on the Slavery Issue

Benjamin F. Butler never forgot that the Northern press lauded him for his actions following the Baltimore riot. He kept in his pocket a folded clipping from the *New York Times* that cited "his sudden encampment at the Relay House; his noble march to Baltimore; his posting cannon upon the hill overhanging the city; and his wise proclamation to the people of Baltimore." The commission soon given to him by President Lincoln, however, was far more important. Despite having been a Democrat most of his life, he became the Union's first major general of volunteers in 1861.[1]

As a result of his taking extraordinary steps to save Maryland for the Union, Butler was widely publicized very early in the war. Placed in command of Fort Monroe on the Virginia peninsula, he was then embarrassed by defeat in a skirmish at Big Bethel Church in June 1861. Proud of his past success and angry at his humiliation, Butler was mentally and emotionally prepared to do something unexpected. Whether he sought such an opportunity or stumbled upon it as a result of his legal experience is unknown.[2]

Weapons, ammunition, cotton, corn, horses, clothing, quinine, and many other articles seized from secessionists were treated as contraband of war. That meant they would never be returned and the former owners would receive no compensation. In contrast, Federal officers routinely returned runaway slaves to their owners, as required by the Fugitive Slave Law.[3]

THE SOLDIER IN OUR CIVIL WAR

At Big Bethel, three thousand Federals were met by eighteen hundred Confederates; after nearly three hours, the Rebels were victorious.

A veteran criminal lawyer, Butler pondered this paradox in the treatment of property belonging to secessionists. If property in the form of essential supplies constituted contraband of war, he reasoned, why should property in the form of slaves—potentially useful to the enemy—be treated differently?[4]

When three black men showed up unexpectedly at Fort Monroe, they were identified as "field hands belonging to Col. Charles Mallory, now in command of secession forces in this district." One of them said that he had overheard their master talking about shipping them to North Carolina to work on fortifications. As a result, they ran away from their owner and sought the protection of soldiers in blue.[5]

The runaways were given temporary permission to remain at Fort Monroe, and soon an officer who identified himself as Major Carey demanded their return. Citing the Fugitive Slave Law, he insisted that the law was clearly on the side of the owner. Butler is said to have squinted at his visitor and replied, "Virginia now claims to be part of a foreign nation—and the Fugitive Slave Law applies only within the United States of America. Get your state back in the Union, sir, and Mallory may have his slaves back!"[6]

Col. Theodore Winthrop, Butler's secretary, sensed the importance of the incident. Since it seemed to establish a precedent, he quickly sent an account to the *Atlantic Monthly* magazine. Readers of the periodical learned that "as General Butler takes as contraband all horses used in transport of munitions of war, so he takes black men who carry powder to the carts and flagellate the steeds."

Winthrop, a graduate of Yale College, was aware that his commander's actions contradicted the official national policy as it was defined by the president. Winfield Scott initially threatened to countermand this decision concerning runaways, yet when consulted about runaways who had helped to erect Confederate batteries, Scott chose to support his subordinate.

Soon abolitionist Montgomery Blair became involved. Writing to Butler concerning his action, the postmaster general congratulated Butler for having "declared secession [slaves] contraband of war." Simon Cameron, the U.S. secretary of war, had already notified Butler of his approval. At least for the present, Lincoln decided not to become involved. Summarizing events at Fort Monroe for his cabinet, he referred to the decision made there as "Butler's fugitive slave law."[7]

At the Virginia fortress Capt. James Haggerty took charge of the fugitives suddenly labeled "contrabands." A longtime acquaintance of the general, Haggerty in private termed him "a natural-born gadfly who knows just when to bite at the right spot." Abolitionists everywhere, impatient with the president or openly angry that he showed no signs of attempting to do away with slavery, rejoiced upon hearing of Butler's actions. Although not yet accepted as a legal term, "contraband" came into general use in the North to designate a runaway belonging to a secessionist. Runaways of Union masters in Delaware, Maryland, Missouri, and Kentucky were not contrabands; hence they were returned to their owners.

Within days after the spur-of-the-moment decision by which all property of secessionists was labeled contraband of war, other slaves took refuge at Fort Monroe. Soon there were a dozen of them within the fortress. News spread through the plantations like wildfire. By May 27, sixty-seven blacks were being housed and fed. Six months later, forty-five arrived on a single day. Soon a newspaper correspondent reported that one thousand flocked into Hampton, Virginia, during a twenty-four-hour period. Butler's pronouncement had started a stampede.[8]

Soon after Butler accepted the first contrabands, Washington issued orders forbidding fugitives to reside in military camps around the capital or to accompany troops on the march. This made warships and other vessels of the U.S. Navy particularly inviting places of refuge. So many contrabands flocked to navy yards that the secretary of the navy, Gideon Welles, authorized putting them to work at any jobs they could perform. Naval records include a large number of reports and letters that deal with the status of contrabands, their labor, and their pay.[9]

In December the secretary of war suggested that the labor of contrabands "might be useful to us." In the fall, Brig. Gen. John E. Wool, then commanding Fort Monroe, had began to pay black workers. Men who labored "for the department" received eight dollars per month, and women half as much. His actions were widely copied and extended, and within a few months many former slaves who had not helped to erect Confederate fortifications were at work on Federal projects.

Men "in public service" usually got about ten dollars per month and one food ration daily. Women and boys between twelve and sixteen years of age were paid four dollars per month and a daily ration. Children under twelve received one food ration. There was no uniform rate of pay for contrabands who worked for private employers, and a minority objected to being used as laborers for public or for private tasks.[10]

It took time for the press of the Northeast to take notice of Butler's treatment of runaway slaves. Meanwhile, he smiled with delight when he thought of a newspaper not far away. According to the *Richmond Examiner,* his actions of May 24 made him "the beastliest, bloodiest poltroon and pickpocket the world has ever seen."

For a man who craved publicity, it was a triumph to be castigated in a secessionist newspaper. At least for the moment, this seemed almost to make up for his humiliation at having been removed from action and ordered to supervise eighty-acre Fort Monroe deep inside the Confederacy.

MANY FEDERAL COMMANDERS FAILED to share Butler's glee at having transformed runaway slaves into contraband of war. Maj. Gen. John A. Dix, another Democrat temporarily in command at Baltimore, issued a statement saying that slaves were not his business. Should they come to him, he said, he would promptly send them away.

Rushed to Missouri a few weeks later and ordered to restore peace there, Maj. Gen. Henry W. Halleck echoed the verdict of Dix. Brig. Gen. Don Carlos Buell, who was beginning to discover firsthand

HARPER'S HISTORY OF THE GREAT REBELLION

Col. William T. Sherman, later a major general, never relaxed his opposition to the use of black soldiers.

how high tensions ran in Kentucky, took a similar position. So did a then-obscure colonel, William Tecumseh Sherman.

Some aides may have believed the president to be secretly pleased with Butler's actions, but even those most intimately acquainted with Lincoln never could read his mind accurately. Later, it became clear that he agonized over the possibility that Butler's unauthorized actions might antagonize all-important Kentucky and other border states.

Lincoln realized that if the North in general or Congress in particular should take him at his word, he would be in deep trouble. Voicing long-held convictions, he made it clear that he opposed territorial extension of slavery while pledging to uphold it where it existed. Ready to fight to preserve the sacred Union, he denied that Virginia or any other state had actually withdrawn from it. Therefore the property-based Fugitive Slave Law, which he repeatedly sanctioned, remained valid in Virginia, though perhaps not on Federal soil at Fort Monroe.

Late in September the president angered abolitionists by revoking Maj. Gen. John C. Frémont's proclamation that offered freedom to slaves of Missouri. His action seems to have been based upon political considerations and his insistence that his preeminence as commander in chief must be respected. Not long afterward, the chief executive countermanded Maj. Gen. David Hunter's similar proclamation in South Carolina.[11]

Gen. David Hunter proclaimed freedom for the slaves of South Carolina—but was also ordered by Lincoln to withdraw his order.

LOSSING, *PICTORIAL FIELD BOOK*

When some of the hundreds of slaves in the District of Columbia learned what was taking place not far to the south, they headed for the nearest Federal military post. Brig. Gen. Irvin McDowell, who had been placed in command of forces gathering for a possible battle, was bewildered when blacks began converging upon his camps.

Soon he received cautious guidance from General Scott. President Lincoln, said the general in chief, wondered if it would be well "to allow owners to bring back those which have crossed the Potomac with our troops." Then Scott hastened to warn that Lincoln's name "should not at this time be brought before the public in connection with this delicate subject."

Butler's decision to treat runaway slaves as contraband of war served to divide Republicans in Congress. This division within the ruling party indicated that the sectional struggle was entering a new phase. If the war escalated, as expected, it would be Republicans who were waging it against slavery, no matter what Lincoln might say.

Lawmakers who were staunch abolitionists were already angry that Lincoln showed no intention of making universal freedom a war goal. Others were wary of arousing antagonism in the border states.

Democrats usually opposed any action that could be construed as restricting the rights of slave owners.

On August 6, 1861, a controversial statute was approved under which any and all property, which included slaves, was made subject to confiscation if knowingly employed "in the service of the rebellion." Slaves who were confiscated would not automatically gain their freedom, however; the lawmakers stipulated that this issue would be decided later by Congress or the courts.[12]

This legislation, later known as the First Confiscation Act, did not mention persons then called contrabands. Yet nearly everyone in the capital knew that Butler had prevailed. This occurred despite the president's frequently expressed personal solution for the slavery issue: gradual emancipation with compensation to owners, followed by colonization of freedmen.

Two days after Congress acted to take up the crusade he had started, Butler received another rebuke. Brig. Gen. John E. Wool, then stationed at Troy, New York, was ordered by General Scott to take command of the department in which Fort Monroe lay. He arrived on

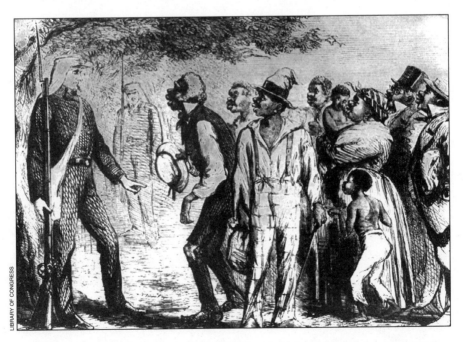

Runaway slaves who came to Federal posts very early expected to be returned, so they pled for sanctuary.

Federal commanders quickly began putting contrabands to work as menial laborers.

August 17 and assigned Butler to command volunteer forces operating in the field outside of the fort.

Nothing could stop the avalanche Butler had started. Refugees flocked to Federal installations in great numbers; tens of thousands were put to work as stevedores, blacksmiths, roustabouts, servants, canal diggers, and general laborers. Instead of diminishing, the problem of what to do with contrabands kept growing larger. As a result, in July 1862 Congress took additional action in the form of a second and more comprehensive Confiscation Act. Compared with promises made by Lincoln when he assumed the mantle of power, it was radical to an extreme. Lincoln signed it, however, and issued a proclamation of warning to secessionist slave owners.[13]

Under the terms of the new statute, Confederates who failed to surrender within sixty days were to be punished by having freedom conferred upon their slaves. Rebel-owned slaves who escaped or were captured, the new act stipulated, "shall be deemed captives of war, and shall be forever free of their servitude."

Even this giant step was not enough to satisfy Butler and his admirers. Significantly, however, it was taken during the period when a troubled president found himself forced to consider framing a statement designed to confer freedom upon blacks in Confederate territory. When he issued the Emancipation Proclamation in late 1862, it was strictly for military purposes and was probably the single most effective war measure he adopted.

Well before that time, however, contrabands became a major problem in Union territory. Some camps established for them had death rates comparable to most prisons. In Illinois, the state from which Lincoln went to the Executive Mansion, constitutional restrictions against free blacks were strengthened. Gov. John A. Andrew of Massachusetts refused to let contrabands enter his state, offering the explanation that he "did not want them to suffer from the climate."

During Sherman's March to the Sea in late 1864, so many contrabands followed his armies that they became a constant nuisance. At Ebenezer Creek, not far from Savannah, a pontoon bridge was built so Federal troops could cross. Once the men in blue were back on solid ground, the bridge was pulled up, and scores of contrabands drowned or were left wailing on the western bank of the stream.[14]

Increasing hordes of escapees first treated as contraband of war by Democrat Butler forced the first Republican president to modify his position concerning the form of property known as slaves. As a result, the announced goals of his administration were altered and expanded. Radical as it proved to be, this change of stance was not Lincoln's first. The man who offered Confederates at Charleston a pair of equally unpalatable choices concluded that he had been wrong to promise so-called seceded states that they would never be invaded.

22

The Tremendous Loss of Life Begins

IRISH-BORN STEPHEN CLEGG ROWAN was frustrated and angry. He believed his vessel, the USS *Pawnee,* should have had the honor of helping to hold Fort Sumter after the president decided to supply Major Anderson and his men. Delays and snarled communications dogged the relief expedition, and as a result, the warship did not arrive off the Charleston bar until the artillery duel was under way.

This time, Rowan wanted no nonsense—and no delay. Having been ordered to Alexandria, Virginia, the warship anchored without incident on the night of May 23. John A. Dahlgren, Washington naval yard commandant, elevated by Lincoln over the heads of other men, considered the *Pawnee* invulnerable to fire from any Virginia shore batteries. Its heavy broadside, he noted with satisfaction, "is just suitable for the case, for it would overawe all opposition."

About daylight on May 24, Rowan reported, steamers approached Alexandria from the navy yard. They were known to be transporting "the Zouave regiment, for the purpose of landing and occupying" the Potomac River city about eight miles south of Washington.[1]

Although Rowan did not know it, the man who planned the ill-fated expedition to relieve Fort Sumter was on hand to watch the action. Now chief clerk of the Navy Department, Gustavus V. Fox was aboard either the *Baltimore* or the *Mount Vernon,* which with the *Guy* was loaded to the gunwales with Zouaves.[2]

Eager to prevent secessionists from learning the goal of the secret expedition, Rowan directed Lt. R. B. Lowry to go ashore to demand

PAGEANT OF AMERICA

Alexandria, Virginia, was described as "elegantly quiet" before hostilities began.

the surrender of Alexandria. Lowry's report to Rowan said that he reached the wharf about 4:20 A.M. Carrying a white flag, he found Maj. George H. Terrett in command of Virginia militia and presented him with an ultimatum: "I demanded the surrender of the place, saying that we were prepared to seize it. In your name I said it would be useless to resist, since you were actuated simply by a desire to spare the shedding of blood of women and children."[3]

Having accosted Terrett in an open street filled with members of the Virginia militia, Lowry received a brusque reply. Refusing to surrender, Terrett promised not to take hostile action if not attacked. He agreed to evacuate the city about 8:00 A.M.

Satisfied, Lowry turned back to the river. Just as he reached the wharf, he saw companies of Col. Elmer Ellsworth's Fire Zouaves disembarking. Virginia sentries fired a few muskets, which were answered by a volley from the troops aboard the transports. Lowry raced to the side of Ellsworth, identified himself, and explained what had taken place.

"I have been on shore, demanding the surrender of the town. The commanding officer is already evacuating. He promises to make no resistance. The town is full of women and children."

According to the naval officer, Ellsworth replied, "All right, sir; I will harm no one."

Leading Lt. J. C. Chaplin and a detachment of men from the *Pawnee,* Lowry hurried to the railroad depot to seize it, along with some "burden [freight] cars that stood on the tracks." Back on the streets of Alexandria, he found that Ellsworth was no longer at the head of his regiment. After a brief wait, Lowry "hoisted the American ensign on a street flagstaff, and also upon the custom-house."

Returning to the depot, he discovered that infantry who had come from Washington by land had the location firmly secured. Since he had seen small bodies of men marching away from Alexandria, he assumed that the mission had been completed without casualties.[4]

IN HIS INAUGURAL ADDRESS, Lincoln had promised that there would be no invasion of states claiming to have seceded. When batteries were erected at strategic points in Virginia, however, it appeared that the Potomac River might be closed to Federal vessels. Promise or no promise, it was imperative that the capital not be cut off from the rest of the world. Plans were therefore made for the first incursion into secessionist territory that was authorized in Washington.

Three branches of the military were involved. As in the case of the Fort Sumter expedition, communication became snarled. A troop of cavalry rode across the Chain Bridge and headed toward Alexandria soon after midnight. Beginning about 2:00 A.M. on May 24, two major bridges became crowded with infantry and special units. Members of the Fourteenth New York Regiment, the Fifth New York, and

PHOTOGRAPHIC HISTORY OF THE CIVIL WAR

John A. Dahlgren, inventor of the gun that bore his name, was in charge of the naval contingent.

the Twenty-eighth New York used the Aqueduct Bridge. So did Col. Michael Corcoran and 250 unarmed workmen. Col. Daniel Butterfield led the Twelfth New York across the Long Bridge. The First Michigan and the Twenty-fifth New York followed.[5]

According to one estimate, greatly exaggerated, about thirteen thousand Federals began converging upon the Virginia city whose garrison consisted of fewer than seven hundred members of the state militia. Some defenders of Alexandria had no weapons; others had modified 1812 muskets, but few or no cartridges.[6]

Col. Ephraim Elmer Ellsworth, whose Zouaves moved upon Alexandria by steamers, was the first officer to reach the heart of the city. A twenty-four-year-old native of Saratoga County, New York, he had worked as a dry goods clerk and newsboy before going to Chicago in 1857. There he took lessons from a French fencing master and from

THE SOLDIER IN OUR CIVIL WAR

Men of Zouave units wore colorful uniforms somewhat like those used by French troops in the Crimean War.

Young and good looking, Col. Elmer Ellsworth was high on the list of Lincoln's favorites.

J. C. BUTTRE ENGRAVING

him learned about Algerian troops who won lasting fame in the battle of Solferina.

Intrigued with these colorful fighting men known as Zouaves, he organized a company of volunteers and drilled them at least a dozen hours each week. Each man wore what their commander termed "authentic Moorish dress" that was described as being "very elegant."[7]

Under Ellsworth's leadership, the Chicago Zouaves won first place in a national drill contest. At this time, or shortly afterward, Ellsworth came to the attention of a midstate attorney.[8]

After their first encounter, Abraham Lincoln called Ellsworth "the greatest little man I ever met." Through Gen. John Cook, head of the Springfield Grays, he invited the leader of the Chicago Zouaves to read law in the Springfield office of Lincoln and Herndon. Within weeks he was treating him more like a colleague than an apprentice.[9]

Still calling himself Colonel Ellsworth, although briefly without a command, after six months the easterner accompanied Lincoln on his eleven-day journey from Springfield to Washington. When the new chief executive failed in his effort to create a special military post for

A Rebel flag flew defiantly from Alexandria's Marshall House hotel when invaders reached the town.

LOSSING, PICTORIAL FIELD BOOK

his young favorite, Ellsworth went to New York and recruited a regiment of Zouaves from among the firemen of the city.

On May 7 he and his men were mustered into Federal service, despite having left New York before complying with all regulations. Lincoln always wanted Ellsworth to have the best, so he may have arranged for his protégé to win new fame in the invasion of "the sacred soil of the Old Dominion."[10]

Edward H. Howe, a reporter for the *New York Tribune,* received permission to accompany Ellsworth and his men on the expedition. After seizing the telegraph office, Howe said later, Ellsworth momentarily left the head of his column to investigate the city's only hotel of any size. He was not sure from a distance of four blocks, but it seemed that he glimpsed a rebel flag on the rooftop pole of the Marshall House hotel.[11]

Ellsworth took only a few strides toward the hotel before he saw that his eyes had not betrayed him. Drawing his sword, he rushed to the front door, pushed or broke it open, and from a man in shirt sleeves demanded an explanation for the presence of the rebel flag. Identifying himself as a guest, the fellow shook his head wordlessly.

Accompanied by Pvt. Francis E. Brownell and Howe, the Zouave leader climbed hurriedly to the third floor. There, by means of a ladder, they managed to reach the roof and the flagpole. Once ropes were cut, it was easy to haul down the offending banner. Triumphantly carrying the flag, Ellsworth neared the first landing of the stairway without incident.

Suddenly the man he had accosted earlier jumped from hiding and leveled a shotgun. A single blast caught the Zouave in his chest, killing him instantly. Brownell responded with a point-blank rifle shot and a series of bayonet slashes at the man, who proved to be hotel owner James W. Jackson. Both Ellsworth and Jackson died in their second confrontation, which lasted less than sixty seconds.[12]

MOST VIRGINIA FIGHTING MEN escaped from Alexandria by means of the Orange and Alexandria Railroad, burning bridges behind them. Col. William T. Sherman's battery of light artillery managed, however, to capture a troop of cavalry. As a result, Capt. John A. Dahlgren faced a new dilemma. Addressing a telegram simply to "Navy Department," he said: "The *Baltimore* has returned from Alexandria with thirty-six prisoners of war taken this morning, of which one is a captain and another a lieutenant. Will the Department please direct me what to do with them?"[13]

THE SOLDIER IN OUR CIVIL WAR

Shot dead by Jackson, Ellsworth dropped his pistol; Pvt. Francis E. Brownell then killed Jackson.

No prisoners had been taken when Fort Sumter surrendered, so there were no precedents on which to base an answer. The secretary of the navy, Gideon Welles, decided that the first prisoners taken in the yet undeclared war should be retained at the navy yard "until further instructions were issued."

On May 28 a group of Federal officers began an inspection of the captured town. Irvin McDowell, a brigadier general since May 14, had on the previous day been made commander of the Army and Department of Northeastern Virginia. If the ninety-day militia now under him were to fight at all, they would have to meet secessionists within five or six weeks. Otherwise, the men of many units would be out of uniform and on their way home without having smelled powder. In order to fight, volunteers who had responded to the president's call would have to invade Virginia again. It was hoped that one decisive encounter would put the rebellion to rest so that Lincoln's promise of a brief struggle would be kept.

HOTEL OWNER JACKSON WAS soon buried in an obscure grave, and a public subscription campaign was launched. In time, the fund provided thirty thousand dollars to his widow and children.[14]

The death of Ellsworth led to great bitterness in the North. Dozens of poems, songs, sermons, and editorials praised his heroism and labeled him a martyr. He was incorrectly reported to have been "killed by John T. Day, John B. Farrar, and others." This story may have contributed to widespread belief that he was assassinated.[15]

Ellsworth's body was carried from the hotel to the Alexandria railroad depot on a litter of muskets. Transported to the navy yard where it lay overnight, it was draped with American flags and crepe and was guarded by Zouaves. Hours earlier every flag in the capital had been lowered to half-staff. One of Lincoln's secretaries called the "hideous tragedy" at Alexandria "a sensational climax of deeper import than Sumter and Baltimore."[16]

When Lincoln heard the news from Alexandria, he wept uncontrollably and gave orders that Ellsworth should be brought to the Executive Mansion to lie in state in the East Room with lilies on his chest. With the doors and windows of the Executive Mansion draped in black, the president went to his desk and penned a May 25 letter of condolence to Ephraim and Phoebe Ellsworth. His personal affliction that their son was the first commissioned Union officer to die, he told them, was "scarcely less than your own."[17]

No artist or photographer succeeded in capturing the grief shown by the president when he learned of Ellsworth's death.

When the funeral service was about to begin, the sobbing president exclaimed, "My boy! My boy! Was it necessary that this sacrifice be made?"[18]

SIX WEEKS EARLIER, THE commander in chief of the U.S. armed forces had carefully crafted a booby trap for the Confederates at Charleston. Instead of leading to a quick end to hostilities, his scheme backfired and launched a series of increasingly severe strikes and counterstrikes, as well as the enlargement of the Confederacy. The first Federal invasion of the Confederacy brought the consequences of war into the Executive Mansion.

Still grieving, the president insisted upon movements that he believed would end the conflict quickly. Instead, they resulted in defeat at the battle of First Bull Run.

Even in the midst of his planning, Abraham Lincoln was unable to forget the image of his young protégé's flower-covered body. He did not then imagine that the East Room funeral foreshadowed four years of increasingly ferocious war and the deaths of 623,000 men. Tens of thousands of them were loved fully as much as he loved Elmer Ellsworth.

Conclusion

IN 1860 A THREE-WAY SPLIT in the long-dominant Democratic Party guaranteed the election of the nominee of the new Republican Party. Most contenders for the nomination favored an attempt at compromise with the South, despite their party's official stance regarding the abolition of slavery.

Abraham Lincoln's victory at the Republican national convention stemmed partly from the fact that his views were not widely known. Most of his leading opponents had expressed opinions that were believed likely to alienate blocks of voters.

As the choice of the Republican Party, Lincoln was automatically the subject of suspicion and hostility in the South. Although he was personally in no way committed to abolition, the platform of his party was enough to give eager secessionists an excuse to act. Their seizures of scores of federal installations left Fort Sumter as the most prominent symbol of the federal presence in the seceded states.

Totally committed to the preservation of the Union, in his first inaugural address the new chief executive made his position clear. Denying the possibility of secession, he said that he would hold and repossess all federal facilities and collect the revenues and duties that weighed heavily upon the South. His public promise clearly pointed toward Fort Sumter, now the focal point of decades of sectional controversy.

Lincoln soon sent a carefully crafted offer to Charleston. Actually a trap, it was set to spring on the secessionists regardless of what they did or did not do. Once the blame for having fired the first shot was placed on the Confederates, the president implemented a plan under which he called for seventy-five thousand volunteers from state militia units to enter Federal service. He expected these men with little or no combat experience, plus naval vessels of the blockade, to quickly end the sectional schism. A March 9, 1861, dispatch by Seward said, "the President entertains a full confidence in the speedy restoration of the harmony and the unity of the government."[1] Under the terms of the Whiskey Rebellion legislation, the men of the militia units could not serve for more than thirty days after Congress had assembled.

Instead of causing secessionists immediately to reconsider their views, the call for militia led to an 80 percent enlargement of the Confederacy and a rapid escalation of the conflict that soon engulfed the nation. Confederate President Jefferson Davis responded to Lincoln by licensing privateers to prey on Northern commerce. In turn, Lincoln reacted by announcing a blockade of questionable legality that could only partially be implemented at once.

No one died during the artillery duel at Charleston, and members of the garrison were not detained. After the Confederate triumph at the Southern port, there were a few minor clashes on land between small groups of armed opponents. Ship-to-shore exchanges took place at Gloucester Point, Virginia, on May 9. A similar burst of gunfire erupted at Sewell's Point, Virginia, nine days later.[2]

Still, the first significant bloodshed of the war occurred when soldiers struggled with civilians in the streets of Baltimore on April 19 and in Saint Louis on May 10. A May 7 riot in Knoxville, Tennessee, had left one person dead and an undetermined number injured.[3]

Northern women were drawn into the struggle because the U.S. Army was not prepared to deal with large numbers of wounded. In the South, women showed great versatility and skill in improvising substitutes for scarce commodities. They also took an active role in such projects as "gunboat fairs," by which money was raised to begin to build a Confederate navy. Wartime entrance of women into the workplace and into active roles in their communities marked the beginning of the modern women's movement.

Just six weeks after having won a great psychological victory at Charleston, the president was thrown into the depths of grief as a result of tragedy linked with the first invasion of Confederate soil. To most military officers, his expectation of a short and almost bloodless victory over secessionists was by this time clearly unrealistic. Yet five weeks after the death of Elmer Ellsworth, he requested lawmakers to give him "the legal means for making this contest a short, and a decisive one." Five months later, in his first annual message to Congress, he told lawmakers that he hoped to prevail without a "remorseless, revolutionary struggle."[4]

Lincoln's passion for the Union caused him to refuse to consider compromise. Had any other contender for the Republican nomination won in 1860, there is little likelihood that Charleston would have become the focus of armed struggle. Delay and compromise were genuine alternatives for every major contender for the presidency except Lincoln.

Despite his sorrow at the death of a young man killed in Alexandria, Virginia, Lincoln gave no hint that he felt any personal responsibility for Ellsworth's fate. Insisting that events controlled him, he eventually convinced himself that he played no part in launching the war. The conflict began, he wrote in 1864, when insurgents fired upon the *Star of the West*. Once he took the oath of office, the sixteenth president said, he simply "accepted the war thus commenced."[5]

Lincoln refused to consider an armistice and demanded unconditional surrender of the Confederates. Capable of agonizing over the impending execution of a single deserter, he did not hesitate to make decisions that sent hundreds of thousands to their deaths.

His notion that he did not play a decisive role in the conflict was bolstered by a long-standing and deep-rooted conviction that he was an instrument of God. This viewpoint made the Almighty responsible for what took place. Hence it may account for the fact that Lincoln's prepresidential bouts of acute depression were infrequent during the war years.

Multitudes in the North knew no details about events that led to the Confederate assault upon Fort Sumter. Most or all accepted the president's assurance that his secret expedition was designed only to take food to starving men. Since secessionists fired first, they were reviled for having dishonored the U.S. flag and starting the war.

Lincoln was thus insulated from the heat of battle by his belief that the war commenced in January 1861 and by his conviction that he was a relatively passive instrument, serving the purposes of God or of fate.[6] He never tried to define the meaning of such terms as "God," "the Almighty," "Fate," and "Necessity." Yet it was no accident that in 1864 U.S. coins began carrying the inscription "In God We Trust" for the first time. By then the president described the nearly ended conflict as a "mighty convulsion, which no mortal could make, and no mortal could stay [stop]."[7]

Today many people see the course of the conflict as having been determined by larger-than-life generals, their armies, and their weapons. Lincoln has become mythologized as the Great Emancipator who waged war for social justice. During 1861–65 few informed observers adopted these views. In the North, as well as in the South, those caught up in the conflict saw things from a different perspective. Many, if not most, at that time knew that the president of the United States was the most dynamic factor in shaping the course of the "short and decisive blaze"—actually an all-consuming firestorm—that he ignited in Charleston.

Perhaps the greatest paradox of the Civil War is the fact that Lincoln's failure to achieve a short and practically bloodless military victory had far-reaching social and political consequences. Had his well-crafted plans succeeded, there is no reason to believe that an Emancipation Proclamation would have been issued. Nothing in Lincoln's writings suggests that the Fugitive Slave Law would have lost its impact had the "so-called seceded states" quickly returned to the Union. How long it would have taken for America's slaves to gain emancipation and citizenship and voting rights in the reunited nation is an open question.

Neither is it possible to assess accurately the rapidity with which change would have occurred in the state-nation relationship. While Lincoln was avowedly an ardent admirer of Thomas Jefferson and his philosophy, when the sixteenth president took the oath of office, he became chief executive and commander in chief of what can only be termed "a Jeffersonian democracy." In sharp contrast with the principles of the Federalists whom Jefferson opposed and mastered, Jefferson espoused strong states and a comparatively weak central government. Lincoln—who perhaps leaned toward this point of view—was forced by the exigencies of a long and bitter war to exercise more and more personal power. At the same time, war measures served to concentrate power in Washington at the expense of the states. By the time peace came in 1865, the states had yielded so frequently to the central government that no one could have halted this pattern of acquiescence had he tried to do so.

Today, many political aspirants campaign on an anti-Washington platform. In 1996, voters in at least two states approved measures that had more than a little in common with the states' rights movement of the decades that preceded the Civil War. Whether the trend toward relegating more authority to the states concerning such issues as welfare and health care is a result of this movement or a consequence of it is debatable.

At least one significant factor in contemporary American life is not in question. Here and throughout much of the world, the United States is frequently billed as the only "superpower" on earth. Regardless of whether this is good or bad in the long run, the United States would not be a superpower if fifty strong and separate states made all the significant decisions. Bombastic attacks upon "the concentration of power in Washington" do not take into account the fact that the United States became *one nation* in the real sense of that term as a result of the failure of Lincoln's plan to conduct a little war.

Notes

IN CITING WORKS IN the notes and bibliography, short references have been used generally. Works frequently cited have been identified by the following abbreviations:

AAC	*American Annual Cyclopedia,* 1860–1861
AL	Nicolay, John G., and John Hay. *Abraham Lincoln: A History*
B&L	Buel, Clarence C., and Robert U. Johnson, eds. *Battles and Leaders of the Civil War*
CDC	*Charleston Daily Courier*
CM	*Charleston Mercury*
CMH	Evans, Clement A., ed. *Confederate Military History*
CV	*The Confederate Veteran* magazine
CW	Basler, Roy P., ed. *The Complete Works of Abraham Lincoln*
CWC	Wilcox, Arthur M., and Warren Ripley. *The Civil War at Charleston*
CWR	Harwell, Richard B. *The Confederate Reader*
CWT	*Civil War Times* and *Civil War Times Illustrated*
DAB	Johnson, Allen, and Dumas Malone, eds. *Dictionary of American Biography*
DxD	Miers, Earl S., ed. *Lincoln Day by Day*
EC	Current, Richard N., ed. *Encyclopedia of the Confederacy*
ESH	Roller, David C., ed. *Encyclopedia of Southern History*
HE	Lossing, Benjamin J., ed. *Harper's Encyclopedia of U.S. History*
JSHS	*Journal of the Southern Historical Society,* 1876–1944
CM	*Charleston Mercury*
MOLLUS	Publications of the Military Order of the Loyal Legion of the United States. Various cities and dates.
N-OR	U.S. Navy Department. *Official Records of the Union and Confederate Navies in the War of the Rebellion*
NYH	*New York Herald*
NYT	*New York Tribune*
OR	U.S. War Department. *The War of the Rebellion: A Compilation of the Official Records of the Union and Confederate Armies*
PH	Miller, Francis T., ed. *Photographic History of the Civil War*
RR	Moore, Frank, ed. *The Rebellion Record*
S	*Supplement to the Official Records of the Union and Confederate Armies*
WKS	Nicolay, John G., and John Hay, eds. *The Complete Works of Abraham Lincoln*
WWW	Sifakis, Stewart. *Who Was Who in the Civil War*

Chapter 1: A Southern Officer and a Southern Fort

1. Thomas, Special Orders No. 137, *OR,* 1:73.
2. Doubleday, *Reminiscences,* 18–22.
3. *WWW,* 11.
4. Doubleday, *Reminiscences,* 41ff.
5. Anderson to Cooper, *OR,* 1:74–76.
6. Swanberg, *First Blood,* 161–64; Nevins, *Emergence of Lincoln,* 366; Stern, *Prologue,* 236ff.
7. Doubleday, *Reminiscences,* 31–37.
8. Anderson to Cooper, *OR,* 1:84; *CWC,* 7.
9. Cooper to Anderson, *OR,* 1:83.
10. Anderson to Cooper, *OR,* 1:89.
11. Meredith, *Storm,* 52; Buell, memorandum of verbal instructions, *OR,* 1:89f; *ESH,* 1085b.
12. Crawford, *Genesis,* 140–46.
13. Doubleday, *Reminiscences,* 44, 76–80; Crawford, *Genesis,* 108–12.
14. *CWC,* 8; Crawford, *Genesis,* 102–5, 108–12.
15. Crawford, *Diary,* 10.
16. Ibid.; Swanberg, *First Blood,* 90–95; *HE,* 6:303.
17. Anderson to Cooper, *OR,* 1:112f.
18. *CM,* December 27–30, 1860.
19. Swanberg, *First Blood,* 105; Doubleday, *Reminiscences,* 58–64; Crawford, *Genesis,* 110–12; Crawford, *Diary,* 11.
20. *CM,* December 27–30, 1860; Meredith, *Storm,* 24ff.
21. Crawford, *Genesis,* 102ff.
22. *NYH,* December 28–29, 1860; Crawford, *Diary,* 15; *RR* 1, doc. 9ff.
23. Nicolay, *Outbreak,* 29f.
24. *CM,* January 4–6, 1861.
25. Swanberg, *First Blood,* 7.
26. *RR,* 1, docs. 8, 51.
27. Doubleday, *Reminiscences,* 76–80; Crawford, *Genesis,* 108–12.
28. Mosocco, *Chronological Tracking,* 1–8; Hendrickson, *Sumter,* 160–61.

Chapter 2: No Foreign Presence

1. *CWC,* 4.
2. Roman, *Military Operations,* 1:24–25.
3. Foster to De Russy, *OR,* 1:108f; Anderson to Cooper, *OR,* 1:3f.
4. *CWT,* May 1992: 48.
5. *Charleston Daily Courier,* December 28–30, 1860; Capers, "Journal," *S,* 1:62.
6. Mosocco, *Chronological Tracking,* 1.
7. *CM,* December 28, 1860–January 3, 1861.
8. *CDC,* January 1–3, 1861.
9. Humphreys to Maynadier, *OR,* 1:5–9; Pickens to Cunningham, *OR,* 1:7; *CWC,* 6.
10. *CMH,* 6:6–9; Anderson to Cooper, *OR,* 1:114.
11. Prime to Totten, *OR,* 1:329.

12. Slemmer, Report, *OR*, 1:333–42.
13. Reno to Maynadier, *OR*, 1:327; Reese, Report, *OR*, 1:329f; Patterson to adjutant general, *OR*, 1:327.
14. Elzey to Cooper, *OR*, 1:322f.
15. Whiting to Totten, *OR*, 1:318f.
16. Haskin, Report, *OR*, 1:489–90.
17. Smith to Larned, *OR*, 1:493.
18. Totten, Report, *OR*, 1:638, 43; *RR* 1, doc. 17.
19. McKinstry, Report, *OR*, 1:646f.
20. Grant and Farrar, Reports, *OR*, 1:649f.
21. *WWW*, 58; Harney and Blair, Reports, *OR*, 1:667–69.
22. Dyer, *Compendium*, 2:582.
23. Warner, *Generals in Gray*, 312; Twiggs to Scott, *OR*, 1:581.
24. *CMH*, 15:12–26.
25. Bennett to Drum, *OR*, 106:451–52.
26. Cooper to Van Dorn, *OR*, 1:623f.
27. Hendrickson, *Sumter*, 160–62; Gorgas to Bartow, *OR*, 127:298; list of seized arsenals, *OR*, 122:60–61.
28. Anderson, *Concise Dictionary*, 917–23.
29. *HE*, 6:494–96.
30. Hardee to Walker, *OR*, 1:453.
31. McPherson, *Battle Cry*, 264; Sandburg, *War Years*, 1:212; Randall, *Lincoln the President*, 1:317; *WKS*, 2:301; Current, *Speaking of Abraham Lincoln*, 62; Davis, *First Blood*, 72–73, 166–67.

Chapter 3: Washington Humiliated

1. *CM*, December 28–29, 1860; Meredith, *Storm*, 80.
2. *CM*, December 28, 1860, et seq.
3. *NYH*, December 28, 1860.
4. Lay to the President of the United States, *OR*, 1:111.
5. Meredith, *Storm*, 84; Thomas, memorandum of arrangements, *OR*, 1:128f.
6. Anderson correspondence, *OR*, 1:132–43.
7. Doubleday, *Reminiscences*, 94f; Stern, *Prologue*, 258–59.
8. Scott to Dimick, *OR*, 1:119; Swanberg, *First Blood*, 127.
9. Scott to Buchanan, *OR*, 1:114.
10. Thomas, memorandum of arrangements, ibid., 128f.
11. Swanberg, *First Blood*, 145; Scott to Dimick, *OR* 1:119; Meredith, *Storm*, 88; Stern, *Prologue*, 255–56.
12. Hendrickson, *Sumter*, 102–9; Thomas to Scott, *OR*, 1:130; Thomas to Anderson, *OR*, 1:132.
13. Thomas to Anderson, *OR*, 1:132.
14. Meredith, *Storm*, 80; F. W. Pickens, *S*, 1:66.
15. Stern, *Prologue*, 258; *CDC*, January 8, 1860; *Savannah Daily Morning News*, January 8, 1860.
16. Doubleday, *Reminiscences*, 101.

17. Hendrickson, *Sumter,* 99–101; Meredith, *Storm,* 86f; Nicolay, *Outbreak,* 33; Stern, *Prologue,* 256; *CWT* October 1976, 14; Musicant, *Divided Waters,* 11.
18. Yulee to Finegan, *OR,* 1:442f.
19. *CM,* January 6–8, 1861.
20. *CDC,* January 10–12, 1861.
21. McGowan, Report, *S,* 1:69–70; *CWC,* 8–10.
22. Crawford, *Genesis,* 186; *CDC,* January 23, 1861.
23. Hendrickson, *Sumter,* 100–102; McGowan, Report, *S,* 1:69–71.
24. *Harper's Weekly,* January 26, 1861.
25. Doubleday, *Reminiscences,* 101–5; Swanberg, *First Blood,* 94f; Stern, *Prologue,* 261–63; *RR* 1, doc. 19; Musicant, *Divided Waters,* 12.
26. McGowan, Report, *RR,* 1:21.
27. Clarkson, "Story of the Star of the West," *CV* 21:234–36.
28. Stern, *Prologue,* 266ff.
29. Foster to Totten, *OR,* 1:138–39, 146–48; Roman, *Military Operations,* 1:28.
30. Doubleday, *Reminiscences,* 117; Meredith, *Storm,* 112–15.
31. Doubleday, *Reminiscences,* 118–19.
32. *WWW,* 43–44.

Chapter 4: A New Commander in Chief

1. *CW,* 4:170–71.
2. Lamon, *Life of Lincoln,* 508; *WKS,* 2:112; Sandburg, *Lincoln,* 1:38.
3. *WKS* 2:138–51; Neely, *Lincoln Encyclopedia,* 280.
4. Randall, *Lincoln the President,* 1:282.
5. *CW,* 4:205.
6. Hendrickson, *Sumter,* 163–67; Leech, *Reveille,* 37–45.
7. *CW,* 1:250, 4:251.
8. Ibid., 4:254.
9. Ibid., 4:262–71.
10. *RR,* 1, doc. 39; *CW,* 4:261; *WKS,* 2:184f.
11. Capers, "Journal," *S,* 1:63.
12. Anderson to Cooper, *OR,* 1:191.
13. Miers, *Lincoln Day by Day,* 3:26; Swanberg, *First Blood,* 222; Nicolay and Hay, "Lincoln and His Cabinet," 421f; *OR,* 1:182–90; quoted in Lincoln, *Autobiography,* 237.
14. McPherson, *Battle Cry,* 267; *AL,* 3:375–449; Nevins, *War for the Union,* 1:30–56.
15. *CW,* 4:279; Nicolay and Hay, "Lincoln and His Cabinet," 423.
16. Washington to Walker, *OR,* 1:263f.
17. Current, *Speaking of Lincoln,* 64.
18. Lincoln, *Autobiography,* 233–34; *OR,* 1:196; *CW,* 4:284f.
19. Cameron to Lincoln, *OR,* 1:197; *CW,* 4:285; Hendrickson, *Sumter,* 167–68; Lincoln, *Papers,* 1:478.
20. *CW,* 4:289–90, 291.
21. Ibid., 4:288–90, 299.
22. Leech, *Reveille,* 51.
23. *CW,* 4:301.
24. Basler, *Touchstone,* 61.

25. Current, *Lincoln Nobody Knows*, 194; Lamon, *Life of Lincoln*, 503.
26. Current, *Speaking of Lincoln*, 182.
27. Neely, *Lincoln Encyclopedia*, 248a; McPherson, *Second American Revolution*, 43; Mitgang, *Lincoln*, 345.

Chapter 5: He Says We Don't Exist

1. Anderson to Cooper, *OR*, 1:78–79, 87–88.
2. Nicolay, *Outbreak*, 26–27; Swanberg, *First Blood*, 61.
3. D. F. Jamison, Ordinance, *OR*, 1:110.
4. Roman, *Military Operations*, 1:26–27; Swanberg, *First Blood*, 83; *AAC, 1861*, "South Carolina," December 29, 1860.
5. Crawford, *Genesis*, 148; Doubleday, *Reminiscences*, 82; Swanberg, *First Blood*, 109; Nicolay, *Outbreak*, 31.
6. Crawford, *Genesis*, 150.
7. Davis to Whiting, *OR* 1:258.
8. Swanberg, *First Blood*, 117.
9. Meredith, *Storm*, 102.
10. Crawford, *Genesis*, 153–55; Swanberg, *First Blood*, 119f.
11. *RR*, 1, docs. 42, 49.
12. McPherson, *Battle Cry*, 268.
13. Current, *First Shot*, 54.
14. *RR*, 1:51.
15. Swanberg, *First Blood*, 226–32, 239.
16. *RR*, 1:181b; *Cincinnati Daily Press*, November 21, 1860.
17. Brooks, *Abraham Lincoln*, 253; Long and Long, *Civil War*, March 3, 1861.
18. Roman, *Military Operations*, 1:32ff; McPherson, *Battle Cry*, 269.
19. *RR*, 1:51a.

Chapter 6: Keep Your Slaves and Come Back

1. Dumond, *Southern Editorials*, 12–188.
2. *AL*, 3:260, 271; *CW*, 2:409; 3:15, 145–46, 192, 233–34; McPherson, *Second American Revolution*, 129; Hoerner, *Lincoln and Greeley*, 200; Thomas, *Lincoln*, 229f.
3. *CW*, 3:1–201.
4. Current, *Speaking of Abraham Lincoln*, 100–103.
5. *CW*, 2:461–69.
6. Basler, *Touchstone*, 76; Fehrenbacher, *Prelude*, 70–95; Simon, *House Divided*, 20.
7. Randall, *Lincoln the President*, 1:104f; McPherson, *Second American Revolution*, 32–112.
8. *Journal of Negro History*, 4:7–21, 37:418–53; Staudenraus, *African Colonization;* Quarles, *Lincoln and the Negro;* Vorenberg, "Abraham Lincoln and the Politics of Black Colonization," *Journal of the Abraham Lincoln Association*, 14, no. 2 (1993): 23–45; *The Liberator*, September 12, 1862; *CWT* May-June 1990, 54ff; *RR*, 2:68a; Nevins, *War for Union* 1:337; *RR*, 5, doc. 59.
9. *RR*, 5, doc. 65a; Nevins, *War for Union*, 1:339n; 2:233; *CW*, 5:370–71.
10. Vorenberg, "Colonization," 41; *RR*, 6, doc. 21a; Greeley, *American Conflict*, 257; Nevins, *War for Union* 2:241.

11. *WKS,* 2:114, 220–21, 6:111; *CW,* 2:294; Hoerner, *Lincoln and Greeley,* 106; Randall, *Lincoln the President,* 1:236.
12. *WWW,* 700.
13. Perkins, *Northern Editorials,* 1:394–95, 420–21; Neely, *Encyclopedia,* 215, 338.
14. *NYH,* December 24, 1860; Current, *Lincoln Nobody Knows,* 80.
15. Hoerner, *Lincoln and Greeley,* 234; Perkins, *Northern Editorials,* 1:246, 356, 365; 2:835.
16. Randall, *Lincoln the President,* 1:234; Neely, *Encyclopedia,* 296, 302; Sandburg, *Lincoln,* 1:16.
17. Neely, *Encyclopedia,* 54, 270; Randall, *Lincoln the President,* 1:321; *Detroit Free Press,* February 19, 1861; Mitgang, *Lincoln,* 261; Perkins, *Northern Editorials,* 1:336; Lincoln, *Papers,* 2:456f.
18. Perkins, *Northern Editorials,* 1:186–87, 330, 336, 338, 346, 358, 368.
19. Hoerner, *Lincoln and Greeley,* 188–90, 289; Lincoln, *Papers,* 354–55; Neely, *Encyclopedia,* 58.
20. Thomas, *Lincoln,* 305.
21. Lincoln, *Autobiography,* 309; Hoerner, *Lincoln and Greeley,* 263–67, 275.
22. *CW,* 4:249–71; Neely, *Encyclopedia,* 148.
23. Weems, *Washington,* 216–22.
24. Current, *Lincoln Nobody Knows,* 237–40; McPherson, *Second American Revolution,* 40–45, 114–16.
25. *CW,* 4:316–18; Current, *Speaking of Lincoln,* 12.
26. Current, *Speaking of Lincoln,* 96; Neely, *Encyclopedia,* 280.

Chapter 7: Bread Enough for Five Days

1. *EC,* 2:448–53.
2. Crawford, *Diary,* 42; *WWW,* 172; Meredith, *Storm,* 122; Jamison, *OR,* 1:261.
3. Hendrickson, *Sumter,* 27.
4. Doubleday, *Reminiscences,* 120.
5. *MOLLUS,* 2:317.
6. Roman, *Military Operations,* 23–40.
7. *RR,* 1, docs. 40–41.
8. Doubleday, *Reminiscences,* 110.
9. Meredith, *Storm,* 116–17, 128; Cummings Point sketch, *OR,* 1:244.
10. Holt to Anderson, *OR,* 1:182–83.
11. Meredith, *Storm,* 157.
12. Chester, "Inside Sumter," 52–54, 60–61.
13. *CDC,* March 26–April 8, 1861.
14. Snyder to Anderson, *OR,* 1:213–16.
15. *CM,* March–April 1861.
16. Swanberg, *First Blood,* 72–73; Meredith, *Storm,* 109; Cameron to Anderson, *OR,* 1:213–16.
17. Crawford, *Diary,* 80; Doubleday, *Reminiscences,* 133, 141.
18. *DxD,* 3:28, 29, 33.
19. Swanberg, *First Blood,* 247–49; Crawford, *Diary,* 49.
20. *OR,* 1:197; Fox, *Confidential Correspondence,* 1:13; McPherson, *Battle Cry,* 268; Meredith, *Storm,* 133; Doubleday, *Reminiscences,* 130–34; Randall, *Lincoln the President,* 1:329.

21. Swanberg, *First Blood,* 249, 251.
22. Crawford, *Diary,* 50, 54; McPherson, *Battle Cry,* 269.
23. Swanberg, *First Blood,* 255; Cameron to Fox, *OR,* 1:235–36.

Chapter 8: An Intolerable Offer

1. *AAC, 1861.*
2. *WWW,* 404; Doubleday, *Reminiscences,* 105.
3. Swanberg, *First Blood,* 278ff.
4. Cameron to Talbot, *OR,* 1:245; *CW,* 4:323–24; Swanberg, *First Blood,* 280; Catton, *Fury,* 301.
5. *RR,* 1, docs. 40–41.
6. Current, *Lincoln and First Shot,* 51; Lincoln, *Papers,* 1:476.
7. Talbot to Cameron, *OR,* 1:251–52.
8. Swanberg, *First Blood,* 276.
9. Current, *Lincoln and First Shot,* 118.
10. Pryor, *Reminiscences,* quoted in Stern, *Prologue,* 493; Swanberg, *First Blood,* 289; Catton, *Fury,* 302–4.
11. *CW,* 4:249–71.
12. Lincoln, Message to Congress in Special Session, *CW,* 4:421–41; *WKS,* 2:303.
13. Eisenschiml and Newman, *American Iliad,* 15, 19.
14. Crawford, *Genesis,* 422–25; Chesnut, Lee, and Chisholm to Maj. D. R. Jones, *OR,* 1:59.
15. Swanberg, *First Blood,* 296; *B&L,* 1:76; Eisenschiml and Newman, *American Iliad,* 16; *CWC,* 13–16.
16. *CWC,* 13–15; Swanberg, *First Blood,* 292; Anderson to Beauregard, *OR,* 1:13.
17. Walker-Beauregard correspondence, *OR,* 1:300–302.
18. Meredith, *Storm,* 130.
19. Swanberg, *First Blood,* 298–301, 318–20; *CDC,* April 8–12, 1861.

Chapter 9: Success in Failure

1. *WWW,* 59.
2. *DxD,* 3:28.
3. Fox, *Confidential Correspondence,* 1:6; Fox to Scott, *RR,* 1:212; Eisenschiml and Newman, *American Iliad,* 28; Swanberg, *First Blood,* 168, 200, 233ff; *DAB,* "Fox."
4. Current, *First Shot,* 60.
5. Fox, *Confidential Correspondence,* 1:8ff; Meredith, *Storm,* 134; Sandburg, *Lincoln,* 1:190.
6. Fox, *Confidential Correspondence,* 1:3.
7. Joseph G. Totten, Memorandum for the President and Cabinet, *OR,* 1:198–200; Nevins, *War for Union,* 1:44; Scott, Memoranda for the Secretary of War, *OR,* 1:200–204; Cameron to Lincoln, *OR,* 1:196–98; *CWT,* October 1976, 24; Eisenschiml and Newman, *American Iliad,* 13.
8. Fox, *Confidential Correspondence,* 1:11ff; Lincoln to secretary of war, *OR,* 1:226–27.
9. Fox, *Confidential Correspondence,* 1:8; Anderson to Thomas, *OR,* 1:211.
10. Preliminary orders, Navy Department and War Department, *OR,* 1:227; Cameron to Anderson, *OR* 1:235.

11. *RR,* 9, docs. 213–14; Lincoln to the Brooklyn Navy Yard commandant, *OR,* 1:229; Current, *First Shot,* 61, 97.
12. Stern, *Prologue,* 483.
13. Welles to Mercer, *OR,* 1:240, 368–69, 406; Fox, *Confidential Correspondence,* 20–24.
14. Meigs to Seward, *OR,* 1:368.

Chapter 10: A Continuous Bombardment

1. Swanberg, *First Blood,* 280.
2. Ibid., 286; Crawford, *Genesis,* 421.
3. Meredith, *Storm,* 152; *CM,* April 9–12, 1861.
4. *CDC,* April 7–10, 1861; Crawford, *Genesis,* 396–98; Pickens to Walker, *OR,* 1:292–93; Doubleday, *Reminiscences,* 148; Roman, *Military Operations,* 1:39.
5. Walker to governors, *OR,* 1:290–91.
6. Bronze marker at Fort Sumter, erected 1932.
7. *CWR,* 7.
8. *RR,* 1, doc. 49; Greeley, *Conflict,* 67–68.
9. *NYH,* April 9–11, 1861; Fox, *Confidential Correspondence,* 1:27, 35.

Chapter 11: The Heroes of Fort Sumter

1. Swanberg, *First Blood,* 298; Eisenschiml and Newman, *American Iliad,* 21; Craven, *Ruffin,* 217.
2. Davis, *History,* 58; Catton, *Coming Fury,* 314.
3. Doubleday, *Reminiscences,* 145–46; Meredith, *First Blood,* 168; Eisenschiml and Newman, *American Iliad.*
4. *CDC,* April 6–14, 1861.
5. *CM,* April 14, 1861.
6. Swanberg, *First Blood,* 314–16.
7. Eisenschiml and Newman, *American Iliad,* 25.
8. Simons to Beauregard, *OR,* 1:37–39.
9. *RR,* 1, doc. 56a.; Meredith, *Storm,* 172.
10. *RR,* 1, doc. 82; Nicolay, *Outbreak,* 63.
11. Swanberg, *First Blood,* 320–24, Roman, *Military Operations,* 1:431.
12. Roman, *Military Operations,* 1:431.
13. Foster, "Journal," 25.
14. Chisholm, "Notes," 83.
15. Meredith, *Storm,* 190–91.
16. *CWC,* 15.

Chapter 12: Point of No Return

1. *RR,* 9, docs. 208–12; Stern, *Prologue,* 523–27; Fox, Report, *N-OR,* 4:244–51.
2. *CW,* 4:350; Roman, *Military Operations,* 1:426; Lincoln to Fox, *N-OR,* 4:251.
3. *DAB;* Doubleday, *Reminiscences,* 151; Meredith, *Storm,* 192.
4. *Pittsburg Daily Gazette,* April 18, 1861.

5. *AL*, 3:322, 4:63; Browning, *Diary*, July 3, 1861; Neely, *Lincoln Encyclopedia*, 38, 82; Current, *President*, 120–21; Randall, *Lincoln the President*, 1:344; Nevins, *War for Union*, 1:76.
6. *AL*, 4:44.
7. Fox, *Confidential Correspondence*, 43f; *CW*, 4:350–51.
8. Current, *First Shot*, 99, 184; *AL*, 4:63; Randall, *Lincoln the President*, 1:343.
9. *CW*, 5:212f, 8:332.
10. *CW*, 4:271.
11. Ibid., 4:272–91.
12. Thomas, *Lincoln*, 232–34; *CW*, 4:279–80; *DxD*, 3:26–27.
13. *CW*, 4:292–93.
14. Ibid., 4:291f.
15. U.S. Statutes at Large, 1:424; Richardson, *Messages and Papers*, 1:158f; Randall, *Lincoln the President*, 1:354–55; *Cases in the Supreme Court of the United States*, Martin v. Mott, 1827.
16. Hyman, *More Perfect Union*, 60–61.
17. *HE*, 183–85; Craig, Statement of Arms Distributed by Sale, *OR*, 122:52.
18. Leech, *Reveille*, 56.
19. *AL*, 4:65.; *DxD*, 3:33; Randall, *Lincoln the President*, 1:361; Horan, *Matthew Brady*, 116.
20. *AL*, 4:65ff; Leech, *Reveille*, 53–57; Current, *First Shot*, 207.
21. Sandburg, *Lincoln*, 1:226–27.
22. *OR*, 122:55–67.
23. *CW*, 4:429.
24. Sandburg, *Lincoln*, 1:213–14, 224–27.
25. Stern, *Prologue*, 531.
26. *DxD*, 3:35.
27. *Washington Star*, April 15, 1861; Thomas, *Lincoln*, 257.

Chapter 13: The Call

1. Richardson, *Messages and Papers*, 1:158.
2. Seward, Proclamation by the President, *OR*, 122:67–68, 417–18; *WKS*, 2:246–48; *CW*, 4:331–33; Richardson, *Messages and Papers*, 6:13–14; *RR*, 1:63.
3. U.S. Statutes at Large, 1:424; Act of 1795, sec 2.
4. *OR*, 122:68.
5. *CW*, 4:330.
6. *OR*, 122:68–69.
7. Leech, *Reveille*, 55.
8. *OR*, 122:70–76; Sandburg, *Lincoln*, 1:220.
9. Randall, *Lincoln the President*, 1:360; Ellis to Cameron, *OR*, 1:486; Letcher to Cameron, *OR*, 122:76; Jackson to Cameron, *OR*, 122:82–83.
10. Greeley, *American Conflict*, 80; Hoerner, *Lincoln and Greeley*, 220; Eisenschiml and Newman, *American Iliad*, 33; *RR*, 1, docs. 61–64, 178.
11. Lincoln, *Papers*, 2:572; Perkins, *Northern Editorials*, 2:749.
12. Nevins, *War for Union*, 1:75.
13. Mitgang, *Lincoln*, 267; *Daily Missouri Republican*, April 19, 1861; Dumond, *Southern Editorials*, 179ff; Hyman, *More Perfect Union*, 62; *RR*, 1:171.

14. *Mobile Advertiser,* April 16, 1861.
15. *New Orleans Daily Picayune,* April 18, 1861.
16. Sandburg, *Lincoln,* 1:211; Thomas, *Lincoln,* 260.
17. Note to Table of Quotas, *OR,* 122:69; *Senate Executive Document No. 1,* 37th Cong., 1st sess., 21.
18. *New York Times,* April 18.
19. Stephens, "Verbatim Diary," April 16–18, 1865; *CV,* 1:169–70; Dumond, *Southern Editorials,* 476–77; Thomas, *Lincoln,* 230.
20. *HE,* 8:104–6.
21. *Louisville Journal,* quoted in the *Madison (Wis.) Daily State Journal,* April 19, 1861.
22. Sandberg, *Lincoln,* 1:225.

Chapter 14: War on the Water

1. *EC,* 1:373; 2:480; 3:979, 1269.
2. *CM,* May 8, 1861; *National Intelligencer,* May 27, 1861.
3. W. F. Colcock, register of commissions issued to applicants for letters of marque and reprisal, *N-OR,* 2:1(28):346–47; Davis, Letters of Marque and Reprisal, *OR,* 116:680; *New York Times,* May 18, 1861.
4. *CW,* 4:338–39; *OR,* 122:89–90; *RR,* 1, doc. 78; *NYH,* May 20, 1861; *New York Times,* May 20, 1861.
5. *CW,* 4:346–47; *OR,* 122:122; *RR,* 1, doc. 161.
6. Wenzell to Welles, *N-OR,* 1, 1:17, 26; Letters of Marque and Reprisal, *N-OR,* 2, 1:325–429.
7. *JSHS,* 1:155.
8. Scharf, *Confederate Navy,* 433.
9. Ibid., 431.
10. *N-OR,* 2, 1:27–246.
11. *CM,* May 13, 1861.
12. *New York Times,* June 16, 1861.
13. *OR,* 116:1, 2, 4–6, 29–31, 412–45, 160, 219, 229, 393, 611, 680, 689, 692, 780;
14. *Boston Journal,* May 17, 1861; *NYH,* May 18, 1861; see *OR,* 116:24, 38, 69–71, 77–79, 84–89, 91–95, 114–117, 143, 243, 37, 397, 611, 719.
15. *JSHS,* 1:153–55.
16. Boatner, *Dictionary,* 175–76; Faust, *Encyclopedia,* 165–66; Warner, *Generals in Blue,* 93–94; *WWW,* 143–44; *RR,* 3, docs. 23, 74; *RR,* 5, docs. 60, 63; *PH,* 7:25, 29.
17. Davis, Commission of the *Savannah, OR,* 116:680; Howell Cobb, act recognizing the existence of war between the United States and the Confederate States, *OR,* 127:281–85; Townsend, General Orders No. 100, *OR,* 124:150.
18. Black, *Reports,* 2:635–99; Neely, *Lincoln Encyclopedia,* 33; Hyman, *More Perfect Union,* 141–42; House Rep. No. 262, 43d Cong., 1st sess., 2–3.
19. Scharf, *Confederate Navy,* 10f; *N-OR,* 1, 1:818–19; *EC,* 3:1269; Faust, *Encyclopedia,* 604.

Chapter 15: Citizen Rights Suspended

1. *CW,* 4:347; *WKS,* 6:258; Neely, *Liberty,* 3–8.
2. *CW,* 4:344.

3. Neely, *Liberty*, 8.
4. Randall, *Constitutional Problems*, 144–45.
5. Carmen and Luthin, *Lincoln and Patronage*, 56; Neely, *Liberty*, 8–11.
6. Parker, *Habeas Corpus*, 12–67; *EC*, 2:727.
7. *CW*, 4:364–65; *RR*, 1, doc. 232a.
8. *CW*, 4:419; *RR*, 1, doc. 3, 56b.
9. Neely, *Liberty*, 14–18; *AAC, 1861*, 360b; *AAC, 1864*, 422–23; Miller, *Photographic History*, 7:198.
10. *CW*, 4:430.
11. Neely, *Liberty*, 115; *CW*, 5:436–37; *AAC, 1864*, 422–23.
12. *CW*, 6:451–52, 460.
13. *AAC, 1861*, 361; Miller, *Photographic History*, 7:208.
14. *DxD*, 3:38, 41, 49, 51, 71, 73, 80, 141, 142, 200, 207, 270, 315.
15. Neely, *Lincoln Encyclopedia*, 247; *CW*, 7:281; Browning, *Diary*, April 3, 1864.
16. Schwab, *Confederate States*, 186; *PH*, 7:212; *OR*, 108:482.
17. *PH*, 7:199; *N-OR*, 2, 3 (124):121–24, 132–33; *EC*, 2:728.
18. Schwab, *Confederate States*, 170–192; *Richmond Examiner*, February 3, 1864; *Raleigh Progress*, April 6–7, 1864.
19. *PH*, 7:197–99, 212; *EC*, 2:729; *AAC, 1864*, 424–25.
20. *WKS*, 6:263–65; *CW*, 4:353–54; *RR*, 2, doc. 14.
21. Congressional Globe, 37th Cong., 1st sess., 16, 223, 265, 393.
22. *AAC, 1864*, 421.

Chapter 16: The Loss of a General

1. Lee, *Recollections*, 24; Freeman, *Lee*, 1:430; Horn, *Lee Reader*, 92; "Robert E. Lee," 24.
2. Horn, *Lee Reader*, 92.
3. Freeman, *Lee*, 1:425; *WWW*, 380.
4. Sandburg, *Lincoln*, 1:223; Davis, *Gray Fox*, 8; Freeman, *Lee*, 1:425; Horn, *Lee Reader*, 91.
5. Freeman, *Lee*, 1:427–28; Davis, *Gray Fox*, 8.
6. Freeman, *Lee*, 1:429.
7. Leech, *Reveille*, 27; Davis, *Gray Fox*, 9–10; Freeman, *Lee*, 1:432–33, 636–37.
8. *AL*, 4:98.
9. Sandburg, *Lincoln*, 1:223; Horn, *Lee Reader*, 94.
10. Freeman, *Lee*, 1:633–36; Thomas, *Lincoln*, 259–60; Leech, *Reveille*, 57f; *AL*, 4:97–100; Katcher, *Source Book*, 279.
11. "Robert E. Lee," 25.
12. Freeman, *Lee*, 1:437.
13. Horn, *Lee Reader*, 94.
14. Ibid., 36–90; Warner, *Generals in Gray*, 180f; Lattimore, *Lee*, 15, 18–22.
15. Katcher, *Source Book*, 278; Warner, *Generals in Gray*, 160; *WWW*, 346.
16. Freeman, *Lee*, 1:440; Davis, *Gray Fox*, 15; Lee, *Recollections*, 25.
17. Freeman, *Lee*, 1:441–42; Horn, *Lee Reader*, 94; "Robert E. Lee," 24–25; Davis, *Gray Fox*, 16.
18. Davis, *Gray Fox*, 17.
19. Freeman, *Lee*, 1:446, 637f; Davis, *Gray Fox*, 19; Nevins, *War for Union*, 1:110.

20. Roman, *Military Operations,* 1:21; *WWW,* 43; *CV,* 21:236; *S,* 1:65.
21. Nevins, *War for Union,* 1:108–9.
22. *DxD,* 709.

Chapter 17: Four More States Are Lost

1. *New York Times,* April 15, 1861.
2. *RR,* 1, doc. 70.
3. *CW,* 4:332.
4. *Richmond Dispatch,* April 18, 1861; *RR,* 1, doc. 70.
5. Nevins, *War for Union,* 1:77.
6. Current, *Speaking of Lincoln,* 67; Horau, *Brady,* 140.
7. *OR,* 2:714, 794, 798, 895, 902, 916, 940, 948, 955–56, 961; see also "Virginia, militia," and "Virginia, policy of."
8. Washington to Walker, *OR,* 111:133–34.
9. Thomas, *Abraham Lincoln,* 540.
10. *DxD,* 3:32; Randall, *Lincoln the President,* 1:326–27, 347; Nevins, *War for Union,* 1:47; Foote, *Civil War,* 1:46.
11. McPherson, *Battle Cry,* 271; Current, *First Shot,* 96–97; *AL,* 3:424.
12. *DxD,* 3:34; *CW,* 4:329–31; *RR,* 1, doc. 61; Sandburg, *Lincoln,* 1:222.
13. Walker to Bragg, Bragg to Walker, Bragg to Davis, *OR,* 1:468.
14. Samuel Cooper, General Orders No. 5, *OR,* 127:224; Toombs to Stephens, *OR,* 111:18.
15. Nevins, *War for Union,* 1:77; *OR,* 108:22; Horau, *Brady,* 142; *OR,* 127:294.
16. *ESH,* 1085b; for proclamations and official secession documents of Arkansas see *OR,* 1:111, 127; Tennessee, *OR,* 4:127; North Carolina, with official secession contingent upon the popular vote, *OR,* 1:108, 127.
17. *AL,* 3:418.
18. Randall, *Lincoln the President,* 1:358–59.
19. *CW,* 3:427, 431f.

Chapter 18: The Loss of an Armory and a Naval Base

1. Nicolay, *Outbreak,* 83; *CMH,* 2:51.
2. *ESH,* 577a; *OR,* 2:6.
3. *ESH,* 577a; *RR,* 10:320–22.
4. Imboden, "Jackson at Harpers Ferry," 111f.
5. *DxD,* 3:35.
6. Boatner, *Dictionary,* 423.
7. Imboden, "Jackson at Harpers Ferry," 117.
8. Boatner, *Dictionary,* 418; *Virginia Cavalcade,* Summer 1979, 14–21; *RR,* 10, doc. 321; Davis, *History,* 75.
9. *RR,* 2, docs. 3–5.
10. Horau, *Brady,* 144.
11. *RR,* 1, doc. 72b; Letcher, Report, *OR,* 127:392; *New York Times,* April 21, 1861.
12. Maynadier to Cameron, *OR,* 2:5–6; Cameron to Jones, *OR,* 2:5; Letcher, Report, *OR,* 127:392.

13. *America's Civil War,* January 1994, 20; Nicolay, *Outbreak,* 95; Sandburg, *Lincoln,* 1:223; *CMH,* 2:51.

14. *RR,* 2, docs. 784, 787, 824; Nevins, *War for Union,* 1:81; Boatner, *Dictionary,* 433; Leech, *Reveille,* 65.

15. *CMH,* 4:124.

16. Taliaferro, Report, *N-OR,* 1, 4:306–9.

17. *CMH,* 4:124.

18. Soley, *Blockade,* 48.

19. McCauley correspondence, *N-OR,* 1, 4:219, 221, 228, 241, 265, 270–77, 179, 288.

20. *CMH,* 124.

21. Scott to Wright, *OR,* 2:23; Wilkes, Report, *N-OR,* 1, 4:293–96; *RR,* 1, docs. 119–20; Soley, *Blockade,* 51; *CMH,* 4:125; Greeley, *Conflict,* 112a.

22. Alden, Report, *N-OR,* 1, 4:299–302; abstract log, USS *Pawnee, N-OR,* 1, 4:292–93; Soley, *Blockade,* 47f, 54–55; Nicolay, *Outbreak,* 96; Horau, *Brady,* 144; Leech, *Reveille,* 60.

23. Paulding, Report, *N-OR,* 1, 4:305; *CMH,* 4:125; Soley, *Blockade,* 53.

24. Wright to Townsend, *OR,* 2:21–23; *CMH,* 4:125.

25. *RR,* 1, doc. 120.

26. Nicolay, *Outbreak,* 97.

27. Wright, Report, *N-OR,* 1, 4:296–98; Peters to Letcher, *N-OR,* 2, 2:110; Soley, *Blockade,* 53.

28. Taliaferro, Report, *N-OR,* 1, 4:306–9; "List of Guns Sent from Norfolk Navy Yard," *N-OR,* 1, 5:806; *New York Times,* April 26, 1861; Soley, *Blockade,* 54.

29. Greeley, *Conflict,* 114f; *CMH,* 4:125.

Chapter 19: Many Lives Are Lost in Baltimore

1. Randall, *Lincoln,* 1:362.

2. Davis, *First Blood,* 23.

3. Emory, "Baltimore Riot," 781.

4. Catton, *Coming Fury,* 340.

5. *Baltimore Sun,* April 1–15, 1861.

6. *Washington Evening Star,* April 19, 1961; Davis, *First Blood,* 23; Emory, "Baltimore Riot," 782.

7. Jones, Report, *OR,* 2:7.

8. Nicolay, *Outbreak,* 85; Catton, *Coming Fury,* 341.

9. *RR,* 1, docs. 787–79; Norris, Statement, *OR,* 114:631; Nicolay, *Outbreak,* 86.

10. *NYH,* April 20, 1861; Davis, *First Blood,* 24.

11. *NYH,* April 20, 1861; Nicolay, *Outbreak,* 86.

12. Emory, "Baltimore Riot," 777–80; Nicolay, *Outbreak,* 86.

13. Brown, Message from the Mayor of Baltimore, *OR,* 114:15–20; Davis, *First Blood,* 23; Emory, "Baltimore Riot," 784.

14. Howard, Extract from the Report of the Baltimore Police Commissioners, *OR,* 2:9–11; Kane, Report, *OR,* 114:628–30.

15. Catton, *Coming Fury,* 343.

16. Randall, *Lincoln the President,* 1:363; Davis, *First Blood,* 24; Kane, Report, *OR,* 114:628–30; Emory, "Baltimore Riot," 785–86.

17. *Philadelphia Public Ledger,* April 20–22, 1861; Brown to the President, *OR,* 114:564.
18. Jones to Clemence, *OR,* 2:7–9; Randall, *Lincoln the President,* 1:362.
19. Goss, "Going to the Front," *Century War Book,* 20.
20. Randolph, *Lincoln the President,* 1:363; *AL,* 4:140; *Washington Evening Star,* April 19, 1861; Davis, *First Blood,* 26; Ketchum, *Picture History,* 85.
21. Nicolay, *Outbreak,* 89–90; Emory, "Baltimore Riot," 789–90; Gill, Statement, *OR,* 2:20–21; Brown, Report to the General Assembly of Maryland, *OR,* 2:12–13; Kane, Report, *OR,* 114:628–30; Davis, *First Blood,* 26; Brown, Report, *OR,* 2:14; Hicks to Lincoln, *OR,* 114:564; Catton, *Coming Fury,* 344.
22. Nicolay, *Outbreak,* 90f.
23. *NYH,* April 20, 1861.

Chapter 20: Personal Safety Is Lost in Saint Louis

1. Sherman, *Memoirs,* 1:184–86; *WWW,* 590.
2. Parker to Price, *N-OR,* 1, 24:418–20; Nicolay, *Outbreak,* 120; Grant, *Memoirs,* 1:150; *ESH,* 846.
3. Catton, *Coming Fury,* 371; Nicolay, *Outbreak,* 116; Ketchum, *Picture History,* 86.
4. Catton, *Coming Fury,* 373.
5. Sherman, *Memoirs,* 1:187; Nicolay, *Outbreak,* 116.
6. Grant, *Memoirs,* 1:155–56.
7. *WWW,* 58, 284; Catton, *Coming Fury,* 373.
8. Blair to Cameron, *OR,* 114:106; Warner, *Generals in Blue,* 286; Thomas, Special Orders No. 74, *OR,* 114:106.
9. Nicolay, *Outbreak,* 116; Blair to Cameron, *OR,* 114:106; Lyon to Thomas, *OR,* 114:107–9.
10. Frost to Lyon, *OR,* 114:109.
11. Nicolay, *Outbreak,* 117; Catton, *Coming Fury,* 374–76; *B&L,* 1:265.
12. Frost to Lyon, *OR,* 114:113.
13. *RR,* 1, doc. 235a; Lyon to Thomas, *OR,* 114:107–9.
14. Sanderson to Sanderson, *OR,* 114:107.
15. *RR,* 1:234b; Nicolay, *Outbreak,* 119; Ketchum, *Picture History,* 87; Sherman, *Memoirs,* 1:191–92; Sanderson to U.S. War Department, *OR,* 114:107; Catton *Coming Fury,* 379.
16. *Saint Louis Republican,* May 11, 1861; Ketchum, *Picture History,* 63; *B&L,* 1:265; *OR,* 3:9.
17. *Saint Louis Republican,* May 12–18, 1861.
18. Warner, *Generals in Blue,* 287.
19. *B&L,* 1:265; *WWW,* 261.
20. Grant, *Memoirs,* 1:152–53, 156–57.
21. Ketchum, *Picture History,* 86; *B&L,* 1:264.

Chapter 21: Lincoln Loses His Reins on the Slavery Issue

1. Warner, *Generals in Blue,* 57; *WWW,* 93b.
2. Scott to Butler, *OR,* 2:640–41; Butler to Cameron, *OR,* 2:641–42.
3. *EC,* 2:648–50; Randall, *Constitutional Problems,* chaps. 12–16.
4. *ESH,* 1:293b; Catton, *Coming Fury,* 394; *ESH,* 293b.

5. Butler to Scott, *OR*, 2:648–51; *EC*, 2:648–50; Catton, *Coming Fury*, 394; McPherson, *Battle Cry*, 355.

6. Victor, *Southern Rebellion*, 191; James Parton, *With Butler*, 127f; Catton, *Coming Fury*, 395.

7. Welles, *Diary*, 1:127; *NYT*, May 31, 1861; Butler, *Autobiography*, 259–61; Nevins, *War for Union*, 1:398.

8. Letter to Gentlemen of Yorktown, *OR*, 2:966; Catton, *Coming Fury*, 396; *RR*, 2, doc. 44.

9. *RR*, 2, docs. 33, 61; Miller, *Photographic History*, 6:70; *EC*, 3:1,444; see *N-OR*, 1, vols. 4–8, 12–14, 16–19.

10. *WWW*, 731; *AL*, 5:127; *OR*, 9:369–70; *RR*, 2, doc. 63; *Ohio Statesman*, August 2, 1861.

11. Lincoln to Frémont, *CW*, 4:530–31; Lincoln to Browning, *CW*, 4:530–31; Randall, *Lincoln the President*, 2:21; *WWW*, 237b.

12. Faust, *Encyclopedia*, 162a; McPherson, *Battle Cry*, 356; Catton, *Coming Fury*, 422–24; *EC*, 1:405; *RR*, 1, doc. 475.

13. *CW*, 5:341–42; *RR*, 5, doc. 562.

14. Miller, *Photographic History*, 7:17; *OR*, 103:393, 441, 450.

Chapter 22: The Tremendous Loss of Life Begins

1. Rowan to Welles, *N-OR*, 1, 4:478.

2. Dahlgren to Welles, ibid., 477.

3. Lowry, Report, ibid., 479.

4. *RR*, 1, doc. 78; Lowry, Report, *N-OR*, 1, 4:480–81.

5. Sanford to Scott, *OR*, 2:37–39.

6. *New York Times*, May 25, 1861; Nicolay, *Outbreak*, 110; Terrett to Lee, *OR*, 2:43–44; Taylor to Cocke, *OR*, 2:26–27.

7. Ketchum, *Picture History*, 363.

8. Nicolay, *Outbreak*, 111; Davis, *First Blood*, 63.

9. Faust, *Encyclopedia*, 240.

10. Davis, *First Blood*, 83; Read to Cameron, *OR*, 1:188–89; *CW*, 4:333; *DxD*, 3:40; Nicolay, *Outbreak*, 112.

11. *New York Times*, May 25, 1861; Davis, *First Blood*, 64.

12. Faust, *Encyclopedia*, 240; *New York Times*, May 25, 1861; Nicolay, *Outbreak*.

13. Dahlgren to Navy Department, *N-OR*, 1, 4:482.

14. *Richmond Examiner*, November 14, 1861.

15. Ibid., May 26–30, 1861; Catton, *Coming Fury*, 500b; Nevins, *War for Union*, 1:146; Horau, *Brady*, 162; Farnham, Report, *OR*, 2:41f; Allen to Porter, *OR*, 115:1289–90; Nicolay, *Outbreak*, 110, 113.

16. Leech, *Reveille*, 80–82; *New York Times*, May 25, 1861; Nicolay, *Outbreak*, 114.

17. *CW*, 4:385–86.

18. *DxD*, 3:44, 45; Davis, *First Blood*, 162.

Conclusion

1. Scharf, *Confederate Navy*, 429.

2. *DxD*, 71, 75; Mosocco, *Chronological Tracking*, 12–13.

3. *DxD,* 71; Mosocco, *Chronological Tracking,* 12.

4. Lincoln, Message to Congress in Special Session, *CW,* 4:431; Lincoln, Annual Message to Congress, *CW,* 5:35–53.

5. Lincoln to Schermerhorn, *CW,* 8:1.

6. *CW,* 4:190, 194, 208–09, 234–35; 5:185–86; 6:332–33, 496–97; 7:431–32, 533–34; 8:55–56; Hoerner, *Lincoln and Greeley,* 127–71; Mitgang, *Lincoln,* 227; Handlin and Handlin, *Lincoln and the Union,* 181; Hertz, *Letters and Documents,* 2:897, 964; Richardson, *Messages and Papers,* 6:36, 172; Randall, *Lincoln the President,* 1:279.

7. Hertz, *Letters and Documents,* 1:122; *CW,* 7:535.

Bibliography

Adams, Elmer C., and Warren D. Foster. *Heroines of Modern Progress*. New York: Macmillan, 1926.

American Annual Cyclopedia and Register, 1860–61. New York: D. Appleton, 1866–67.

Anderson, Wayne, ed. *Concise Dictionary of American History*. New York: Scribner's, 1940.

Andrews, J. Cutler. *The South Reports the Civil War*. Pittsburgh: University of Pittsburgh Press, 1970, 1985.

Baltimore Sun, April 1861.

Basler, Roy P. *A Touchstone for Greatness*. Westport, Conn.: Greenwood, 1973.

Bates, Edward. *Diary*. Edited by Howard K. Beale. Washington, D.C.: Government Printing Office, 1933.

Black, J. S. *Reports of Cases Argued and Determined by the Supreme Court of the United States at December Term 1861*. New York: Banks, 1903.

Boatner, Mark M. *The Civil War Dictionary*. Rev. ed. New York: David McKay, 1987.

Bolton, Sarah K. *Lives of Girls Who Became Famous*. New York: Crowell, 1949.

Braden, Waldo W. *Abraham Lincoln, Public Speaker*. Baton Rouge: Louisiana State University Press, 1988.

Brooks, Noah. *Abraham Lincoln and the Downfall of American Slavery*. New York: Putnam's, 1894.

Browning, Orville H. *Diary*. Edited by Theodore C. Pease and James G. Randall. Springfield: Illinois State Historical Library, 1933.

Bruce, Robert V. *Lincoln and the Riddle of Death*. Fort Wayne, Ind.: Bruce, 1981.

Buckmaster, Henrietta. *Women Who Shaped History*. New York: Collier, 1966.

Buell, Clarence C., and Robert U. Johnson, eds. *Battles and Leaders of the Civil War*. 4 vols. New York: Century, 1884–88. Reprint, Secaucus, N.J.: Castle, 1985.

Butler, Benjamin F. *Autobiography*. Boston: Thayer, 1892.

Capers, Ellison. "Journal and Notes." In *Supplement to the Official Records of the Union and Confederate Armies*. 1:62–65.

Carmen, Harry J., and Reinhard J. Luthin. *Lincoln and the Patronage*. New York: Columbia University Press, 1943.

Catton, Bruce. *American Heritage Picture History of the Civil War*. New York: Wings, 1982.

———. *Coming Fury*. Garden City, N.Y.: Doubleday, 1961.

Causey, B. G., and Malcolm Causey. *Fort Sumter-Fort Moultrie*. Mount Pleasant, S.C.: Supplemental, 1966.

The Century War Book. New York: Century, 1894.

Charleston Daily Courier. December 1860–May 1861.

Charleston Mercury. December 1860–May 1861.

Chase, Salmon P. *Diary and Correspondence*. 2 vols. Washington, D.C.: Government Printing Office, 1903.

Chester, James. "Inside Sumter in '61." In *Battles and Leaders of the Civil War,* ed. Robert U. Johnson and Clarence C. Buell, 1:50–73.

Chesnut, Mary Boykin. *A Diary from Dixie.* Edited by Ben Ames Williams. Boston: Houghton Mifflin, 1905.

Chisholm, A. R. "Notes on the Surrender of Fort Sumter." In *Battles and Leaders of the Civil War,* ed. Clarence C. Buell and Robert U. Johnson, 1:82–83.

Civil War. 1982–1996.

Civil War Chronicles. 1991–92.

Civil War Times and *Civil War Times Illustrated.* 1959–1996.

Clarkson, H. M. "Story of the Star of the West." In *Confederate Veteran,* 21:234–36.

Confederate Veteran, 1892–1932.

Colman, Edna M. *Seventy-five Years of White House Gossip.* Garden City, N.Y.: Doubleday, 1925.

Cooke, Jacob E., ed. *Frederick Bancroft, Historian.* Norman: University of Oklahoma Press, 1957.

Craven, Avery. *Edmund Ruffin.* New York: Appleton, 1932.

Crawford, Samuel W. *Diary.* In *Supplement to the Official Records of the Union and Confederate Armies,* 1:8–61.

———. "The First Shot Against the Flag." In *Annals of America,* 320–29.

———. *The Genesis of the Civil War.* New York: Webster, 1887.

Current, Richard N., ed. *Encyclopedia of the Confederacy.* 4 vols. New York: Simon and Schuster, 1993.

———. *Lincoln and the First Shot.* Philadelphia: Lippincott, 1963.

———, ed. *The Political Thought of Abraham Lincoln.* Indianapolis: Bobbs-Merrill, 1967.

———. "Lincoln, the Civil War, and the American Mission." In *The Public and the Private Lincoln,* ed. Davis et al. Carbondale: Southern Illinois University Press, 1979.

———. *The Lincoln Nobody Knows.* New York: McGraw, 1958.

———. *Speaking of Abraham Lincoln.* Urbana: University of Illinois Press, 1983.

Dannette, Sylvia, ed. *Noble Women of the North.* New York: Yoseloff, 1959.

Davis, Burke. *Gray Fox.* New York: Rinehart, 1956.

Davis, George B. *The Official Military Atlas of the Civil War,* 1891–95. Reprint, New York: Grammercy, 1983.

Davis, Jefferson. *Messages and Papers of Jefferson Davis and the Confederacy.* Edited by Mark E. Neely Jr. New York: N.p., 1966

———. *A Short History of the Confederate States of America.* New York: Belford, 1890.

Davis, William C., ed. *First Blood.* Alexandria, Va.: Time-Life, 1983.

Dodge, Bertha. *Story of Nursing.* Boston: Little, Brown, 1954.

Doubleday, Abner. "From Moultrie to Sumter." In *Battles and Leaders of the Civil War,* ed. Robert U. Johnson and Clarence C. Buell, 1:40–49.

———. *Journal.* In *Supplement to the Official Records of the Union and Confederate Armies,* 1:78–81.

———. *Reminiscences of Forts Sumter and Moultrie.* Spartanburg, S.C.: Reprint Co., 1976.

Dumond, Dwight L., comp. *Southern Editorials on Slavery.* New York: Century, 1931.

Dyer, Frederick H. *A Compendium of the War of the Rebellion.* 3 vols. Des Moines: Dyer, 1908.

Eisenschiml, Otto, and Ralph Newman. *The American Iliad.* Indianapolis: Bobbs-Merrill, 1947.

Emory, Frederick. "The Baltimore Riots." In *Annals of America,* 775–800.

Faust, Patricial L., ed. *Historical Times Illustrated Encyclopedia of the Civil War.* New York: Harper & Row, 1986.

Fehrenbacher, Don E. *Prelude to Greatness.* Stanford, Calif.: Stanford University Press, 1961.

Foote, Shelby. *The Civil War: A Narrative.* New York: Random House, 1958–74.

Forgie, George B. *Patricide in the House Divided.* New York: Norton, 1975.

"Fort Sumter—1861." In *Civil War Times,* October 1976.

Foster, J. C. "Engineer Journal of the Bombardment of Fort Sumter." In *OR,* 1:16–25.

Fox, Gustavus V. *Confidential Correspondence.* Edited by Richard Wainwright. 2 vols. New York: De Vinne, 1920.

Fraser, Walter J., Jr. *Charleston! Charleston!* Columbia: University of South Carolina Press, 1989.

Freeman, Douglas S. *R. E. Lee.* 4 vols. New York: Scribner's, 1935–49.

Gibbes, Robert W. *Report.* In *Supplement to the Official Records of the Union and Confederate Armies,* 1:75–77.

Grant, U. S. *Memoirs and Selected Letters.* 2 vols. New York: Literary Classics, 1990.

Greeley, Horace. *The American Conflict.* Hartford: O. D. Chase, 1866.

Handlin, Oscar, and Lillian Handlin. *Abraham Lincoln and the Union.* Boston: Little, Brown, 1980.

Harper's Weekly, January 5–26, 1861.

Harwell, Richard B. *The Civl War Reader.* New York: Konecky, 1991.

Hendrickson, Robert. *Sumter—The First Day of the Civil War.* Chelsea, Mich.: Scarborough House, 1990.

Herndon, William Henry. *Herndon's Life of Lincoln.* Edited by Paul M. Angle. Cleveland: World, 1930.

————, and Jesse W. Weik. *Abraham Lincoln.* 3 vols. New York: Appleton, 1892.

Hertz, Emanuel. *Abraham Lincoln: Letters and Documents.* New York: Liveright, 1931.

————. *The Hidden Lincoln.* New York: Viking, 1938.

Hoerner, Harlan H. *Lincoln and Greeley.* Urbana: University of Illinois Press, 1953.

Horan, James D. *Matthew Brady.* New York: Bonanza, 1960.

Horn, Stanley, ed. *Robert E. Lee Reader.* Indianapolis: Bobbs- Merrill, 1949.

Humphrey, Grace. *Women in American History.* Indianapolis: Bobbs-Merrill, 1919.

Hunter, Alvah F. *A Year on a Monitor and the Destruction of Fort Sumter.* Columbia: University of South Carolina Press, 1987.

Hyman, Harold. *A More Perfect Union.* New York: Scribner's, 1973.

Journal of Negro History. 4:7–21, 37:418–53.

Journal of the Southern Historical Society (1876–1944). Edited by James I. Robertson Jr. 49 vols. Richmond.

Katcher, Philip. *The Civil War Source Book.* New York: Facts on File, 1992.

Ketchum, Richard M., ed. *The American Heritage Picture History of the Civil War.* New York: Wings, 1960.

Lamon, Ward H. *Life of Abraham Lincolon.* Boston: Osgood, 1872.

Lattimore, Ralston B., ed. *The Story of Robert E. Lee.* Philadelphia: N.p. 1964.

Lee, Robert E. *Recollections and Letters.* New York: Doubleday and Page, 1904.

Lee, Stephen Dill. "The First Step in the War." In *Battles of Leaders of the Civil War,* ed. Robert U. Johnson and Clarence C. Buell, 1:74–81.

————. *Journal.* In *Supplement to the Official Records of the Union and Confederate Armies,* 1:72–75.

Leech, Margaret. *Reveille in Washington.* New York: Harper, 1941.

"Letters of Marque and Reprisal." In *N-OR,* 2, 1:325–429.

The Liberator. September, 1862.

Lincoln, Abraham. *Abraham Lincoln Papers Index.* Washington, D.C.: Government Printing Office, 1960.

————. *An Autobiography of Abraham Lincoln.* Compiled by Nathaniel W. Stephenson, Indianapolis: Bobbs-Merrill, 1926.

————. *Collected Works.* 9 vols. Edited by Roy P. Basler. New Brunswick, N.J.: Rutgers University Press, 1953–55.

————. *Complete Works.* 12 vols. Edited by John G. Nicolay and John Hay. New York: Century, 1894.

————. *Complete Works of Abraham Lincoln.* Edited by Roy P. Basler. 9 vols. New Brunswick, N.J.: Rutgers University Press, 1955.

————. *The Lincoln Papers.* Edited by Paul M. Angle. New Brunswick, N.J.: Rutgers University Press, 1955.

————. *The Lincoln Papers.* Edited by David C. Mearns. 2 vols. Garden City, N.Y.: Doubleday, 1948.

————. *New Letters and Papers.* Edited by Paul M. Angle. Westport, Conn.: Greenwood, 1946.

————. *Papers.* Library of Congress microfilm. Washington, D.C.

————. *Uncollected Letters.* Edited by Gilbert A. Tracy. Boston: Houghton Mifflin, 1917.

Long, E. B., and Barbara Long. *The Civil War Day by Day.* Garden City, N.Y.: Doubleday, 1971.

Lossing, Benjamin J., ed. *Harper's Encyclopedia of U.S. History.* 19 vols. New York: Harper, 1901.

McCallum, Jane Y. *Women Pioneers.* N.p.: Johnson, 1929.

McClure, Alexander K., ed. *The Annals of the War.* Philadelphia: Philadelphia Weekly Times, 1878.

McElroy, Joseph. *Jefferson Davis.* 2 vols. New York: Harper, 1937.

McGowan, John. *Report.* In *Supplement to the Official Records of the Union and Confederate Armies,* 1:69–71.

McHenry, Robert. *Webster's Military Biographies.* New York: Dover, 1978.

McPherson, James M. *Abraham Lincoln and the Second American Revolution.* New York: Oxford, 1990.

————. *Battle Cry of Freedom.* New York: Oxford University Press, 1988.

Marshall, Helen E. *Dorothea Dix.* New York: Russell, 1937.

Meredith, Roy. *Storm over Sumter.* New York: Simon and Schuster, 1957.

Miers, Earl S., ed. *Lincoln Day by Day.* 3 vols. Washington, D.C.: Lincoln Sesquicentennial Commission, 1960.

Miller, Francis T., ed. *Photographic History of the Civil War.* 10 vols. New York: Review of Reviews, 1911.

Mitgang, Herbert, ed. *Abraham Lincoln: A Press Portrait.* Athens: University of Georgia Press, 1956.

————. *Lincoln As They Saw Him.* New York: Rhinehart, 1956.

Military Order of the Loyal Legion of the United States. 54 vols. Reprint. Wilmington, Del.: Broadfoot, 1993–95.

Moore, Frank, ed. *The Rebellion Record: A Diary of American Events.* 11 vols. and supplement. New York: Putnam's, 1861–68; Van Nostrand, 1864–68.

Mosocco, Ronald A. *The Chronological Tracking of the American Civil War per the Official Records.* Hampton, Va.: Multi-print, 1993.

Musicant, Ivan. *Divided Waters.* New York: HarperCollins, 1995.

National Almanac and Register, 1860–61. Philadelphia: n.p., 1861–62.

National Intelligencer. December 1860; April–May 1861.

Neely, Mark E., Jr., ed. *The Abraham Lincoln Encyclopedia.* New York: McGraw-Hill, 1982.

———. *The Fate of Liberty.* New York: Oxford University Press, 1991.

Nevins, Allan. *The War for the Union.* 4 vols. New York: Scribner's, 1959–71.

New York Herald. December 1860–May 1861.

Nicolay, John G. *The Outbreak of Rebellion.* Wilmington, Del.: Broadfoot, 1989.

Nicolay, John G., and John Hay. *Abraham Lincoln: A History.* 10 vols. New York: Century, 1886.

———. "Lincoln and His Cabinet Face the Problem of Sumter." *Century Illustrated Monthly.* January 1888.

Nofi, Albert A. *The Opening Guns.* Bryn Mawr, Pa.: Combined, 1988.

Oates, Stephen B. *Abraham Lincoln: The Man Behind the Myths.* New York: Harper, 1984.

Paludan, Phillip S. *A Covenant with Death.* Urbana: University of Illinois Press, 1975.

Parker, Joel. *Habeas Corpus and Martial Law.* Cambridge: Welch, Bigelow, 1861.

Parton, James. *With Butler in New Orleans.* Boston: n.p., 1864.

Perkins, Howard C., ed. *Northern Editorials on Secession.* 2 vols. New York: Appleton, 1942.

Phisterer, Frederick. *Statistical Record of the Armies of the United States.* New York: Scribner's, 1883.

Pickens, Francis W. "Memorandum and Orders." In *OR-S,* 1:65–67.

Pryor, Sara Agnes. *Reminiscences of War and Peace.* New York: N.p., 1904.

Quarles, Benjamin. *Lincoln and the Negro.* New York: Oxford University Press, 1962.

Randall, James G. *Constitutional Problems under Lincoln.* Springfield, Ill.: Abraham Lincoln Association, 1943.

———. *Lincoln, the President.* 4 vols. New York: Dodd, 1945–55.

Richardson, James, ed. *A Compilation of the Messages and Papers of the Presidents, 1789–1897.* 10 vols. Washington, D.C.: Authority of Congress, 1898.

Richmond Examiner, 1860–61.

"Robert E. Lee." Conshahocken: Eastern Acorn, 1983.

Roller, David C., ed. *Encyclopedia of Southern History.* Baton Rouge: University of Louisiana Press, 1968.

Roman, Alfred. *The Military Operations of General Beauregard.* 2 vols. New York: Harper, 1884.

Ross, Ishbel. *Angel of the Battlefield.* New York: Harper, 1956.

St. Louis Republican. May 1861.

Sandburg, Carl. *Abraham Lincoln: The War Years.* 4 vols. New York: Harcourt, 1939.

Savannah Daily Morning News, January 2–11, 1861.

Savannah Republican, January 1861.

Scharf, John T. *History of the Confederate States Navy.* New York: Rogers and Sherwood, 1887.

Schwab, John C. *The Confederate States of America.* New York: Burt Franklin, 1968.

Schurz, Carl. *Abraham Lincoln.* 2 vols. Boston: Houghton Mifflin, 1891.

Schwartz, Bernard. *The Reins of Power.* New York: Hill and Wang, 1963.

Seward, William. *Diary.* Lincoln, Ill.: Gordon and Fledman, 1930.

Shaw, Archer H. *The Lincoln Encyclopedia.* New York: Macmillan, 1950.

Sherman, William T. *Memoirs.* 2 vols. New York: Literary Classics, 1990.

Sifakis, Stewart. *Who Was Who in the Civil War.* New York: Facts on File, 1988.

Simon, John Y. *House Divided.* Fort Wayne: Warren Library, 1987.

Smith, Elbert B. *The Presidency of James Buchanan.* Lawrence: University of Kansas Press, 1975.

Soley, J. R. *The Blockade and the Cruisers.* New York: Scribner's, 1887.

The Statistical History of the United States. New York: Basic, 1976.

Staudenraus, P. J. *The African Colonization Movement.* New York: Columbia University Press, 1961.

Stephens, Alexander H. *Constitutional View of the Late War between the States.* 2 vols. Philadelphia: National, 1868–70.

Stepp, John W., and I. William Hill, eds. *Mirror of War.* Washington, D.C.: Washington Evening Star, 1961.

Stern, Philip Van Doren. *Prologue to Sumter.* Bloomington: Indiana University Press, 1961.

Strozier, Charles B. *Lincoln's Quest for Union.* New York: Basic Books, 1982.

Suppinger, Joseph E. *The Intimate Lincoln.* Lanham, Md.: University Press of American, 1985.

Supplement to the Official Records of the Union and Confederate Armies. 10 vols. Wilmington, Del.: Broadfoot, 1994–95.

Swanberg, W. A. *First Blood.* New York: Scribner's, 1957.

Thomas, Benjamin H. *Abraham Lincoln.* New York: Knopf, 1952.

"Treatment of Prisoners during the War between the States." In *Journal of the Southern Historical Society,* 1:113–330.

Ulrich, Bartow A. *Abraham Lincoln and Constitutional Government.* Chicago: Legal News, 1916.

U.S. Navy Department. *Official Records of the Union and Confederate Navies in the War of the Rebellion.* 31 vols. Washington, D.C.: Government Printing Office, 1894–1927.

U.S. War Department. *The War of the Rebellion: A Compilation of the Official Records of the Union and Confederate Armies.* 128 vols. Washington, D.C.: Government Printing Office, 1880–1901.

Victor, Orville J. *History of the Southern Rebellion.* New York: Torrey, 1861.

Vorenberg, Michael. "Abraham Lincoln and the Politics of Black Colonization." *Journal of the Abraham Lincoln Association* 14, no. 2:23–45.

Warner, Ezra J. *Generals in Blue.* Baton Rouge: Louisiana State University Press, 1964.

———. *Generals in Gray.* Baton Rouge: Louisiana State University Press, 1959.

Washington Evening Star, April–May 1861.

Weems, Mason L. *The Life of Washington.* Edited by Marcus Cunliff. Cambridge: Harvard University Press, 1962.

Welles, Gideon. *Diary.* Edited by Howard K. Beale. 3 vols. New York: Norton, 1960.

————. *The Diary of Gideon Welles.* Edited by Roy P. Basler. 3 vols. New York: Norton, 1960.

Wheeler, Richard. *Voices of the Civil War.* New York: Crowell, 1976.

Wilcox, Arthur M., and Warren Ripley. *The Civil War at Charleston.* Charleston: Post-Courier, 1966.

Wilson, Dorothy Clarke. *Stranger and Traveler: The Story of Dorothea Dix, American Reformer.* Boston: Little, Brown, 1975.

Wright, John S. *Lincoln and the Politics of Slavery.* Reno: University of Nevada Press, 1970.

Index

Illustrations are noted by **boldface.**

abolition, 47, 59, 64, 116, 187, 189–90, 205 [*see also:* slaves and slavery]
abolition, annulled, 189–90
Adams, James H., 15, 52
Albany, N.Y., 42, 63
Alexandria, Va., 142, 146, 195, **196, 197–202,** 206
American Revolution, Second, 60, 64
Amy Warwick, **129**
Anderson, Richard, 10
Anderson, Robert, **8,** 9–16, 29, 34, 44, 47, 51, 54, 73–74, 79, 83, 90–91, 99–104, 107, 124, 138, 146, 149, 195
Anderson, William H., 125
Andrew, John A., 116, **117,** 167, 171, 193
Apalachicola, Fla., 22
Arlington, estate, 141, 145
Army of Northeastern Virginia, 202
Articles of Confederation, 121
Atlantic Monthly, 187
Augusta (Ga.) arsenal, 23

Baker, Edward D., 45
Baldwin, John B., 152
Baltimore and Ohio Railroad, 159, 168–69
Baltimore, Md., 132–34, 153, 167–74, 185, 188, 206
Baltimore riot, 167–69, **170,** 171, **172, 173–74**
Baltimore Sun, 168
Barbour, Alfred M., 157–58, 160
Barnwell, R. W., 52
Barrancas, Fort (Fla.), 22
Bates, Edward, 89, 111, 132

Baton Rouge, La., 178
Baton Rouge (La.) arsenal, 23
battery, iron (Charleston, S.C.), **72,** 97
Beauregard, P. G. T., 38, 47, 69–70, **71,** 74, 78–79, 82, 83–85, 94, 98–99, 101–2, 122, 124, 138, 146
Big Bethel, Va., 185, **186**
Black Hawk War, 10
black soldiers, 188
Black, Jeremiah S., 52, 54
Blair, Francis P., Jr., 24, 60, 176–77
Blair, Francis P., Sr., 142, **143,** 176
Blair House, 143
Blair, Montgomery, 142, 176, 187
Blakely gun, 93, 102
Blandowski, Constantin, 180
blockade, 125–26, 129, 205
Bolivar Heights, Va., 159
Boston Chronicle, 15
Boston, Mass., 167, 172
Botts, John Minor, 137
bridges, burned, 173, **174**
Brilliante, 129
Brooklyn (N.Y.) Navy Yard, 91, 126
Brown, George W., 134, 169, 171
Brown, John, 158, 167
Brown, Joseph E., 22, **23**
Brownell, Francis E., 200, **201**
Browning, Orville, 107
Buchanan, Franklin, 146
Buchanan, James, 11, 12, 20, 30–31, 37–38, 51–52, 54, 87–88, 111
Buell, Don Carlos, 12, **13,** 188
Buffalo, N.Y., 42
Burr, Aaron, 132
Butler, Benjamin F., **153,** 185
Butterfield, Daniel, 198

Calhoun, John C., 27, **28**
Cameron, Simon, 74, 89, 91, 116–17,
    143, 146, 172, 187
Camp Jackson (Saint Louis, Mo.),
    177–79, 182
Camp Verde (Tex.), 26, 31, **35**
Campbell, John A., 56–57
Capers, Ellison, 15, 47
Capitol, U.S., **45,** 112, 171, **173**
Carlisle Barracks, Pa., 160
Carolina Light Infantry, 19
Carpenter, Francis B., 62
Cass, Lewis, **11**
Castle Pinckney (Charleston, S.C.), **10,**
    12, 19–21, 53, 128–29
casualties, 185–86, 201, 205, 207 [*see also:*
    Baltimore riot, Saint Louis riot]
Chaplin, J. C., 196
Charleston, S.C., 9–16, 28–29, **30, 31,**
    32–44, 47, 49, 58, **68,** 69, 70–71, **72,**
    74, **75,** 77, **78,** 79–85, 93–105, 108,
    123–26, 128–29, 152, 165, 174,
    205–6 [*see also:* battery, iron;
    Charleston Harbor; Citadel, The;
    Cummings Point; James Island;
    Johnson, Fort; Morris Island;
    Moultrie, Fort; Mount Pleasant;
    Rattlesnake Shoal; Shute's Folly;
    Sullivan's Island]
Charleston (S.C.) arsenal, 21
Charleston Harbor (S.C.), **85**
Charleston Mercury, 37
Charles Town, Va., 160
Chase, Samuel P., 60, 63, 110
Chatham Artillery, 22
Chesnut, Mary Boykin, 83, 97
Chester, James, 73, 83
Chew, Robert, 78–79, 81–82, 93, 108
Chisholm, A. R., 83
Church, William C., 36
Cincinnati, Ohio, 63
Citadel, The (Charleston, S.C.), 14, 31,
    34, **35**
Clarkson, H. M., 36
Clay, Cassius, 63
Cleveland, Ohio, 42
Clinch, Fort (Fla.), 22–23

Coffee, Titian J., 132
colonization of freed slaves, 60, 191
Columbia, S.C., 77, 161
Columbus, Fort (S.C.), 33
confiscation, 191–92
Congress, Confederate, 128
Congress, U.S., **113,** 115–16, 118–19,
    126, 133–34, 137–38, 151, 153, 155,
    189–91, 205–6
Conner, James, 47
contrabands, 186–90, **191, 192,** 193
Cook, John, 199
Cooper, Samuel, 11, 12, 47, 146
Corcoran, Michael, 128, **129,** 198
Crawford, Martin J., 55–56
Crawford, Samuel, 36, 47, 71, 84, 103
Crenshaw, 129
Crittenden Compromise, 151
Crittenden, John J., **150,** 151
CSS *Virginia,* 164
Cummings Point (Charleston, S.C.), 16,
    38, 41, 101
Cunningham, John, 21
Cushing, Caleb, 62

Dahlgren guns, 162, 164
Dahlgren, John A., 195, **197,** 201
Darby, earl of, 125
Davis, Jefferson, 26, 42, 48, 52, **53,** 55,
    58, 61–62, 69, **70,** 71, 97, 107, 119,
    121–24, 127–29, 152, 162, 165, 206
Davis, Jefferson C., **14**
Davis, Robert C., 135
Davis, Robert W., 171
Davis, Varina, 69
DeBow, J. B. D., 137
Declaration of Independence, 59–60, 64
Democratic Party, 205
Dennison, William, 116
Denslow, H. W., 104
Department of Northeastern Virginia, 202
Department of Texas, 26, 141
Department of the West, 176
deSaussure, William G., 20–21, 30
Dix, John A., 188
Doubleday, Abner, 12, 36, 39, 70, 73, 97,
    103, 107, **108**

Douglas, Stephen A., **59, 114**
Dry Tortugas (Fla.), 27

Ebenezer Creek, Ga., 193
Eight Massachusetts Regiment, **173**
Ellis, John W., 117
Ellsworth, Elmer, 110, 196–98, **199,** 200, **201,** 202, 206, 207
Ely, Alfred, **128**
Elzey, Arnold, 23
Emancipation Proclamation, 60, **62, 65,** 193
Emory, Frederic, 169–70
Everett, Edward, 62, **63**
Executive Mansion, **132**

Faunce, John, 95
Fayetteville, N.C., 161
Fielding, George, 103
Fifth Amendment, 132
Fifth New York Infantry, 197
First Bull Run (Va.), 203
First Infantry, U.S. Army, 26
First Michigan Infantry, 198
First Texas Rifles, 145
First Volunteers, Georgia, 22
Floyd, John, 10, 11–12, 52
Fontaine, F. G., 84
Foote, Andrew H. J., 91
Forsyth, John, **55,** 56, 58
Foster, John G., 10, 11, 16, 38, 41, 73, 83, 101–2
Founding Fathers, 60, 133
Fourteenth New York Infantry, 197
Fox, Gustvus V., 74, 76, 87, **88,** 89–91, 107–8, 111, 152, 195
Freeborn, 90
French, B. B., 45
Frost, Dan M., 178
Fugitive Slave Law, 46–47, 185–86, 189

Gaines, Fort (Ala.), 22
Galloway, Edward, 103
Gardner, John L., 9
Garrison, William Lloyd, 62
General Clinch, 35
Genesis of the Civil War, The, 36

German Artillery, 20
Germans, 171, 175–76, 180–81
Gettysburg Address, 59
Gibbes, R. W., 93
Gibbes, Wade Hampton, 146
Gloucester Point, Va., 206
Gosport Navy Yard (Va.), 157, 162–64, **165,** 166
Gourdin, Robert, 54
Governor's Island, 32, 88
Greaves, John, 171
Greeley, Horace, 62, 64, 84, 95, 104, 118–19
Green, Allen J., 35

habeas corpus, 131–38
Haggerty, James, 187
Hall, Norman J., 13, 54
Halleck, Henry W., 188
Halltown, Va., 160
Hampton Roads, Va., 164
Hampton, Va., 187
Harney, William S., 177
Harp, James, 103
Harpers Ferry, Va. (now W.V.), 157–60, **161,** 162, 165
Harper's Weekly, 60
Harriet Lane, 88, **90,** 91, 95
Harris, Isham G., 118
Harrisburg, Pa., 42
Haskin, A., 23
Hay, John, 108, 125
Hayne, Isaac W., 38, 54–55
Haynesworth, George E., 35
Hiawatha, 129
Hicks, Thomas H., 116, 134, 168
Holt, Joseph, 38, 54–55, 73
Home Squadron, U.S. Navy, 162
hostages, 128
Hough, Daniel, 103
House Divided speech (Lincoln), 60
Howe, Edward H., 200
Hoyle, Isaac W., 104
Humphreys, F. C., 21
Hunt, Henry J., 158
Hunter, David, 189, **190**
Hunter, Robert M., 56

Ida, 22
Imboden, John D., 159
Indianapolis, Ind., 41, 63
Indianola, Tex., 142
invasion, 122, 143, 193, 195–203, 206
Irwin, James, 103
Isabel, 104

Jackson, Andrew, 27, 142
Jackson, Claiborne F., 118, 175, 177, 182
Jackson, Fort (Ga.), 23
Jackson, Henry H., 159
Jackson, James W., 201, **202**
Jackson, Miss., 34
Jackson, Thomas J. "Stonewall", 161, **162**
James Island (Charleston), 47, 72, 97
Jamison, David F., 21, 77
Jeff Davis, 127–28
Jefferson City, Mo., 118
Jefferson, Fort (Fla.), 27
John Frazer and Co., 93
Johnson, Fort (Charleston, S.C.), 13, 21, **22,** 71
Johnson, R. W., 141
Johnston, Albert S., 145–46
Johnston, Joseph E., 144, **145,** 146
Jones, David R., 100
Jones, Edward F., 167–68, 170–71
Jones, Roger, 159–60

Kane, George P., **133,** 134, 171, 174
Kenosha, Wis., 63
Key West, Fla., 27
Kimball, A. N., 34
Kirby-Smith, Edmund, 147
Kirkwood, Samuel J., 117
Knoxville, Tenn., 206

La Patrie, 125
LaFayette Artillery, 20
Lamon, Ward Hill, 75
Lane, Joseph, 63
Lawton, Alexander, 22
Lee, Robert E., 121, 141–46, 157, 162
Lee, Stephen D., 83, 98, 100
Leisenring, George, 171

Letcher, John, 117, **118,** 146, 150, 157, 160–61
letters of marque and reprisal, 123–25, 127, 129 [*see also:* privateers]
Lexington, Mass., 171
Libby Prison (Richmond, Va.), **127,** 128
Liberia, 60, **61**
Liberty, Mo., 24
Lincoln, Abraham, 9–10, **40,** 41–49, 51–66, **66,** 68, 74, 77–82, 87–92, 95, 97, 104, **109,** 110–13, 115–22, 123–24, 126–29, 131–38, **140,** 142, 145, 148–49, 151, 154, **155,** 159, 161, 163, 166, 167–68, 173–74, 176, 183, 185, 187, 189–90, 192, 199–200, 202, **203,** 205–8
Lincoln, Mary Todd, 41, **43**
Little Rock (Ark.) arsenal, 24
Liverpool, England, 93
London *Times,* 72–73
Louisiana State University, 175
Louisville, Ky., 9
Lowell, Mass., 169
Lowry, R. B., 195–96
Lyon, Nathaniel, 177–78, **179,** 180–82

Madison, Wis., 118
Magoffin, Beriah, 117
Magrath, Andrew G., 77
Mallory, Charles, 186
March to the Sea, 193
Marion Artillery, 20
Marion, Fort (Fla.), 22
Marshal House hotel, **200**
Mason, Fort (Tex.), 141
Massachusetts, Fort (Miss.), 21
Maury, Matthew F., 146
McCauley, Charles S., 163–64, 166
McCormick, Cyrus H., 63
McDowell, Irvin, 190, 202
McGowan, John, 34–36
McKinstry, Justus, 24
McRee, Fort (Fla.), 22
Meade, R. K., 12, 19–20, 146
Meagher Guards, 19
Meigs, Montgomery C., 91, **92**
memoirs of U. S. Grant, 182

Mercer, Samuel, 91
Mexican War, 38, 87, 145
militia, 112, 115–20, 124, 132, 149, 154, 173–74, 182, 202, 205–6
Mobile, Ala., 119
Monroe, Fort (Va.), 34, 157, **158,** 163, 185–86, 191
Montgomery, Ala., 47, **54,** 56–58, 69, 71, 81, 83–84, 93, 105, 123, 152, 162
Moore, Thomas O., 23
Morgan, Fort (Ala.), 22
Morris Island (Charleston, S.C.), 33–36, 70, 72, 74, 84, 97, 104
Morris, Gouverneur, 133
Morton, Oliver P., 41–42
Moultrie, Fort (Charleston, S.C.), 9–15, 20–21, 29–31, 36, 38, 51–53, 70, 79, 90, 93, 97, 99, 101
Mount Pleasant (Charleston, S.C.), 12
Mount Vernon, Ala., 22
Mounted Rifles, U.S. Army, 159

Napoleon, Ark., 24
Nashville, Tenn., 47
Nelson, Samuel, 56
Newburyport, Mass., 104
New Orleans, La., 23, 32, 125, 142
New York Chamber of Commerce, 104
New York Evening Post, 36
New York Herald, 29, 62, 73, 84, 92, 119, 166, 174
New York, N.Y., 31–32, 38, 42, 56–57, 61, 63, 76, 79, 82, 88, 90–92, 95, 100, 104, 108, 115, 127, 149, 167, 200
New York Times, 120
New York Tribune, 60, 185, 200
Nicolay, John G., 15, 108, **109,** 110, 125, 174
Nina, 19–20
Ninth Infantry, U.S. Army, 33
Norfolk, Va., 88, 161, 163–66
nullification, 27

Oglethorpe Barracks (Ga.), 23
Oglethorpe Light Infantry, 22
Orange and Alexandria Railroad, 201
Orr, James L., 52

Patch, William, 169
Paulding, Hiram, 163–64
Pensacola, Fla., 22, 27, 95
Peoria, Ill., 61
Pettigrew, Johnson, 15, 19–20
Philadelphia, Pa., 42, 63, 118, 127, 131, 168, 171
Philadelphia Press, 118
Philadelphia Public Ledger, 118
Philadelphia, Washington, and Baltimore Railroad, 169
Pickens, Fort (Fla.), 22, 34, 48–49, 57–58
Pickens, Francis, 20–21, 29, **37,** 53, 70, 72, 75, 77–80, 91, 94
Pike, Fort (La.), 23
Pinkerton, Allan, 44
piracy, 125, 127–28
Pittsburgh, Pa., 42, 107
Pomeroy, S.C., 6
Potomac River, 197
Potter, R. M., 142
Preston, William B., 152
Prime, Frederick E., 21
Prioleau, Charles K., 93–94
prisoners of war, 201–2
Pritchard, John, 103
privateers, 123, **124,** 125, 127, 206 [*see also:* Letters of Marque and Reprisal; piracy]
proclamation (William S. Harney), 178
Pryor, Roger A., 81
Pulaski, Fort (Ga.), 22, **23,** 27

Randall, James G., 154
Randolph, George W., 152
Rattlesnake Shoal (Charleston, S.C.), 96
Reading, Pa., 104, 117
Republic of South Carolina—see South Carolina, Republic of
Republic of Texas, 145
Republican Party, 65, 205
Richmond Dispatch, 150
Richmond Examiner, 188
Richmond, Va., 69, 127–28, 137, 146, 153, 157, 160, 162, 165
Ringold Artillerists, 117
Robertson, John, 146

Rodgers, John, 164
Rogers, Peter, 171
Roman, A. B., 55
Rowan, Stephen C., 92, 195–96
Rowland, Albert G., 171
Ruffin, Edmund, 84, 97, **98**

Saint Augustine, Fla., 22
Saint Clairsville, Ohio, 104
Saint Louis, Mo., 142, 175, **176,** 177–84, 206
Saint Louis (Mo.) arsenal, 24, 175, **177,** 179–81
Saint Louis (Mo.) riot, 175–79, **180,** 181–84
Saint Philip, Fort (La.), 23
San Antonio, Tex., 142
Sandburg, Carl, 120
Santo Domingo, 57
Saratoga County, N.Y., 198
Savannah, **124,** 127–28
Savannah, Ga., 22–23, 34, 95, 104, 125
Savannah Volunteer Guards, 22
Schell, Franck, 172
Schultze, A. C., 32
Schurz, Carl, 79, **80**
Scott, Winfield, 9, 25, 30–31, 33, 38, 44, 46, 48–49, 63, 74, 79, **89,** 110, 112, 118, 131–33, 136, 141, 159, 161, 163, 187, 190–91
Secessionville, S.C., 47
Second Artillery, U.S. Army, 23
Second Cavalry, U.S. Army, 141, 145
seizure of federal installations, 17, 19–27
Seventeenth South Carolina Infantry, 21
Seward, William H., 48, 56–57, 60, 65, **81,** 82, 91, 110, 114, 205
Sewell's Point, Va., 206
Sherman, William T., **145,** 175–77, 180–81, **189,** 201
Ship Island, Miss., 21
Shute's Folly (Charleston, S.C.), 71
Sigel, Franz, 179
Sixth Massachusetts Regiment, 167–69, **170,** 171, **172**

Sixty-ninth New York Infantry, 128
slaves and slavery, 59–66, 109, 116, **136, 137,** 153, 186–90, **191, 192** [*see also:* abolition; abolition, annulled; colonization; contrabands; Emancipation Proclamation; Fugitive Slave Law]
Slemmer, Adam J., 22
Smith, Albert J., 23
Smith, H., 23
Snyder, G. W., 12, 29–30
Solferina, 199
South Carolina, Republic of, 20, 40, 53, 77, 80
Springfield Grays, 199
Springfield, Ill., 40, **42,** 63, 199
Springfield, Mass., 157
Springfield, Mo., 175
Stanton, Edwin M., **135,** 172
Star of the West, 32, **33,** 34–39, 112, 207
Staunton Artillery, 159
Stephens, Alexander H., 61, 119, 121, **122,** 152, 165
Stevens, C. H., 72
Stevens, P. F., 35
Stevens, Thaddeus, 126
Stoddard, William A., 113
Stone, Charles P., 44, 161
Stringham, S. H., 89
Stuart, Alexander H. H., 152
Sullivan's Island (Charleston, S.C.), 9, 12, 29, 47, 74, 93, 97
Sumner, Charles, 125
Sumter, Fort (Charleston, S.C.), 11–15, 20–21, 27–28, 29–40, 47–49, 54–58, 65–66, 68, 69–73, 77–81, 87–89, 93–98, **99,** 100–102, **102, 103,** 104–5, 107–12, 114, 115–16, 120, 146, 149, 152–53, 166, 167, 176, 166, 167, 176

Talbot, Theodore, 38, 77–81, 91, 93
Taliaferro, Alexander G., 162, 165
Taney, Roger B., 62
Tappan, Henry P., 118
tariff, 27, 47, 1–9
Taylor, Fort (Fla.), 27
Terrett, George H., 196

Thirteenth Amendment, 153
Thomas, C. W., 33
Thomas, Lorenzo, 9, 30, 32–34
Toombs, Robert, 93, **94,** 151–52
torpedo, 73
Totten, Joseph G., 89
Tredegar Iron Works (Richmond, Va.), 153
Trescot, W. H., 52
Troy, N.Y., 191
Turner, Ashby, 159
Twelfth New York Infantry, 198
Twenty-eighth New York Infantry, 198
Twenty-fifth New York Infantry, 198
Twiggs, David E., **25,** 26, 141

U.S. Army, 112, 131, 137, 153, 206
U.S. Constitution, 59–60, 121, 133, 136
U.S. Customs Service, 27, 111
U.S. Navy, 123–27, 137, 166, 188
U.S. Revenue Service, 27, 46, 90, 110–11, 124, 205
U.S. Supreme Court, 46, 56, 62, 105, 129, 133, 136, 183
Uncle Ben, 95
Unionists, 121–22, 134, 137, 150–52, 168–69, 175–76, 179–81
USS *Atlantic,* 91, 95, 126
USS *Bainbridge,* 126
USS *Baltic,* 95–96, 104, 126
USS *Baltimore,* 195, 201
USS *Brooklyn,* 30–32, 34–35
USS *Colorado,* 126
USS *Cumberland,* 163–64
USS *Dolphin,* 163
USS *Guy,* 195
USS *Illinois,* **91, 95**
USS *Merrimac,* 163, 165
USS *Minnesota,* 126
USS *Mississippi,* 126
USS *Mount Vernon,* 195
USS *Pawnee,* 88, 91–92, 95, **96,** 107, 163–64, 195–96
USS *Perry,* 127
USS *Plymouth,* 163

USS *Pocahontas,* 88, 91, 107
USS *Powhatan,* 91–92, 95–96, 107

Vigilant Rifles, 34
Villard, Henry, 62
Virginia Military Institute, 161

Waite, C. A., 26
Walker, L. Pope, 47, 83, 94
War of 1812, 16, 61
war powers of the president, 137–38
Washington Artillery, 20
Washington Brigade, 168, 171
Washington, D.C., 29–38, 41, 44–49, 63, 88, 92, 105, 109, 112, 123–24, 126–27, 131, 132, 142, 145–46, 151, 165–66, 168, 171–72, 195
Washington, George, 60, 65, 111
Washington Globe, 142, 174
Washington, L. Q., 48, 151
Webb, W. A., 33
Webster, Daniel, 61
Weems, Mason, 64
Weitfieldt, Ann Amelia, 95
Welles, Gideon, 90–91, 111, 163, 188
West Point (U.S. Military Acadmey), 10, 38, 121, 146
West Virginia, 153
Whiting, William H. C., 22–23
Whiskey Rebellion, 111–12, 115, 120, 124, 205
Wigfall, Louis, 84, 100, **101**
Wilmington, N.C., 125
Wilson, Henry, 138
Winthrop, Theodore, 187
Wise, Henry A., 157
Wood, Fernando, 61
Woods, C. R., 33
Wool, John E., 45, 188, 191
Wright, H. G., 163, 165

Yale College, 187
Yankee, 95

Zouaves, 195–96, **198**

Webb Garrison is a veteran writer who lives in Lake Junaluska, North Carolina. Formerly associate dean of Emory University and president of McKendree College, he has written more than forty books, including *A Treasury of Civil War Tales, Civil War Curiosities, The Lincoln Nobody Knows,* and *Atlanta and the War.*